No Win Situation

Natalia,
Thank you for the support!
Stay Sweet! Jenn.

Copyright 2012 by Jennifer Luckett No Win Situation

All rights reserved. No part of this book may be reproduced in any form or by any electronic or mechanical means, including information storage and retrieval systems, without permission in writing from the publisher, except by a reviewer who may quote brief passages in a review.

First Edition June 2012
Printed in the United States of America

10 9 8 7 6 5 4 3 2 1

This is a work of fiction. Names, characters, places, and incidents either are products of the author's imagination or are used fictitiously. Any resemblance to actual events or locales or persons, living or dead, is entirely coincidental.

No Win Situation

by

Jennifer Luckett

Other Titles by Jennifer Luckett

Caught In The Middle

Dedication
Delbreco L. Williams. Love you!

Acknowledgements

Lord, thank you for blessing me with the talent to be able to pen novels that people can relate to and be entertained by. You have been my helper, guide, and my support system. Had it not been for you in the year 2011, I know for a fact that I wouldn't have made it. I give you all the glory. I'll never say what I can't make it through again because that was the hardest year of my life. Two people that I truly loved were removed from my life but you stood by me and helped me to make it. I owe you big time.

Mom, you love me regardless of my flaws and you've always supported me. I hope that I'm the best mother to my daughter as you have been to me. You're so strong and I truly admire you. Delz, you're my pride and joy. You act so much like me that sometimes we really bump heads. I am so proud of you. And don't get brand new because you're going to high school. You're still my baby! My twin brother Jerome, I hate that we live so many miles apart at times because we were close growing up. I remember when I called you and asked you to come to Mississippi because Delz and I needed you. You showed up exactly when I needed you all the way from Cali. Bruh, that's love! I love you no matter how far apart we are. My li'l cousin Amber, you're all grown up now but you'll always be my li'l cousin in my eyes. You have your own family now and I love you despite you being messy! ☺ My family that has supported me on the Luckett side, including all of my uncles especially Howard and John K. I am so blessed to have you all. The Gordon's, Auntie Ann, Sue, and Charlene you all are so special to me. Jackie Patterson, big cousin I remember when you would babysit me growing up and you always had a great sense of humor. Oh, and we gotta get together on this movie thing that you keep talking about. You're a trip!

LaTasha Patterson, (Nikki) I enjoy your company and I can't wait to have our next road trip. Sheila Green and Blossom Kelly, I feel that y'all are some true patient people and you both care for others. Y'all are like my work fam. Blossom, girl you make us all laugh with your personality (smh and smiling). Only the three of us know why I'm doing that.

My bestie, MeShun Eldridge; Shun when I needed a friend after that tragedy you listened and felt my pain and you understood every word that I spoke. You showed up and even took off of work to be there that day. We don't see each other often but every-time we talk it's always the same and I am so glad that you are my friend. I see you doing big things and I'm happy for you. Stay strong. LaQuandra McWillie and family, I am appreciative and glad to have supporters like you all. Mrs. Joyce Booker, you're so sweet. Jessica Flanagan, girl, remember how we would laugh and clown in class? There was never a dull moment with you. Everyone from Velma Jackson High who purchased my debut novel, thanks a million. Jade, thanks greatly for the cover and I wish you the best of luck!

To all of the authors who have given me guidance along the way, I want to say that it's people like you who make the world a better place. Special shouts to Author Endy, my literary sister. E, whenever I have a concern I know that you are a phone call away. You have shown me how to dust the bullshit off of my shoulders and keep it moving. You don't entertain the craziness in the industry and that has really rubbed off on me. You take care of your daughters and you have a heart that's made of gold. I respect you to the fullest. Author Cash, I wish you continued success as an author. Congrats. Author Victor L. Martin, I appreciate your friendship and I hope that you and your career continue to shine. You've never "ego-tripped" and that alone speaks volumes. Stay up. Oh, and like I told you, your book "The Game of Deception" was the truth!

Author Shelia Lipsey, you have so much talent and you are truly one of God's special children. You're always speaking positive and I like that about you. Continue to push your pen, and I know good things will continue to happen in your life.

Beneficial, you lightened my heart at a time when it was heavy, and so for that you'll never be forgotten. My Facebook supporters are a big help, including Thomasena M. You're so supportive and loving, and I will always remember you. Kendra Littleton, Kedra Byrd, Destiny Smith, Charnitra, Patricia Taylor, Novie, Ryan Chaunte Ivory (thanks for encouraging me after that situation). I'm happy to have met you through mutual associates), Sharlene Minus, Kinetra Horton, Romonica Bass, and others ,I want to say thank you ladies for encouraging me to continue to move my pen! Y'all pretty girls rock.

BAB Bookstore and all book clubs that've walked with me through my literary journey, you all are great! And, I mean that from the bottom of my heart. Now, to Victoria Canady, you are now my family, and I truly believe that God has placed you in my life for a reason and not just for one season. We've talked, laughed, and have almost cried together. You have a tender heart, and you're so comforting. You've called me at times when I thought no one cared, and that right there shows me that you're real. We have gone through some drama together, and we always had each other's back until all the dust settled and the smoke cleared. Then, we'd burst out laughing and we're ready for something new to pop off! But seriously, you've given me the best advice and I know you want to see me happy and successful. I wish you and your husband many more years of happiness together. I am blessed to have you around to help me when the times get rough, and I'm here for you as well. Dominique Luckett, love you, cuz, and I wish you the very best. I wish I could see you more.

LaTonya Jones, I wish you peace and prosperity, and I hope that the boys will be as strong as you have been. Twyla James, Vanna, and Jersona Murphy, you all have always been so sweet to me and my daughter. When I resided in Milwaukee you all welcomed me with open arms. Remember how I kept y'all on pins and needles? LOL Especially you godmother! You all will always have a special place in my heart.

Kelvin and Cherrie Luckett, thank you two for being part of Delz life. She has really been blessed by having you two around. I appreciate the realness.

Delbreco Williams, not one day goes by that I don't think of you and the impact you have had on my life. You taught me how to grind and stay independent, and like you would say, "When you have your own you don't have to ask nobody for shit." Regardless of how hard you were, you had a caring side that showed through a lot of your actions. Even though you passed so soon, I understand that God has the final say so. I hope that you're in heaven smiling down on me and Delz. I know that your soul is finally in peace now without the everyday heartaches and pains. I hope to see you whenever I make my transition. Losing you was the hardest thing I've ever experienced, but when you left this world, a lot of things were revealed to me that I needed to know. You still live on through my memories of you. You are a soldier and a legend in my book. See you on the other side.

Readers, I have learned a lot from people's actions lately and the things that go on no longer surprise me. Let me say this, I have learned what the true meaning of loyalty is and I respect those who have love and respect for me. I can't be fake because that's too time consuming and I'd rather just keep it real so that I can be happy with who I am. Life is too short to wake up with any regrets. So I'll love those who treat me with respect, and in return, I'll give the same. For the ones who can't give respect, I will forget them. Also, true love is not easy to find, and it shouldn't be hidden. If a person loves you, they will never disrespect you, because when you hurt they should hurt too, and feel your pain. I wish everyone happiness! With that said, I'm out.

Lookin' for Baller Status
Kay-Kay

The Milwaukee night quickly became warm, sticky, and humid after the water drops stopped tumbling from the clouds. My mother, Tamela Jean Butler, betta known as "Tammie," glanced over her shoulder wandering out the front door. "I need to leave here so I can get a fix. I'll holla at y'all later," she explained. She would do anything to get high. She would give head and put pussy on the market. She always vanished around nine o' clock every night. It was that woman's normal routine. She was a certified crackhead.

Hell, it didn't make me a bit of difference though 'cause all I wanted to do was party like a rock star at the club down the street where all the d-boys hung out. Mama normally didn't get back home 'til around three or four in the morning anyway, but hey, that suited me just fine. Me, and my younger sister, Alize, were used to her absence anyway. The only way I could leave her place and move up was to find a shot caller who would hold me down and save me from the slums, that's what I was in search of.

Alize and I got spruced up in our tight booty shorts with our coochie prints showing, with halter-tops, and dipped down the street with our neighbors Monique and Shay who met us at our apartment. They were sisters too, and their mama and ours were good friends. Prob'ly cause their mama, Lacey, was a dopehead too.

No Win Situation

We all sashayed down the street. One dude in a pearly-white Suburban on twenty-six inch chrome wheels drove slowly alongside us talking hellified noise, trying to work his game, and get his dick wet. I could tell what was on his mind by the way he stared us down like eye-candy. He was a dark chocolate dude with dreadlocks. I ain't gon' lie; dude was cute, around twenty-one or two, but he had HO written all over his forehead.

"What's up, cuties?" he asked us. He smiled, showing off his platinum grill, covered with sparkling diamonds. I kept on kickin', ignoring the hell outta him like he didn't exist.

"Shorty, in the tight blue shorts, where you headed?"

"To the club," Alize answered, pointing up the street.

"Club? You don't look old enough to get in that club."

"I'm sixteen, but I'ma try my best to get in there," she said as we kept on walking.

"You got to be twenty-one or older to dot them doors. Give me yo' number and let me call you later on before you run up in there wit' them squares who gon' be up in there touching all over you."

"Ain't nobody gon' be doin' nothin' to me that I don't let them do. I ain't easy. I don't just let er'body I meet feel on me," Alize retorted with sass. She could be naive but most of the time she was up on her game.

"Don't take it the wrong way, but you kno' they gon' be in there drinking and getting high. So, when they see that biggo ass squeezed up in those tight shorts, they gon' be ready to cop a feel."

"Uh-huh," she responded crossing her arms as we all continued walking towards the club.

"So, are you gon' give me yo' digits or what?" the dude called out from the car, still driving at a creep alongside of us.

"I don't even kno' yo' name or nothin'."

"Well, come here and step to the truck, boo. Don't be scared." The truck came to a stop at the curb.

"Oh, I ain't never scared," Alize immediately stated.

Alize went up to his truck while we stood and waited for them to get through conversing. My li'l sister stood at the vehicle for 'bout five or six minutes until I rudely cut their conversation short when damn near twenty insects formed a circle around us.

"Ay, Alize, come on here. These bugs over here wilding out," I shrieked. I hit one and killed it. "Worrisome bastard," I muttered to myself.

Shay yelped, "Come on, Alize. Ain't nobody trying to be out here fighting these bugs."

Alize placed her index finger up, her way of telling us to hold on.

"Put yo' finger down and c'mon," I ordered.

"Dag," she growled.

She and the dude said their goodbyes and he crept off making the pipes on his Suburban roar.

Alize walked back toward us as we began walking.

"Damn. He was super fine," Alize said.

"Yeah, he was cute. On a scale from one to ten I'll give him a nine," I said.

"I wanna bend some corners in that pretty truck," Alize sang out.

I looked at her like she was stupid. "You kno' he got some baby mamas somewhere, and if one of them ho's catch you in his ride they gon' be ready to fuck you up on sight," I kidded.

"Yeah, he said he got three kids and two baby mamas, but ain't nobody whoopin' this," she said and touched her butt.

"What? You gon' be baby mama number three?" I teased, laughing.

We all started hen cackling.

Monique cautioned, "You betta be careful. He looks like he's packing. You might not be able to walk for a week when he gets through wit' you. He may have you 'roun' here walking gap legged."

"Well, you just gon' have to push me in a wheelchair 'cause I will give him some."

Monique snickered. "You so crazy."

Monique was the oldest of us. She was twenty-one and her sister, Shay, was seventeen like me, and Alize was the youngest at sixteen.

I knew that I was underage and didn't have no business outside that club trying to shake my rump, but since it was my cousin Boo Man and his partner Money's club, I figured I'd beg Boo-Man to let us in. The line was long as hell. We made it there at nine-thirty on the dot. There had to be at least a hundred people ahead of us. When we finally made it to the door about thirty-five minutes later, Boo Man was taking the money at the door.

"I'ma let you li'l rugrats in here this time, but don't bring y'all's young asses back up here no mo'. Ain't trying to get my goddamn license taken away for y'all. The age is twenty-one and up."

"Stop trippin'. We ain't gon' stay long. I promise we ain't," I explained, trying to reassure him.

"Hold up! Hold up! I changed my mind. I'm not letting y'all in unless this dime piece right here blesses me with her number," he said, eyeing Shay down. She may have only been seventeen, but older dudes was constantly sweating her, thinking she was legal.

Shay shot him a blushing smile.

"Shay." I turned to her. "Give my freak nasty cousin yo' number so we can get in."

Boo Man was six two, medium build, chocolate Hershey's Kisses complexion, and handsome. The women were always jocking him, and from the look my girl, Shay was giving him, I knew that she was no different.

"Oh, I'ma sho' her how freaky I am." Then he flicked his tongue at her.

"Man, I don't want to see yo' nasty tongue. Lick at her when y'all in private," I insisted.

"Stop hatin' Kay-Kay. You ain't supposed to be up here no way. Where Aunt Tammie at?"

"I don't kno'. Prob'ly somewhere smoking dope. You kno' how she gets down."

"That's fucked up," Boo Man commented, shaking his head.

"To her it's not. C'mon, let us in and stop trying to hold a conversation. We tryin' to party, not stand here, and talk to you."

Boo Man held his hand out for our money.

"Damn, we got to pay?" I asked, surprised.

"You damn right you got to pay, and hurry up 'cause you holding up my line."

"How much is it? Five dollars?" I guessed.

"Hell, naw. It ain't five; it's ten. But Shay ain't got to pay."

They were just smiling and staring at each other as if they were on some love at first sight type of foolishness.

I disrupted them with, "Why she ain't got to pay?"

"'Cause she looking sexy, and she gon' give me her digits, that's why."

"Ugh, here." I passed him ten dollars; it was all the money I had. I walked in the club first.

The place was jam packed, which was normal for Club Hip Hop. Ballers were er'where. I felt like I was in Thug Heaven. The thugs were turning around checking me out, and my girls were following behind me. I added a li'l sexy to my walk as I went over and stood up against a wall. Smoke and loud music fumed the air.

I knew I was the shit that night. I'm what you'd call a red-bone, a fine one at that. People say I favor the R&B singer Alicia Keys. I'm five-six, fair skinned, with long, wavy hair, a hundred forty pounds and thick, but definitely not fat. All of my weight was in my hips and phat ass, which is where it needed to be. I allowed my hair to dangle down my back. Dudes in the club couldn't stop turning around gawking. The busted up bitches wouldn't stop with the rolling of the eyes and grittin' on me. Me and my girls were posted up against the wall when Mario's song, "Break Up", featuring Gucci Mane and Sean Garrett, rang out through the air. Me and my crew started dancing. I rolled my hips to the beat and sung along. "Loving you, loving you, loving you, when I'm loving you…why would you wanna break up?"

Then one of my favorite parts came on. When Gucci began rapping, I started poppin' my ass a li'l faster while rapping his part, too.

"Now, baby girl done dumped me. She no longer wants me…"

The whole club was straight flippin' out. The center of the floor was full of people dancing. Me, Alize, Monique, and Shay turned around, positioned our hands on the wall, and started rolling our hips seductively like four strippers. The crowd of dudes beside us acted like they loved it. Shay was big-boned, but that didn't stop that heifer from doin' her thing and puttin' her dance moves in.

"Work it, Shay." I egged my girl on.

By now, Mario was bursting through the atmosphere. I started back singing, I kno' I be, I kno' I be, I kno' I be, saying I'll be right back…"

I heard a male's voice in my ear say, "Shake that shit, Li'l Mama." That really had my head on swole.

I dropped my phat booty to the floor and spiraled my hips back up not missing a beat. I was so caught up in the song that I didn't notice that dude was dancing behind me until, I felt him push his hard erection against me and rock to the beat. I enjoyed every second of his attention.

When the song ended, me and my girls turned away from the wall and pressed our backs against it. Some goons, standing a few feet across from us, were staring. I saw one of 'em motion his hand at me. I scanned his lips. 'Let me get yo' number.'

I just nodded.

"What's yo' name, boo?" The guy who I had been dancing with asked.

"Kay-Kay."

"Oh, okay, cool. I see you got a lot of dudes' attention up in here. How old are you?"

"I can't tell you."

"Why?" he wanted to kno'.

"Cause I ain't supposed to be in here," I admitted raising my voice over Beyoncé's tune, "Halo."

"So you must be under twenty-one?"

"Yep."

The blank expression on his face told me he was surprised.

"How much under twenty-one?" he grilled.

"I'm seventeen," I said. My lip was turned up as if to ask "so what?"

"Dude didn't card you at the door?" he asked, with a dumbfounded look.

"Nope," I lied.

"Oh, okay, I feel you. You and yo' girls want a drink?"

"Yeah," the four of us answered in unison.

"What do y'all want? They got Budweiser, Bud Lights, and some wine coolers."

"They don't have liquor?" I asked, sucking my teeth.

"Naw, they only have beers and wine coolers," he replied with a smirk.

"Okay, we'll take strawberry wine coolers."

"I'll be back in a sec," he said before heading to the bar.

Twenty minutes later, he came back and gave each of us an ice-cold strawberry wine cooler.

We stood chitchatting. "So where yo' man at tonight?" he pried.

"I don't have a man, and what's yo' name anyway?"

"Er'body calls me Killa."

"Killa? Oh shit. I'm scared of you. So what, you just go 'roun' killing mufuckas?" I made a face like a white girl in a scary movie.

He laughed. "Girl, naw. I kill if I have to, but naw I don't just go 'roun' killing mufuckas cause I want to."

Killa was fine. He appeared to be at least five-nine, one hundred seventy-five pounds, caramel skin tone, wearing a white Akoo polo and a pair of short black Akoo jeans. He was fresh to def 'til I got to his shoes. He had on a white pair of Air Force One's, and they were old and worn out. Nothin' turned me off more than a dude wit' a dirty pair of kicks on.

I took a few sips of my wine cooler and whispered to my girls that I wanted to go stand by the crowd of thugged-out looking dudes who were staring earlier. Before following up on that, I turned to the guy who had bought us the wine coolers and called out some phony digits, hoping that would be enough to send him on his way because I did not want him stuck up under me the rest of the night; I had grander dreams than what he looked capable of providing.

"So you about to leave?" he yelled out when I walked away.

"Not yet. We 'bout to post up somewhere else for a minute then we gon' leave."

" I'ma get at 'cha some time tomorrow."

"Cool," I told him and left his filthy shoes wearing ass standing solo.

We had to travel through a crowd of people just to get to where the dudes were standing. I wanted to get at the goon who wanted my digits, and I wasn't gonna give him a bogus

one, either. It was gon' be the real deal. As I was gliding through the crowd, some chick shoved pass me. It seemed like she did it on purpose.
"Excuse you," I screamed over the music.
The girl turned around. "Naw, excuse you," she said with attitude.
"Why the fuck did you bump into me like that?"
"Cause you was over there dancing wit' my baby daddy, Charles," she answered.
"Look, I don't kno' no damn Charles," I disputed.
"Don't play dumb. You was just dancing wit' him."
Then I knew exactly who the troll was talkin' bout. "You talkin' bout Killa?" I questioned, confused.
"Killa? That asshole name ain't no Killa. His name is Charles."
"Well, that's what he told me his name was. To keep it real wit' cha I ain't thinkin' 'bout that broke down raggedy bastard. I hope you don't think I want his whack ass."
"Don't even go there, cause you wasn't talking greasy 'bout him when yo' hot yella ass was over there twirkin' all up on him," she said waving her finger in my face. She was tore up from the floor up. I mean ugly, a straight chickenhead and she hadda ghettofied attitude to go with it.
"You betta get yo' finger out my face before I jaw you," I threatened and walked off before I caught a murder charge.
"What the hell is wrong wit' that busted up trick?" Alize asked trailing behind me.

"She said I was dancing with her baby daddy. She betta gon' and chill cause this ain't what she want."

Then I heard the slut yell, "Y'all two gon' be just like yo' crackhead mammy."

I froze, whirled around, and stepped back to her. The crowd suddenly made room for me to get through 'cause niggaz and broads love drama.

"Don't do me. You just mad that you're black, fat, and dumpy. You betta gon' head and fall back before you get dropped."

Her baby's daddy, Charles, came over and snatched her by the arm. "Don't be over here starting no shit!" he shouted over the music. He was all up in her face.

She jerked away from him and bellowed, "Let my goddamn arm go."

Charles didn't bicker back and forth with her, he released her arm and warned, "Now when you get your ass kicked, I'm not helping you because I've told you over and over again about clowning."

With that, he pushed on.

I jumped right in her face. I could smell the liquor on her breath. We were two female pits in skirts, about to pop it off.

"Y'all two bitches; you and yo' punk ass sister gon' be just like yo' dope-smoking, prostitute mammy," she bravely restated.

"You don't even kno' my mama," I argued.

"Oh yeah, I kno' yo' mama 'cause my brother's girlfriend lives in those low income apartments up the street on Wells. I've seen her and kno' exactly who y'all are."

I couldn't believe the boldness of that thing. She had no crew wit' her and was solo poppin' off at the mouth. I thought to myself, *This dummy gotta be wasted.*

"If you let one mo' word come outcha mouth 'bout my mama, it's on," I warned.

The female examined me from head to toe, smacked her lips and squealed, "Yo' mama is a nasty, crackhead ho." Before I could flex on her, Alize pushed me out the way. She shoved me so hard I stumbled. The next thing I knew, Alize punched the girl square in the face.

"Oh, hell to the naw," cried ole' girl. Her hand went to her nose to check for blood.

I gave her a devious smile and something else to check for, like my fist.

As soon as I went in her grill, all of my girls joined in the beat down, because that's how we rolled.

The girl fell down to the floor screaming, "Get up off me."

I kicked her in the head, stomach, and side. She curled up in a ball so I let the toe of my shoe chill. But my li'l' sis went in beast mode. She stomped on the chick's head with no mercy. Then she poured a wine cooler on her.

"Bitch don't know who she's messing with," Alize fumed.

The girl managed to struggle to her feet and we all attacked that ass like a swarm of bumblebees.

A half dozen bouncers ran over and pulled us off the girl. She was tore up. She had shoe prints all over her clothes and a big bump on her head.

We were still trying to get some more of that tore up behind, but the big swole bouncers had us restrained. They tossed us over their broad shoulders and easily carried us through the club.

Boo Man was at the door. "Hold up. What y'all doin' wit' my fam up in the air?"

The bouncer that held on to me responded, "They up in here fighting, bruh."

I interceded, "I'm trying to fight this funk. You need to tell yo' deodorant to hurry up and kick in 'cause it's in slow motion tonight." I stuck my lip up trying to inhale some fresh air instead of fresh onions. Big dude squeezed my leg while holding me above his head. I knew he was heated, but it was true, he smelled foul.

"Ouch. Stop squeezing my damn leg," I wailed.

"Man, don't be squeezing my li'l' cousin leg. Y'all put 'em down and let 'em all walk out," Boo Man urged.

The security team put each of us down, including the female we served some act right. Ole' girl looked like she was weak and hurting. Too unsteady to stand, she dropped to the floor harder than a two hundred pound bag of shit.

Boo Man mean mugged me. "What the fuck is wrong wit' her? Whatchu do to her?"

"Beat her down real good."

"For what?"

"Cause she was talking slick 'bout my mama."

Boo Man waved me off. "Girl, go head on wit' that and don't y'all come back up here no mo'. Kinfolks the worse mufuckas to deal wit'," he fumed.

"You kno' the Butler family gets ratchet when somebody comes at us sideways," I blurted with a cocky tone. "You got that same blood in you."

"Man, gon' go home, girl. Hurry up before y'all get in some mo' trouble. Up in here wit' all this damn fighting and shit," he advised.

All four of us bounced leaving that lame female behind. When we arrived home no one was there, so, we chilled out at my crib, laughing our asses off 'bout pounding that trick. Shay and Monique didn't leave for home 'til almost two in the morning and me and Alize drifted off to sleep on our own two sofas.

Boo Man called and woke me outta my sleep. "Cuz, y'all unleashed on ole' girl so bad security had to carry her to her car."

"That's what she gets for starting some drama that she couldn't finish. Deuces." I hung the phone up on Boo Man, let out a loud yawn and went right back to sleep. She started it and we ended it.

Always Some Shit
Kay-Kay

The next day er'body in the neighborhood heard 'bout our altercation at the club. I could hardly get any sleep because my phone kept ringing with calls from mufuckas wanting to know what happened.

I got up off the couch, where I had crashed last night, looking around on a Saturday morning for Mama. Normally, she was in her bedroom sleeping. So I crept through the house and noticed that Mama's bedroom door was closed. I knocked on the door twice. I didn't hear her respond so I turned the doorknob. To my astonishment, she wasn't in the bed, which was unusual. Even though she did her thing in the streets she always came back home in rain, snow, sleet, or hail. I began to worry.

I darted back in the living room. Alize wake up," I cried.

My li'l sister sat straight up scared to death because I had woke her up outta her sleep. We had stayed up talking until the wee hours in the morning, and both of us had been too tired to go to our rooms.

"What the hell?" she answered sounding like a frog.

"Mama ain't in her bedroom."

Alize wiped the sleep from her eyes. "You yelling like the po-po's 'bout to raid this joint. Calm down. She's good, she's prob'ly working overtime suckin' some nigga off fo' a rock," she commented waving me off.

I stood silent for a minute then turned and walked into the kitchen.

"Yeah, maybe she is, but most times she's home by now," I tried explaining while opening the refrigerator door in search of something to eat.

"Ain't 'bout to get myself upset worrying over her. For what? She don't give a fuck 'bout us. She would rather chase down a piece of crack than stay at home wit' us. And when she is at home, she up in here snappin' and cussin' all the time 'cause she's fiending." Alize's response came from the living room.

"No matter what she does she's still our mama." I didn't hasten to remind her.

"I'm like Harpo in The Color Purple. She ain't my mammy," Alize replied laughing hysterically.

"Girl shut up," I said cracking up along with her.

I reached in the back of the refrigerator and pulled out some eggs, bacon, and white bread for toast to get breakfast going.

"Whatchu 'bout to hook up back there in that kitchen?" Alize inquired.

"Why? You lazy and ain't gon' get up and help wit' it."

"Naw, I'ma eat it, though. You kno' cookin' ain't my thing."

"You ain't gon' never get a husband if you won't even try to learn how to cook." I cracked open four eggs open and poured them into the skillet. Then I started frying the bacon.

"Well, I guess I won't ever get one. This is the year twenty-ten anyway. Ain't nobody hardly slaving in a kitchen trying to cook fo' no man that's what Wendy's and all those fast food restaurants for."

"What?" I couldn't help giggling. "You gon' make yo' husband eat fast food every day?" I took the fork and started scrambling my eggs.

"Hell, yeah. Ain't gon' get him full as a tick so he can run out and fuck another bitch on a full stomach," she said and I shook my head.

"Alize, get up, and come fix yo' plate."

Just as I saw Alize get up, the front door burst open. In came Mama strutting through the door with her hair all over her head. A tall, medium build thug-looking nigga followed closely behind her. Mama was stumbling so I knew she was twisted.

Dude and Mama walked right past us toward Mama's bedroom. "What the hell you back there cookin' girl?" she stopped to ask.

"Breakfast you want some?" I replied, wondering who the nigga was that was with her.

"Hell naw. I been getting my drank on. That 2-11 got me right. I ain't trying to eat no food. It'll calm my high down."

"I'm starving like a mufucka," the guy interceded. "Whatchu back there cookin', li'l mama?" He began rubbing his stomach like he was starved out. I ignored him.

"Kay-Kay," Mama hollered. "Can you hear? Whatchu cookin'?"

"Toast, eggs, and bacon," I mumbled.

"Gon' hook me up," the dude begged.

"You got two hands and two feet that God blessed you wit'. Fix yo' own plate."

He walked in the kitchen and fixed a big plate leaving a small portion of food behind. Mama leaned against the living room wall. She was definitely drunk and she was grinning for no apparent reason.

"You took almost all of the food wit' chu. Don't be coming up in here trying to get yo' stomach full fo' the free. You shoulda went to a breakfast buffet somewhere," I yelled.

Mama interrupted, "Just fix some more, and shut up."

Alize rolled her eyes, expressing my feelings exactly.

"Whatever," I mumbled at Mama. She ignored my obvious attitude and led her company back to her bedroom.

I was tight about that but Alize seemed to pay it no mind. Mama's BS never bothered Alize like it bothered me.

Tears spilled from my eyes. Alize came into the kitchen and held me. I rested my head on her shoulder.

"Don't cry, big sis; we gon' be alright." She consoled me.

"I kno', but I'm tired of this shit. I'm tired of having a drunk and dope fiend fo' a mama and men coming in and out the house all the time. I'm just tired of all of it," I complained.

"It's gon' get one day Kay-Kay. We just got to be strong for each other."

"Yeah, I kno'," I sobbed.

An hour later, Mama and dude came outta her bedroom. Mama escorted him to the door and he bounced. I had finished my bowl of cereal when Mama flopped down on the sofa where I was sitting. Alize sat across from me watching television. Mama grabbed the remote and turned the TV off, placing her feet on top of the coffee table that sat directly in the middle of both sofas.

"Why the hell y'all ain't cleaned up, yet?" Mama called herself scolding us.

"I'ma clean up in a minute. The only thing I got to do is wash the dishes. I cooked, but barely ate any of it." I didn't have to remind her why.

"Why didn't you cook you some more if he didn't leave you enough?"

"I was scared he was gonna eat all of that, too."

"Why you keep whining 'bout that? That was my company and it's all good if he wanted to eat somethin'."

"Why different men always gotta be comin' in and out the house all the time. I get so sick and tired of that." My mouth was tight.

"Well, if you don't like what I do up in here then you can get out. It's just that simple. I'ma grown thirty-six year old woman, and you ain't gon' control my life and who I have running in and outta here."

"Do whatcha do then, but when somethin' jump off 'roun' here I hope I'm not in yo' crib."

"Ain't nothin' gon' happen in here and get up outta my business. I got this. You just get yo' tired ass up and wash them dishes."

I hopped up from the sofa and stomped my way in the kitchen pissed off. Alize followed. I washed the dishes and Alize mopped the floor while Mama sat her lazy behind on the sofa, chillin'.

Moments later, I heard several knocks. Mama got up, peeped outta the blind, and quickly stepped back from the window.

I could tell from her expression and body language that it was somebody that she wasn't pleased to see. "Who is it?" I whispered.

"Choppa," she murmured descending two steps away from the door.

"Dope-boy Choppa?"
"Yeah."
"Why he comin' to the door?" I pried.
"I owe him money."

Choppa knocked three more times and shouted, "Tammie, I kno' you up in here so if you don't want me to bust this mufuckin' door in you betta come to it."

Choppa was a twenty-five year old ghetto-superstar in the hood. He had come up in the dope game about a year ago. He had a trap around the corner from our house that did big numbers, so his name was ringing. He was tall, kinda buff, and very pleasing to the eye. And he wasn't the one to test. It was well known that Choppa went hard when it came to his dough. Anybody that owed him paid either his or her debt, or their family paid the undertaker. I understood, instantly, why Mama was stalling to open the door.

"Mama, just answer the door," I urged. Nothin' makes a hustler madder than when a fiend tries to duck when they owe 'em.

She stepped back up to the door and hollered, "Yeah, what's up, Choppa?"

"You kno' what's up. Where my duckets, Tammie?" he yelled from the other side.

"I don't have it right now, but you kno' I'm good fo' it. I'ma have it to you by tonight."

"You betta. Don't make me act a fool 'roun' these parts and don't be duckin' and dodging me either," he warned.

"I ain't dodging you. I gotchu, Choppa. Make yo' way back 'roun' here tonight."

"Aight, I'ma see how real you is."

"Aight, Chop."

I didn't hear Choppa say nothin' back, so Mama and I crept back to the blinds and saw him get into his dark blue Cadillac Escalade and drive off. Alize looked at us both, shook her head and plopped back down on the couch, covering her head with a blanket.

"Whew, that was a close call," Mama sighed.

"You could have gotten all of us killed. You kno' Choppa don't play. He'll murk you on everything I love. That dude is throwed off for real and you messing with his money?"

"I owe him a couple of dollars. I'ma holla back at him wit' his dough." She downplayed the debt.

"You betta if you kno' what's good fo' you," I advised.

"Will you shut the fuck up Kay-Kay? I got this shit you just go on to college and make something outta yo'self so you can do betta than me. That's what you do."

"Oh I kno' I'ma do betta than you, but I ain't going' to no college. College ain't for me."

"Oh yeah you goin' to college," she said as if she could run my life when she was doing a piss poor job of running her own.

"No, I'm not. I'ma just get me a job and move out yo' house, get me a car, and be happy." I walked back into the kitchen. I wanted to avoid an argument even though I knew the conversation was 'bout to blow up.

"You need to try to get an education, Kay-Kay, that's what's goin' to make you happy. People can take yo' house and yo' car, but they damn sho' can't ever take yo' education and knowledge from you. Do you understand?"

Blah, blah, blah, who gives a care 'bout whatchu talkin' bout. I began daydreaming about a nice place I wanted in the future. My place would be totally decked out with the nicest furniture, carpeted floors, and it would be peaceful. No dope boys knocking on my door threatening me. No loud smell of piss that hit my nostrils every time I opened the front door, and definitely no mo' drama like what happens in the hood. I wanted the finer things in life and I didn't need college to get 'em. All I needed was the right dude to come and sweep me off my feet and buy me whatever my heart desired. My train of thought was broken when mama interrupted.

"Kay-Kay, stop daydreaming and listen to what I'm trying to tell you."

"What, Mama?"

"Get an education," she pronounced slowly so that each word could marinate through my brain, like I'm special or something.

"I got this. I kno' what I'm doin' with my life. I got it all mapped out and I'ma be cool, I don't need no advice."

Mama threw her hands up in the air. "Aight, baby girl, since you think you so grown and you kno' 'erthang. I'm gon' let you fly through life with the mindset that you got, and watch where it lands you-flat on yo' back." Mama marched in her bedroom and slammed the door.

I realized that I was only seventeen and would prob'ly make some bad choices in life, but I figured my choices couldn't possibly be as terrible as the ones she had made. I most definitely wouldn't be a dope fiend with a cheap beer in my hand, believe that.

Same Thing, Different Day
Kay-Kay

It was seven o'clock on the dot and Mama started pacing the floor that night after her half of day nap. "I need some sweets. You and Alize go to the store fo' me," she called out from her bedroom.

I don't know why, but when dope fiends start fiending they usually crave sweets.

"Whatchu want?" I asked, stepping all the way up in her bedroom. The closer I got to her, the more she looked spooked and crazy as ever. Her eyes seemed to be bulging outta her head and her mouth was twisted.

"Get me a honey bun, some Laffy Taffy chews and a soda." Mama dug around in her pockets, pulled out some money, and handed me a ten-dollar bill. Normally she was broke because every dime she got a hold of was usually spent on crack. "Dude that came here earlier hooked me up wit' this," she explained, correctly reading the expression on my face.

I thought it was scandalous for her to bring a trick home and screw him with us in the house. I didn't see or hear her having sex, but I knew how she got down especially when she wanted to suck on her glass dick.

"Lemme get me some chips and a coke outta the change that's left?" I asked.

"Hell, naw. You gon' have to getta job 'cause I got somethin' to do later on."

I thought to myself, *You ain't got shit to do, but get high or die tryin'.*

"Dag, Mama. You can't let me get two or three dollars?" I scoffed.

"I told yo' ass naw one time, girl. Don't make me tell you twice. You seventeen- years old. Old enough to find you a job somewhere. Go to Mickey D's, Wendy's, or Checker's and getcha a job."

"Looks like I'm gon' have to go somewhere and earn some funds since you ain't trying to help me." I knew I had slipped up and said the wrong thing when she shot me a dirty look.

"I can't believe you fixed yo' mouth to say that to me after I raised you. You ain't got nothin', but a piece of a sorry daddy, but I don't see you tellin' him he ain't helpin' you."

"Cause he's locked up. That's why I ain't asked him fo' nothin'. You always flip the script on me. I asked you fo' two dollars and now you gettin' all dramatic."

"You damn right I'm getting dramatic because I sent yo' fast, hot ass to elementary, middle, and high school. I put food on the table and clothes on you and yo' sister back and now I'm through." She paused for a minute before she got hell in her again. "Sooner or later you gon' have to get a job and getcha own place or go to college 'cause I can't do yo' jazzy tongue."

I rolled my eyes. "Let me go on to the store for you." I just wanted to get outta that apartment and get some fresh air and a break from listening to her flap her tongue about me attending college.

"Hurry back wit' my stuff 'cause I'm finna be leaving soon as you get back."

"Aight," I said over my shoulder as I left outta her bedroom wondering why she couldn't just stop by the store herself if she planned to leave out soon.

I put on my all white Air Max with no socks and headed toward Lucky Seven's, the corner store over on 26th and Kilbourne. Alize came along.

Everybody loved Lucky Seven's burgers, chicken, and fish sandwiches. A black couple owned it named Mr. and Mrs. Taylor. I guess they were pro'bly in their late fifties. Mr. Taylor ran the cash register and Mrs. Taylor did all the cooking. Seemed like no matter what time a day or day of the week I came to Lucky Seven's, I would spot her in what looked like a small kitchen area behind the counter.

As we neared 26th I decided to share with Alize what was heavy on my mind.

"Sis, I'm gon' have to try to find my own crib. I'm tired of mama's bullshit. I don't kno' how I'm gon' do it, but I just kno' I got to before me and her bump heads."

"I kno' you ain't gon' just up and dip out on me and leave me there wit' her," Alize replied.

"Well, I ain't old enough to have guardianship over you. I ain't even old enough to get my own apartment. Hopefully, somethin' will come through soon and I'll have a game plan on getting me a crib."

There was a silence between us. I could tell by the look on Alize's face that she was saddened by me talkin' bout leavin' without her, and it hurt me just as much as it hurt her. I knew somethin' had to give. I could no longer stand to see my mama slowly deteriorate and dry up because of drugs.

I broke the silence. "I want you to finish school, and then if you wanna live with me you can. But I'm gon' have to move on to bigga and betta. I don't want to end up being just another hood chick living in low income, not doing shit with my life."

"Yeah, but you ain't gotta leave me behind. You can stay until I get outta school then we can leave together," she suggested.

"I don't kno' if I can last that long in that apartment, but I'll try. I been thinking 'bout taking a massage therapy class. It only takes about eight, no more than twelve months."

"Ain't that when you rub all over people's bodies and burn candles in the room and turn the lights down and play soft music?"

I giggled. "Yeah, pretty much."

"That's a freak's job. Do you rub their booty when you massaging them?"

"I don't kno'. But, I ain't gon' be rubbing on nobody's butt, not unless they pay me extra." I couldn't help it; I laughed at my own self. "I'ma up the price on 'em real quick if they question me on some rubbing they crack," I responded, while still laughing.

"When I finish high school I'm gon' enroll in a business course. I'd love to become a concert promoter/party planner/wedding planner. I love entertaining people and I kno' I have the artistic skills to come out on top wit' that kinda stuff. Whatchu think?" she asked.

"I think, you'll do good with all of it," I said.

"You gon' be proud of me, Big Sis when I getchu autographs from Li'l' Wayne, Plies, and all them rappers that's gon' show up at the parties? On the other hand, who knows? I may just become a teacher; I love kids." She seemed very undecided about what profession she would pursue but I believed that Alize would succeed at whatever she chose to do.

"Yeah, I'ma be proud of you. I'm proud of ya now," I said sincerely.

She smiled at me and I placed an arm around her shoulder and gave her a big hug.

We were approaching Choppa's trap spot. His Cadillac Escalade was parked directly in front of the house. Parked behind it was a jet black Charger sitting on twenty-fours with black tinted windows.

"Balling," I uttered, the same way Jim Jones rapped on his cd.

Alize burst out laughing. "You a nutcase."

"Girl, Choppa and his mans are caked up, they stay on the grind, trappin'."

"Twenty-four seven," Alize agreed.

Soon as the words rolled off our tongues, Choppa stepped outta the house and his eyes locked with mine. "Dag, he done spotted us, Alize." I didn't want her to see that I was scared, but I sho'ly was, specially when six of his goons came out behind him. All of 'em dressed in their dope gear, designer jeans, chains dangling low, and jeans sagging.

The sound of Gucci Mane's song, "I'm A Dogg" poured over into the streets from a stereo playing inside the house.

"What's up, Shorty, with that long wavy hair?" Choppa yelled out to me.

I looked his way, but continued walking.

"Yeah, I'm talking to you. Come holla at me."

Alize whispered, "You gon' talk to him?"

"I don't kno'," I answered.

"Hold up," he hollered.

Me and Alize stopped walking immediately. I watched while Choppa made his way down the steps and swaggered up to us.

All I could smell was weed and his cologne. I spotted a blunt in his right hand. He took a long puff off it, inhaled, and then slowly exhaled before he passed it to one of his boys.

"What up, ladies?" he said.

"Hey," both of us replied.

"Where you headed?" he asked staring into my eyes like he was trying to hypnotize me with his gaze.

"Lucky Seven's." I pointed up the street.

"Oh, aight. What's yo' name?"

"Kay-Kay."

He nodded. "I swear you look like Alicia Keys. Damn, shorty, you got a frame so tight, you'll stop traffic." He sweated me from head to toe. "I be seeing y'all come through here on a regular. Where you live?"

"Right around the corner. You came to our house this morning spazzing out."

He gave me a puzzled look. "You sho'?"

"Yeah. Tammie is our mama."

He nodded. "I hope you ain't feeling no kinda way about that but she does owe me some cheddar and I'm out here hustling trying to eat myself. You feel me?"

"Yep, I feel you," I agreed crossing my arms.

He turned his attention to Alize. "So what's yo' name, Li'l' Mama?"

"Alize."

"Alize, what a name." I saw him smile. "How you get that name?"

"It was one of my mama's favorite drinks," she admitted.

"It's all to the good." Then he redirected his attention toward me. "How about I come round there, and holla at chu sometimes?"

"Okay," I quickly agreed. Then I wondered if I had sounded too thirsty.

Choppa didn't seem to take my eagerness outta context. He was eyeing me like I was wifey material.

He asked, "When can I slide through to see you? I don't kno' yo' schedule and I don't want yo' man showin' up while I'm there."

I knew that was his way of asking if I had a man.

"I don't have a boyfriend. I only have friends," I said.

"You mean you just got a couple of dudes you fuck wit' when you feel like it, right? Niggas who cake you off?"

I put my hands on my hips and replied, "Now did I say anything like that? Ain't no nigga doing nothing for me...trust."

"I hear you, Shorty. But you're cute as hell; it's hard to believe that you ain't being sponsored by somebody."

"Well, I'm not."

"It don't even matter because I'm boss with my shit. A nigga ain't but twenty-three years old and gettin' that paper like a Big Dog. Got a laced whip, a fly crib, and stacks on deck," he boasted.

"That's good. Pretty soon I'm gon' have to find me a job so I can do big things. I recently graduated from high school so now I'm trying to find a job and move out on my own. You know....do grown woman things."

"If you get on a real dudes team you ain't got to work. That nigga will look out fo' you as long as you keep it one hunnid wit' him."

I popped my lips. "Well, I ain't found that dude, yet."

"Shid, you lookin' at him right here."

Alize interrupted, "Choppa, who is that wit' those dark blue shorts on?"

I turned to the house's direction to see who she was inquiring about and yes indeed the dude she was peepin' out was a cutie for real.

"That's my li'l' bro', Nine." Then he called, "Ay, Nine, c'mere. I got somebody that want to meet chu."

It suddenly occurred to me that Choppa and his brother Nine had been nicknamed after guns. But as long as they didn't use their choppa and nine on me I was good.

Nine walked over toward us with a blunt in between his fingers. "What up? Who wanna meet me?"

Choppa pointed to Alize then introduced her to Nine.

Nine took a long puff off the blunt and passed it to his brother. Choppa hit the stick of weed. He started coughing real hard, which told me that what was inside that blunt was some grown man.

"Are you okay?" I asked.

Nine burst out laughing. "That's that Purp. Nigga you ain't built for that shit, it's gon' fuck around and collapse your lungs.

Choppa beat his chest three times, trying to catch his breath. "Yeah, I'm good, Mama."

After about ten more seconds of him choking on weed smoke, he finally caught his breath and straightened up his composure trying to get his grown man on.

Choppa passed the blunt back to Nine who inhaled the smoke once again then turned to Alize. "You wanna hit this?"

"Yeah, I'll hit it. I ain't never smoked no weed before though."

I cut in before my little sis hit the blunt. "You sho' that's just Purp up in there?" I asked Nine.

"Hell, yeah. We don't lace our shit. We don't even get down like that, homegirl, if that's what you trying to ask me," Nine replied apparently offended.

"Just asked."

Nine gave Alize a shotgun and she too coughed like a fool for a couple of seconds.

"It's burning my damn chest. That's some strong shit," she explained between breaths.

Choppa asked if he could walk to the store with us and I readily agreed. We stayed in front walking while Alize and Nine lingered behind us talking.

"So, how much money does my mama owe you?" I asked Choppa outta curiosity.

"I really don't want to put her on blast since that's your mama and all."

"You didn't feel that way this morning when you were pissed off at her and talkin' loud."

"Business is business. Shit you kno' how that goes down. I'm out here trying to maintain just like er'body else. Sometimes I gotta step up my game and put people in check when they start fuckin' wit' my pockets, that's all. I gotta eat, too."

"True."

When we made it to the corner store, Choppa opened the door for me and I stepped in first. The smell of food cooking made me hungry as hell.

"Whatchu gotta get outta here?"

"My mama wants two honey buns and some Laffy Taffy's."

"Aight. Get her shit and get whatever you want, too," he offered.

"Okay, thanks."

I went through the store picking up bags of chips, ice cream, and candy. I got mama her favorite junk food. Me and Choppa made it to the checkout counter. Choppa pulled out his bank and paid for everything. He even ordered both of us a big hamburger and fries. I had never seen a knot that big in my life. That fat ass knot made my kitty tingle. I decided right then and there that I was gonna play my position and make him mine.

Nine paid for Alize's burger and fries, and then the four of us bounced.

"See you young folks later," Mr. Taylor said, smiling.

"Okay," Alize and I said at the same time.

Alize untwisted the cap off her bottled water and gulped it down like that was goin' to be her last drink.

"My mouth so dry and I feel like I'm walking on air. What's wrong with me?"

"You just high. Calm down and relax," Nine said and held her. "If you don't calm down you gon' get paranoid."

"My heartbeat is racing," Alize told him placing her hand over her chest, like she was scared.

"Just chill, baby. You aight," he tried to reassure her.

"Okay," said Alize though she didn't look as reassured as she tried to sound.

"You okay, Alize? You betta snack on somethin' to calm that high down before we get back 'roun' there with mama." I told her.

She ate a handful of fries.

"Yeah, just keep munching on them fries and you gon' be good," Nine said while smirking at her.

We got back up the street and stopped in front of Choppa's dope spot. "Shorty, I'ma go get back on my grind. What time can we fall through y'all crib?" asked Choppa, licking his lips like he couldn't wait to taste me.

I wasn't quite ready to take it there but neither could I take my eyes off of him. "How about eleven-thirty?"

"That's cool." He leaned in and placed his sexy lips against my cheek. "I'll get up with you tonight."

"That's fine."

To my left Nine was saying goodbye to Alize.

I ain't gon' front, I liked Choppa and I could tell that my li'l' sis was feelin' Nine. They told us they'd holla and we left heading home.

By the time we arrived home, it was almost dark. Mama sat on the end of her bed rockin' back and forth with her arms folded and legs crossed. Without saying a word, I passed her the bag of goodies along with the ten-dollar bill that she had given me.

"You didn't have to use it?" she asked grabbing her honey bun outta the bag.

"Naw."

"Why?"

"Choppa bought my food for me."

Mama popped her lips. "Humph. Whatever."

"Why you sayin' whatever?" I asked standing in front of her.

"I just said it. Did he mention anything about comin' around here tonight fo' his money?"

"Nope. But, he is comin' back round here to chill with me tonight. He's bringin' his brother to see Alize."

"Well, you need to work yo' mouthpiece and see about him reducing that bill I got," she said with a mouthful of honey bun.

"How do I work my mouthpiece?"

"Damn, through conversation. What the hell you think I'm talkin' bout?" She looked at me like I was as green as a fresh head of lettuce.

"I didn't understand what you meant by that. That's why I asked," I explained defensively.

"You having sex?" she blurted.

She had not asked me that since I first began growing hair on my kitty at twelve years old. "I have had sex before, why? I kno' you not 'bout to try to give me a talk about the birds and the bees." I giggled.

"I'm sure you already kno' 'bout all that by now. I'm 'bout to school you on some real deep shit." She looked around the room as if she had something to say that only the two of us needed to hear. "Where's yo' sister?"

"In the living room sitting down."

"Okay, now I can talk to you. Close the door."

I did as she instructed and waited to hear what was so hush-hush.

"Sit down," she whispered. She was acting like she was about to disclose to me information that would free us from poverty. I covered my mouth to stifle a laugh.

I sat down, pulled out my hamburger and soda outta my bag, and began eating.

Mama took a small bite outta her honey bun.

"Since you have made up yo' mind that you don't want to attend college you need to kno' that these li'l' penny paying jobs ain't gon' cut it. You a pretty, nice shaped young lady like I used to be and you got a blessing that every man gonna want."

I stopped chewing to listen intently.

"What's my blessing?"

"Pussy," she answered. "It can control the world and you got one so you betta learn when to use it. Don't give it up for free when there are sucka's lingering around who willing to pay."

My mouth was wide open trying to absorb what my own mother was saying to me.

"So you are sayin' that I should sell my body to get what I want outta life?"

"That's exactly what I'm sayin' to you." Mama put no cut on it but I was offended.

"I don't have to sell my body just to make it in the world." A frown was plastered across my face. *How dare Mama come at me sideways.*

"I'm not sayin' that you should just go around selling yo' body, but don't fuck wit' no lames who can't help you, when you got some out here that are willing to pay to play."

I let out a long sigh, rolled my eyes, and said, "C'mon, Mama, this is not an appropriate conversation to be having wit' cha daughter."

"I'm trying to give you the heads up on life and spit some knowledge in yo' ear. Sometimes we have to do bullshit that we don't want to do in order to survive and stay ahead. See, you think you kno' everything and can't nobody tell yo' hard head ass shit."

"I see where you comin' from, but you shouldn't encourage me to use my body to get ahead."

"You betta use it while you young and pretty, and these dudes want 'cha. Wish somebody had of told me all of this when I was yo' age. Instead, I had to learn the hard way. I stayed with y'all daddy when he got locked up and I was lost. I was always looking for love instead of juicin' dudes fo' they money then leaving them alone. Cause love don't love don't pay no bills, honey."

"Yeah, you right about that. But I want a family one day. I want to settle down with one man and live happily ever after."

"Gurl, you betta snap outta it. You live in a real world. This ain't the Cinderella story where you meet a Prince and live happy forever."

"It can happen if I believe in it," I argued.

"You so young and gullible," she voiced shaking her head at me. "You betta get wit' the program and stop actin' like you ride the short bus."

I didn't even respond to that. I finished off my burger and fries, stood up, and told Mama, "I'm done with the whole conversation. I'm not no trick."

"One day you'll wish you hadda listened to my advice. Wait until you realize that chasing love don't get you shit but a wet ass and some fatherless children," she retorted.

I wasn't trying to hear that off the wall shit she was talking. Therefore, I dismissed myself right up outta her room and strutted in the living room to check up on Alize. She was sittin' up on the sofa lookin' like she'd seen a ghost.

I walked over to her." Why you lookin' like a zombie?"

"Cause I'm high," she grinned.

Her eyes were red as a ripe tomato.

"You need to go lie down or try to eat somethin' else to calm that down."

She gestured for me to come closer to her. I made a couple of steps toward her.

"What?" I asked confused.

"Sit by me," she insisted and patted the seat twice.

"Sit by you for what?"

"I'm scared."

"Scared about what? Ain't nobody after yo' silly ass."

"I feel like it."

"You just trippin' out."

"I'm dead serious." She rubbed her belly. "I'm still hungry."

"You want some of my chips? I can go in there and get 'em from Mama."

"Yeah, go get 'em. I'm hungry as a hostage."

"You got the munchies, that's all." I got up, and went back to Mama's room and grabbed my bag of junk food off the bed. Mama was changing her shirt gettin' ready to hit the streets pro'bly.

She turned around lookin' at me. "Whatchu gettin' up outta here?"

"My bag that I left. You 'bout to go in a minute, huh?"

"Yep. I'ma try to get Choppa his money too while I'm out."

I knew exactly what that meant. She was goin' to turn a trick.

"Do whatchu do," I responded.

"If he asks you, tell 'em I'm trying to get him his money."

"You gon' fool around here and get hurt for not paying people what you owe 'em."

"I said I'm gon' try to pay him and you stay outta my business. I got this."

"Evidently you don't have it if he gotta run you down for it."

"Since you so concerned, why won't you get him to reduce my bill?"

"How am I gon' get him to reduce somethin' that has nothin' to do wit' me? Ain't in that. That's between y'all."

"But I'm yo' mama. You ain't gon' try to help me out?"

"How?" I asked annoyed.

"If yo' game was tight you'd have him eatin' out yo' hands. Peep game. Give that dude some good poo nanny, make him think you care for him, and start gettin' him to break you off wit' some dough."

"I just met him. I'm not about to lay down with him to clear your debt. And you should be ashamed of yourself for asking me to do something as foul as that. I cannot believe you!"

Mama shook her head at me like I just didn't understand.

"You got to get to kno' him first, play wit' his mind, then he'll pop through and slide you a li'l cake. Then, hopefully, he'll start feelin' you and throw me a li'l' sum, sum er' now and then." She cracked a smile. "Whew weeee, then

I can get high for free," she stated holding her head back with a smile like she was imagining gettin' high without paying for it.

I placed my hand on my hips disgusted. "I wonder what other parents give bad advice the way you give it to me. You sho' ain't a good role model."

"Tell me somethin' I don't kno'."

The alarm clock on her nightstand had 8:59 P.M. on it and there was only one minute 'til Mama would be leaving to walk the ho stroll. For me, it would be the perfect opportunity to get to kno' Choppa when he came over and I couldn't wait.

Stepping Out
Tammie

I stepped outta my apartment at nine o'clock that night. I shut the door behind me and tapped on Lacey's door. She lived two doors down from me, and we were both into the same fucked up things, and neither one of us was trying to get outta them. Crack had us too far gone for us to think about changing our lives, no matter how much hell we had to go through to support our addictions.

Each night we strolled up and down Wells Street turning trick after trick to chase a high that had stolen our dignity and self-respect. Nothing was beneath either of us when we were after those dollars that we needed to cop our next rock.

After my third knock, Lacey's twenty-one year old daughter, Monique, came to the door.

"Mama's in the bathroom, she'll be right out."

"Okay, that's fine."

"You wanna come in and wait for her?" Monique offered.

"Naw, I'm good. I'll just stand outside the door until she comes out."

Monique was brown skinned and ghetto thick. Her sister, Shay, wasn't quite as thick but she was very leggy, with a butt that was steadily rounding into an eye catcher. She was kinda cute and she had the prettiest white smile.

"What's Kay-Kay and Alize up to over there?" asked Monique.

"Girl, nothin'. Their asses supposed to be having some company come over."

"Oh, who's comin' to see them?"

"Some dudes they met today."

Monique gave me a huge smile. "Ooh wee, I'ma gon' have to get over there later and see who them niggaz is."

"I kno' one of 'em caked up." I was referring to Choppa.

"Ooh. Now them paper chasers gon' have to hook me up wit' one of the homeys."

"You betta be trying to find somebody that's gon' help you instead of hurt cha."

"I hear you on that," said Monique.

"Good. I'm glad somebody hears me. I tried to tell Kay-Kay that same thing earlier. She was up there talkin' some make-believe shit."

"Like what?" she burst out laughing. I guess she already knew that Kay-Kay had pie-in-the-sky dreams that only came true in the movies.

"She actually thinks that she's gon' fall in love wit' one of these niggaz 'roun' here and live happily ever after."

"What nigga she gon' find in this hood to live happily ever after wit'?" She raised her eyebrows and top lip. "Nobody 'roun' here. Trust and believe that."

"I tried telling her that. Y'all some young girls, so y'all betta work whatchu' been blessed wit' between them thighs."

"Humph. She betta wake up outta that dream. Trust. . . I work my nookie," Monique admitted.

"Shid. Yo' ass betta, girlfriend. Because er'body should know that love don't love no damn body."

"Sho don't," she agreed.

"I had to learn that the hard way. I been in the streets fo' a minute. So, it ain't too much a mufucka can run by me trying to be slick wit' out me catching on to it," I said rubbing my nose.

"Yeah, 'cause these dudes got a lot of game. That's why I ain't trying to be in love and get played."

"Yeah, it's either be used or be the user and guess what?"

"What?"

"I ain't trying to be used by no body."

"I kno' that's right, Tammie."

"That's how I survive these streets. I'm the user," I boasted.

By the time I finished my statement, Lacey made it to the door. She wore a pair of tight blue jean Capri's and a red tank top with red flip-flops. Lacey favored the way Whitney Houston looked when she was abusing drugs, same shape, and everything. Back in the day, Lacey and I were the finest chicks walkin' around, that is until we turned into fiends. Before I allowed crack to put me in a stranglehold, I was one bad bitch. Jasmine Guy, in her heyday, didn't have a thing on this right here. We had the same features, complexion, and exotic features but I could have loaned her some ass and still had plenty.

Lacey and I headed down the sidewalk to the ho strip between Wells Street and Kilbourne Streets. I was throwing my ass trying to catch some man's attention who would stop his car and pay for a date. Cars passed us while we walked, but to our disappointment, nobody stopped.

We made it up to the strip in no time. The strip was crowded with transsexuals, pimps, and ho's. There was no tellin' what you would see walkin' up and down this street.

"Bitch, you betta work yo' ass a li'l' mo' and make me some mufuckin' guap tonight. If you can't fuck then I can't eat, and if I can't eat then you need to be put to sleep," a pimp wearing a sky blue linen short-sleeved Burberry outfit yelled out to his ho. She was wearing a flamingo colored pink skimpy dress with all her back out and some pink stilettos. Her name was Delicious and her pimp was Gator.

Delicious rolled her eyes prob'ly thinking Gator didn't see her while poppin' the gum in her mouth.

Wam. Wam. Wam. Gator pimp slapped Delicious across her face.

"Dayum," I said aloud. It wasn't unusual to see the pimps chin check their hoes, but Gator had slapped the fire outta Delicious so suddenly that it startled me.

"Now get yo' ass up there by that stop sign befo' both of us end up at the hospital. You gon' be goin' to get this thirteen outcha ass, and I'm gon' be there telling the doctor to hurry up with you so I can get my shoe back," Gator shouted at Delicious.

Delicious held her mouth and slowly made her way down to the stop sign. She looked like she was embarrassed as hell.

"Speed the fuck up," Gator roared after kickin' Delicious in the ass.

Never uttering one word, Delicious sped up and made her way to the end of the street by the stop sign.

Three more of Gator's ho's were standing side by side, looking scared. They already knew what time it was. He was 'bout to go to actin' a fool on them.

Lacey and I moved off the sidewalk and let him deal with his stable. If a woman on the strip saw a pimp coming her way, it was a rule that a ho and a pimp couldn't walk on the same sidewalk or it was disrespectful to the pimp. If you were new to the game, and didn't kno' the rule, you'd wish you hadda when a pimp smashed you upside the head real good.

"What y'all bitches huddled up fo'? Scatter like roaches," Gator ordered his girls. Two went in one direction; the other two went in another.

The night started off slow for Lacey and I until a snow-white, new modeled, Impala eased alongside of us.

The car window came down on the passenger's side revealing a white mid-forties guy behind the wheel.

"Whatchu need, honey?" I asked him, smiling.

"How much for a blow job?" He had cold blue eyes with jet-black hair.

I approached the car window and leaned my head inside. He was wearing a suit.

"Twenty. You want me to do it, baby?"

"Yeah, hop in."

He unlocked the passenger side door. I looked over at Lacey. "I'll be back," I told her.

"Okay, be careful," she said.

"Alright, chick." I got in the car, closed the door, put my seatbelt on, and placed my purse on the floor.

Looking over at him, I questioned, "You ain't the police are you?"

"No."

"So, where you gon' take me?"

"I don't kno'."

"Go up the street and park in the alley," I suggested.

"Okay, honey. By the way, what's your name?"

"Destiny." I never used my real name.

"I'm Bruce," he told me.

Bruce didn't talk much. His eyes were dazed and scary looking. They showed no emotion and neither did he. I dealt with quiet men before so it didn't bother me.

We parked in an alley. Bruce turned the ignition off, leaned back in his seat, unzipped his pants, and pulled his small erection out. A newborn was pro'bly working with more than him.

"Take off your pants," I said.

He got outta his slacks and boxers. He may not have had much, but his testicles were big as tennis balls.

"Do I have to put a condom on?"

"You sho' do, unless all you want is a hand job. But I'm sure you want more than that," I responded. "And it's going to cost you twenty dollars but it'll be well worth it, baby." I plastered a sweet smile on my face.

"How much will you charge to suck me off raw?"

"Oh, no. None of that. The condom protects the both us." I was a fiend but I knew betta than to trick off without protection.

"What if I give you a hundred dollar tip?"

"No. It's either a condom or I can't do it." He was really starting to work on my nerves.

"Dammit," he growled reaching down in his pants. Opening up his wallet, he snatched out a condom. He quickly tore the condom outta the wrapper and rolled it down his shaft.

"Uh, just a minute, sweetie. I have to get paid first." Experience had taught me to get my money before doing anything. I took my seatbelt off, leaned over, and started giving him some neck.

"Damn, baby," he moaned.

I sucked harder, while sliding my hand up and down the length of him.

"Aawwwww. Shiit," he moaned, busting after just a few minutes. Then he placed his hand on mine. "Now, I want some cunt."

"Okay, that will only cost you forty mo'."

"That's fine. I have forty dollars."

"Okay give it to me now," I insisted.

Bruce gave me the money outta his wallet and lodged it back under the seat. I unzipped my black short pants, and pulled them down and revealed my neatly trimmed pussy. I didn't have a lick of drawers on.

Bruce replaced the old condom with a new one. "Get on my backseat," he instructed after wrapping up.

We both climbed onto the backseat of his Impala.

"I want to bang you from the back," he declared with a smile that showed slightly crooked teeth.

I bent over on the back seat, raised my hips in the air, and spread both of my legs. Bruce dived into my wetness pumping hard on my butt cheeks. I was happy that he was enjoyin' his self with all the moaning he was doing, 'cause the only thing I was feelin' were his big balls hittin' up against me. That li'l dick he was workin' with wasn't doin' nothin' but slippin' outta my insides every chance it got. I was wonderin' if he had a girlfriend or a wife. Whichever one he had, I knew she had to be gettin' some sexual relief from some other source besides him. That li'l' Oscar Meyer wiener he toted around was just sad and pitiful. I was actually laughin' on the inside.

He was pumpin' on my ass cheeks hard when his penis fell out again, for what had to be at least the fifth time.

Frustrated he said, "Damn, we got to try something else."

I turned my head slightly to the side still in doggy style position. "I don't kno' what else you could wanna try. Pussy and head 'bout all I can offer."

"No, you have an asshole," Bruce corrected me. But he had to be losing his mind if he thought I was goin' for that. I had done many things in my lifetime but not that one.

"Don't nothin' go in my backdoor. The only thing that comes out is shit. If you wanted anal sex you shoulda picked up a homosexual rather than a female 'cause I ain't the one," I yelled.

I made an effort to rise up, but he quickly pushed me back down on my elbows.

"Give me some service. I already paid you your fucking forty dollars. I want my money's worth."

"Mufucka, if you don't getcha ass away from me I'm gon' be all over you like flies on a shit pile," I forewarned. I was ready to knock the hell outta him.

Wam. My head dropped. He had socked me in the back of the head so hard that I heard ringing in my right ear. It felt like I had been cracked over the head with a baseball bat.

I felt his finger probing at the entrance to my ass hole. "Ughhhh."

He forced his hard little dick in my rear-end. My hole burned something awful. In my back hole, his miniature shaft felt as huge as a log. He pumped harder and faster. The pain caused me to grit my teeth. I squeezed my eyes shut, in an attempt to endure the pain, while bucking like a wild horse and trying to throw his psychotic ass off me. But it was a futile effort because he had me in a vise grip-like hold.

I clenched my teeth and adsorbed the humiliation and pain.

It wasn't long before I felt him stop thrusting his hips forward. Next, he started panting like a bear. "Ooh yeah, baby this is some good brown ass, "he exclaimed. " Ooh yeeeaaahhhh."

He peeled the condom off and shook droplets of semen all over my ass, before collapsing on top of me with his full weight.

I patiently laid there waiting for him to get up. I had a trick up my sleeve for him doin' me dirty. He was playin' wit' the right bitch.

The Beginning
Kay-Kay

It was around midnight and Alize's high had worn off. We both showered and put on our smell goods and sat up in the living room for two hours waiting for Choppa and Nine to show up. It took me thirty minutes to flat iron my hair to get all the waves out. We waited while listening to the radio. I wore some short white booty shorts with a pink tube top. My jeans were tight, gripping my frame with no room to spare. Alize wore a long, fire-red fitted sundress with matching flip-flops. We both were looking cute. Even though Mama did her thing in the streets she made sure, we had nice clothes outta the money she received from her welfare check every month.

Just as I was beginning to grow tired of waiting on Choppa and Nine to arrive my spirits were uplifted by a knock on the door. I jumped up off the sofa and hurried to the door.

"Who is it?" I asked as if I didn't already kno'.

"Choppa."

I looked back over my shoulder and winked my eye at Alize. She smiled and winked back.

"Open the door," she said in a low tone.

I opened the door and the scent of marijuana hit my nostrils hard. Choppa and Nine were positioned on the side with red eyes. I knew they both were high. Nosy ass Monique and Shay opened their apartment door cheesing at us. They both waved. I knew they were just trying to see who was at our door.

"Hey, y'all," said Monique, grinning like she had busted us up to no good.

"Heyyyy," sang Shay.

"Hey," Alize and me greeted back, and then Monique and Shay closed their door.

"Come on in, y'all," I told Choppa and Nine. Choppa stepped in first and Nine followed.

Choppa sat on my empty sofa and Nine sat by Alize.

I closed and locked the door behind them and sat down by Choppa.

"What's good, Ma?" he asked.

"Not much. We just been watching TV and waiting for y'all to show up. Yo' girlfriend must of finally let' cha out the house?" I joked.

"Naw. Never that. You kno' I'm a certified street nigga so I get tied up sometimes. You nah what I mean?"

I nodded. "Yeah, it's cool. Make that money, baby."

"Oh, yeah. If it's some to be made I'ma make it. Believe that."

"By the way, Mama said she's goin' to try to get 'cha yo' money."

"Aight," he said with no expression.

I was looking at him wondering what he would do if Mama didn't get him his money soon. Would he give her a pass now that he and I had met? Not likely, I concluded based on all the rumors I had heard about him.

"Why you staring at me?" he asked.

"Because you're nice to look at."

I was blushing and twirling my thumbs.

Across from us on the other sofa, Nine had Alize smiling so wide it was a wonder her face didn't crack. I overheard a few of his lines; the boy's mack game was official. Before long his arms was around Alize and he was gently sucking her bottom lip. They were getting it in and that made me feel that I needed to step it up a notch. I couldn't let my little sister have all the fun.

I leaned close to Choppa and cooed, "Umm, you smell so good." I was hoping that he would turn up the heat from there, and he did not hesitate.

"You smell good too, Ma. But a nigga wanna see how you taste." He traced my lips with his thumb while staring into my eyes with his baby browns, and then he licked his thumb as if he was savoring my flavor. He was smoother than silk sheets.

Just ten minutes into our first date and I was already his. He just hadn't received the memo yet, but it was on the way. Typically, Choppa wasn't my type. He was dark skinned, tall, and a bit diesel. I liked my dudes a bit lighter and slightly thinner. It was okay though, 'cause his swag was a million and his cheddar wasn't far behind.

He placed my hand in his and brought it up to his mouth. He eased his tongue between two of my fingers and flicked it like it was my G spot.

I blushed. "You so freaky. Stop playin'."

"I'm dead ass serious. A nigga can't wait to make your body quiver."

We were interrupted when his cell phone began ringing. "What it do?" he said into the phone. He listened for a few minutes, ended the phone call without saying a word, then shoved the cell phone down in his front pants pocket.

"You gotta go?" I asked, affecting a pout.

"Naw. I'm straight. That was my ole' lady. She didn't want nothin'."

"What? You didn't tell me you had a woman." Surprise and disappointment was heavily in my tone. I saw Alize and Nine cut their eyes over to us.

"Naw, boo it ain't like that. We on bad terms. She gon' be movin' out real soon 'cause we can't get along."

"You should be over there wit' her trying to work that situation out. I don't wanna be the mistress. I'm trying to be the main girl," I said with a tsk.

"Don't trip, Ma. It's all good. I'm here witchu, ain't it?"

"That don't mean nothin'. What matters is where you lay your head at night." My lip was turned up.

"So whatchu sayin', you want me to bounce?" he challenged.

A part of me wanted to say, *"Hell, yeah."* But, the other part of me wanted to kick it with him regardless of him having a woman at home. She must not have been handling her business or he wouldn't have been cupcakin' me.

"You're good. I just wish you had told me that you have somebody when we first talked," I said.

"You didn't ask. Anyway, never concern yourself with the next chick. All you gotta do is be real with a nigga and hold him down, and the next bitch won't even matter. That's real talk."

"Yeah," I said in a dry manner.

Choppa held my hand. "Trust me, Shorty, I'm not blowing smoke up yo' ass. I'm stepping to you on some real shit. I need a thorough girl in my life. You wanna claim that crown, all you gotta do is show and prove."

"Aight."

I mean, what else was I supposed to say? He was right because if what he had at home was satisfying her man like she was 'pose to then he wouldn't have been looking up in my pretty face.

He used his index finger to turn my head toward him.

"Whatchu thinkin' bout, boo?" he asked gazing in my eyes making me weak.

"You."

"What about me?"

Before I could respond to that question, he leaned in, and started kissing me. His tongue deliciously tangled with mine. My whole body instantly began to heat up. I loved it when a nigga knew how to kiss, because that was a hint that he was prob'ly skilled with his tongue in another way as well.

"Ugh. Y'all need to take that shit to yo' room, Kay-Kay," Alize teased.

She hadn't said nothing but a word. I sucked on Choppa's tongue a while longer, and he licked his lips in that sexy way of his when we ended the kiss.

"Let's go in my room so we can have some privacy," I said.

Choppa wasn't about to protest. The bulge in his pants told me that he was down with my suggestion. I hadn't made up my mind if I was going to let him hit it or not, but the thought was on my mind as he followed me to my bedroom.

"Ooh, y'all gon' get in some trouble back there," Alize called out.

"Don't be a hater," I called back to her. My voice was light with laughter.

Inside my bedroom, Choppa looked around. I had no ideas what he was looking at. I was glad that I kept my bedroom clean and neat because no man wants a nasty woman, and first impressions mean a lot.

Choppa sat down my bed. I went and closed my bedroom door then sat down beside him.

My bedroom was decorated in lavender and white; lavender and white comforter, pillowcase, curtains, shams, and sheets.

We sat on my bed talking about our lives, goals, and dreams. I enjoyed his conversation. I no longer saw him as just another dude driving a fly ass whip trying to play me outta some pussy. Yeah, he was known fo' being 'bout his paper in the streets and playin' no games to get it, but he also had another side to him. If half of what he said was true, he was sweet and loving underneath that cold exterior that he had to have in his line of business. I could see myself falling hard for him. He was a thugged out nigga with some compassion.

After sharing conversation, we kissed and cuddled. Choppa attempted to undress me, but I stopped him. "I'm sorry but I don't want to move too fast," I said tenderly.

"It's all good, Ma. You ain't gotta come off no ass to keep my interest. Just let me hold you. Damn, you soft as hell," he said holding me tight.

My kitty needed two big ass blocks of ice to cool it off. I wanted him. I just didn't want him to think I was the average female that he had been dealing with and give up my goods too fast, which were prob'ly the type of hoodrats he dealt with daily. If I wanted him to be mine I needed to prove to him that I was worthy of being his new woman and he could dump his woman at home. Soon, I'd have to put claims on him, I told myself as I feel asleep in his strong arms.

Sweet Revenge
Tammie

Bruce had been slapping me around on the back seat of his Impala for an hour. I had been beggin' him to let me outta the car for the longest. I had been choked; sucka punched, and threatened more times than I could remember.
"Please let me go. Please," I begged." I have two daughters at home."
"Don't say another word, you black whore."
He snatched me by the hair and pulled my face inches from his. "I hate you good for nothin' women. You all are nothin' but garbage. All of you deserve to be treated like the low-lives that you are." His eyes were full of hatred.
"I haven't done nothin' to you to be treated this way," I cried out.
"Didn't I say hush all of that goddamn noise up?"
I decided to try to comfort him and make him talk about whatever problems he was experiencing in his jacked up life that caused him to go haywire.
Trembling and afraid I asked, "What's wrong, Bruce? What in yo' life has you so angry?"
"Women. We men screw up giving you sluts our hearts and souls and you all turn around and break it."
He turned my hair a loose, and stared at me with a look of death. Whatever woman damaged his mental and left him made him take his frustrations out on me. Here I was

taking the ass whoopin' that she shoulda been getting.

"Baby, I'm not whoever hurt you. I'm sorry she did whatever it was to you that she did. There are plenty mo' fish in the sea. You ain't gotta give up." I wiped a tear from my eye. "I've been hurt before, too. Your heart is not the only one that's been broken. You just need to move past her."

He shot me a grin. Then. . . wham! He punched me dead in the face. My vision became blurred. I cried out for help. That seemed to infuriate him.

His face became a pink mask of hatred. "Just like a whore. Tryin' to play head games with me. You don't kno' anything about me. I can't just up and move at the drop of a hat. I was with her for ten years. She up and left me, took my kids to go marry some nigger."

I was mute.

"Whatchu gotta say about that, bitch?" he screamed.

I was crying and quivering too bad to respond. He raised his fists up as if he were about to swing off on me again. Quickly, I threw my arms up to protect my face. Just as he was about to punch me again, he froze, stared at me, and dropped his fist into his lap.

"I'm not goin' to keep beating the heck outta you. You aren't the woman who hurt me," he said. I wondered if this mufucka was bipolar. In a flash, and for no rhyme or reason, his anger seemed to dissolve.

A few seconds later he said, "I'm goin' to take you home, Destiny. I'm sorry."

"Thank you," I whimpered. *And thank you Lord above.*

We got in the front seats. I rushed to put my clothes back on, got dressed and reached for my purse lying on the floor. Bruce dressed as well. He started his ignition then put his seatbelt on.

I discreetly slid my hand in my purse.

"Where would you like to be dropped off?" he asked.

"The same place you picked me up."

"I'm sorry about all of this. Please forgive me."

I was gonna forgive his ass alright. It was because of slime tricks like him that I never hit the strip without protection. Even when I was down to my last penny and fiending bad, I never sold my little friend that was inside my purse. My hand came outta my purse just as discreetly as it had slid in. I aimed my twenty-five milli toward his chest.

"You sick bastard!" I gritted my teeth as flashes of what he did to me ran through my mind.

His eyes bulged at the sight of the gun. "I'm sorry, sweetie. Just put the gun down and let's talk about it."

My hand trembled. I hadn't ever shot anyone. A sharp pain came from my rectum, sealing this mufucka's fate. I squeezed my eyes shut and pulled the trigger. I pulled it repeatedly until all I heard coming from the gun was a clicking sound. When I opened my eyes, his head was slumped against the steering wheel and the horn was blaring continuously. I could see blood all over him and the driver's seat. My heart pounded fast. I fought to control my breathing. Quickly I reached over his body and searched for his wallet. I found it underneath the driver's seat. I put it inside my purse and bolted.

It was two o'clock in the morning when I unlocked the front door to my apartment. Alize was sleeping on one sofa. Nine was sleeping on the other. They woke up looking startled when I shut the door behind me. I didn't mind my girls having company, but overnight company was a no-no. If I hadn't been traumatized from what had happened a few hours ago, I would've raised pure hell.

"Wassup?" I greeted them. I was trying to act normal, despite having killed a man earlier. The crack that I had smoked after running away from where I left the trick nodded, had somewhat calmed me down.

"Nothin'," Alize said sitting up yawning.

Nine sat up. "Excuse me for laying up on yo' furniture. I dozed off before I knew it."

"You can lie back down," I said.

"Dag, Mama, what happened to you?" Alize asked after she noticed the marks all over my face.

"Oh, nothin'. I got to fighting wit' some female over her nigga," I lied.

"She beat you up bad, Mama. Where that ho at?" asked Alize.

"Watch yo' mouth, girl," I cautioned.

"I'm 'bout to go handle her. Where she at, Mama?" Alize rose up off the sofa.

"Girl, I took care of everything. Sit yo' behind down," I said waving her off. "It's nothin'. Where's Choppa?"

"In Kay-Kay's room," Alize answered.

"I walked over to Kay-Kay's room, and knocked twice before I opened her bedroom door. Her and Choppa were laying on top of the covers asleep. I turned the light on. They both woke up and squinted hard before they sat up.

"Wassup, Mama? We ain't doing nothin'. We both fell asleep."

"That's cool." I reached in my pocket, counted out two hundred dollars, and handed it to Choppa to pay off my debt.

"Aight," he said before counting it.

I stood while he flipped through each bill until he saw that it was accurate.

"'I sho' 'preciate that, Miss Lady."

"No prob."

Kay-Kay asked, "Mama, what happened? Why you all black and blue up under yo' eye?"

"I got into a brawl wit' a skank. I'm good," I tried convincing her.

"Who is she and what y'all was fighting for?"

"Something involving her man, that's all."

"Looks like she got the best of you."

"Please. She's just as hurt as me. I knocked her 'cross her head a couple of times."

"Do you want to go to the ER? You sho' you okay?"

"Yeah, I'm straight."

"I see you been doin' yo' thing tonight. You got a pocketful of money. You rob a bank?" Kay-Kay asked.

"Girl, naw." I looked over at Choppa. "Step outside the door and let me holla at chu on the business tip."

"Holla at him about what?" Kay-Kay butted in.

"None ya."

"What. . . ever." I'm sure she knew that I wanted to cop some drugs from Choppa.

"Don't whatever me."

She rolled her eyes and looked off. Choppa raised up outta the bed and we stepped out in my hallway.

"Wassup witcha?" he asked half sleepy.

"I need to touch down. I hope you have something with you."

"Nah, but I can make a quick run. Look like you already right," he observed.

He was correct but after what I had done, I needed to get higher than the clouds.

"Go and get me something."

I reached in my purse, counted out two hundred dollars and gave it to him.

He ducked his head in Kay-Kay's door, "Ay, I'ma be right back. I gotta make a quick run."

From the doorway I saw Kay-Kay make a face like she was about to protest but she said nothing. Choppa headed towards the front door.

I went in my bedroom, laid down on my bed, and retrieved Bruce's wallet from inside my purse. His driver's license read, Bruce L. Lucas. I looked further and discovered a business card, which had a cross on it and read, *We welcome you to come as you are. God is continuing to answer prayer. Psalm 23: The Lord is my shepherd I shall not want.* At the bottom, it had Deacon Bruce L. Lucas, St. John's Baptist Church.

Oh my God, I thought, *I murdered a deacon.* Behind the card was a picture of him, a woman favoring Tyra Banks, and two biracial young boys. I rose up, opened my dresser drawer, which stood by my bed, and pulled out an old white shirt. I wrapped the wallet in it and tossed it in my wastebasket in my room.

"Kay-Kay," I shouted.

"What?" she answered from her room.

"Come here for a second."

"What's wrong?" she asked after opening my room door.

"Take this garbage out to the dump for me."

"Now? Can't wait 'til later? It's almost three o'clock in the morning," she whined.

"Get yo' sister and Nine to go with you," I suggested.

She grabbed the bag and left out with it. I laid back down wondering if I would be arrested later or if I had gotten away with murder.

Bring It Bitch
Kay-Kay

I wasn't slow. I knew Choppa had left to go get drugs to sell Mama. Often, her drug use bothered me. Unlike Alize, I couldn't just brush it off. I always felt that the things she did reflected on me. At the very least, it embarrassed me. And when she was high it was always something extra with her. Like, why was it so important for me to take her wastebasket outside to the dumpster at this time of morning? I didn't even want to know. I just took the shit on out there without questioning her.

Returning to my bedroom, I plopped down on my bed and sighed as I reached to turn off the lamp on the nightstand. My hand brushed across Choppa's cell phone. I picked it up, about to scroll through his text messages and see what other bitches he had been singing sweet music to. Before I could get all up in his business, the phone rang.

"Hello," I answered in my seductive tone.

"Who is this?" asked a female, sounding vexed.

"Who you wanna speak to?"

"Put Choppa on the mufuckin' phone."

"I can't do that, boo boo. Presently he's busy." Yep, I was being messy as hell.

"Tell that nigga he betta get on this damn phone before I come over there and peel his wig back," she threatened.

"How you gonna do that, Boo Thang? You don't even know who I am or where I'm at. And if you did, you'd get murk'd out."

"Where you at?" she demanded to know.

"Where I'm at, that's where I am. Trust me, you don't want what I got fo' you."

"Yeah, I want it. Tell me where you at ho so I can come get some."

"Now, see I was gon' tell yo' stupid ass that he went after somethin' and he'd be right back 'til you called me out my name. So now when he come back, I ain't gon' tell him you called at all," I said while rolling my neck as if she could see me.

"You ain't got to tell him 'cause I'ma keep callin' 'til he picks this phone up."

"You gon' be hittin' him all night then, because I'm 'bout to turn this phone off. Now lay there and pull your cheap ass weave out while I ride his dick all night. And whenever he makes his way back to you, remember that your ass is gettin' sloppy seconds."

"Bitch, if I ever find out who you are, I'ma mop the streets with that ass. You betta make sho' you keep yo' running shoes on."

"Oh, they stay on. . .because thoughts of me be running through Choppa's head all day long."

I disconnected before she could reply with something slick of her own. *That nigga ain't nothin' but a dog like the rest of them. Prob'ly sold Shorty Girl that same sweet candy he whispered in my ear.* I shook my head, placed Choppa's phone back on the nightstand, and waited for his black ass to return.

High As A Kite
Tammie

Just when the soles of my feet started burning, from pacing back and forth, Choppa returned with my package. I licked my dry lips and bounced from foot to foot as he went inside the pocket of his hoodie and handed me what had become my solace.
"Do yo' thing."
"Oh, I will. Don't worry 'bout that."
He closed my room door and left.
Looking up at all that dope he had gave me, made me happier than a sissy in a dick factory. I opened my purse, pulled out my crack pipe, put my crack pieces in and it was on. I blazed up, took a long pull off it, and felt like I was on top of the world. Dayum. I smoked piece after piece, after piece.
Just as I was about to start on the rest of what I had left I heard Choppa and Kay-Kay in the hallway outside my bedroom shouting at one another.
"These fuckas will mess up a wet dream. Shit," I said, then snatched open my door and stormed into the middle of their chaos.
"Wait one minute," I told them. "I got neighbors. Y'all kno' good and well y'all can't be carrying on like this. Now what's goin' down?"
"She know what the fuck she did," replied Choppa. The scowl on his face was etched on stone. I was praying that Kay-Kay hadn't done anything stupid like go in his pockets.

"Girl, what the hell did you do?" I questioned her. I was agitated that they had disrupted me.

"He left his cell phone on the nightstand while he went to get some drugs to sell you. Some girl called his phone, I answered it and told the skank a thing or two," Kay-Kay shamelessly admitted.

"Why did you that?"

"'Cause I wanted to."

"You betta calm yo' voice down," I shot back

"What. . .ever," she muttered clanking her tongue.

"That was just plain messy," scoffed Choppa. His brows were knitted.

Giving Kay-Kay a severe look I told her, "You kno' you wrong."

"No, I'm not. He left it in my room. Whatever is in my room is not private to me. I can go through whatever I please."

"Kay-Kay, just be quiet." I threw my hands up walking off. "Y'all two pipe blockin'."

"I'm sorry. You right I was outta order for doin' that," Kay-Kay said to him. She turned to me, "Mama do you mind if he spends the night?"

"Hell, he might as well and it's not night it's close to four o' clock in the morning."

"I can't go home tonight after she just did that grimey shit," Choppa said.

"Do what you do. I'm trying to get right," I yelled back and slammed my bedroom door. I hoped like hell they would calm down and stop trippin'.

I picked up where I had left off wit' my crack pipe in hand and lighter in the other. I was gon' get my smoke on. Or, so I thought.

Wet As Water
Kay-Kay

I promised Choppa that I wouldn't answer his phone again, and he calmed down. "I'm sorry for being nosey and for gettin' you in trouble," I added.

"I ain't trippin' that she ain't my bottom bitch no mo', but if you gon' be on my team you gotta learn to respect my shit," he said, wrapping his strong arms around me and easing me down on the bed.

"I'll do that, just don't try to play me."

"Never that, Ma. Watch how I'ma treat you. Like I told you, ol' girl is about to be out."

"I'ma see," I said as he pressed his body down on top of mine, kissed me, and slid his hands under my top.

My nipples hardened at his touch and my kitty jumped against his thigh. This nigga had a way about him that had me gettin' goose pimples all over. It wasn't long before my clothes were strewn on the floor.

When he laid me back down on my pillow, and began playing a melody across my nipples with his tongue, I thought my hair was about to catch on fire. I felt his soft lips travel down my body and come to rest at my moistened vee.

"Hold up, Choppa," I said.

"What's wrong?" he asked gently. Even that got me hotter. The way he could be so damn mean one minute then gentle the next.

"I don't want you to feel like I'm like all the other foot draggers that be tryin' to get at you. I really do like you."

"I like you, too, baby girl. If I wasn't feelin' you I wouldn't be wasting yo' time or mine. And I damn sho wouldn't be about to taste your pussy. Best believe I'm feelin you," he said with what sounded like sincerity.

"I'm diggin' you too, boo." I started feelin' all mushy on the inside. It felt good to hear him say that he was feeling me.

"Lay back then so I can show you how much I'm into you."

I laid back. The feel of his tongue pressed against my clit brought chills down my spine. I have to admit; he knew exactly what he was doin' with that tongue of his. His head game was the best. He was sick wit' it. Up and down, right to left, in and out, his tongue went all over my secret spot. The faster it began to move, the more the feeling of pleasure moved through my body. Like a volcano, I exploded busting off in a matter of minutes.

"Ooh, baby." I let out loud enough for him to hear, yet low enough that nobody else would. I laid there exhausted from the strain of that orgasm he had helped me get. I mean, a bitch was straight out tired, but my pussy was still jumping like a kangaroo.

He stood up, stripped outta his gear, and laid back down. He kissed my lips; slowly he made his tongue slide to my left nipple; taking his precious time, he teased it. He then slid his tongue across my chest making his way to my right breast, sucking on that nipple as well. The warmth from his mouth made my nipples hard as concrete.

I moaned, closed my eyes, and enjoyed the pleasurable sensation my body was receiving. He climbed on top of me. His bone hard erection drummed against my leg while he kissed my earlobe.

"I want you baby," he murmured in my ear.

"I want you, too."

I felt his hardness anticipating my entrance and I damn sho' wanted to feel every inch of him.

"You want this wood inside you?" he asked. Before I could answer, he inserted his firmness.

In and out slowly, he went taking his time. He turned sideways on me, hitting my walls and touching the bottom. He was big and thick, and filled me. Each time he threw the dick to me, I threw my hips back 'til he grunted. He went deep and made it hurt so good. Then he pinned my legs back and showed me that he was that nigga.

I felt his thrusts becoming faster so I knew he was about to bust. My juices erupted for a second time. "Oh my god," I cried out.

Choppa pulled outta me and shot cream all over my stomach.

He softly kissed me on my lips and asked, "You think you ready fo' a nigga like me?"

"I'm ready fo' you if you ready fo' me. I can be yo' ride or die chick. If you wanna take this to the next level, I'm down with it."

"We gon' see just how far you'll ride fo' me. I need a female who gon' be 'bout stackin' them chips like me and willing to get it by any means necessary. Nah mean?"

I nodded. "I'm all of those things, baby. You'll see."

He rolled off me. I got up and peeped in the hallway. All of the lights were off, except for the light in Mama's room. Alize was pro'bly in her bedroom with Nine because her bedroom door was closed, and the living room area was empty.

I slipped to the bathroom and washed off; got a rag for Choppa; soaped it up and brought it back to him. He insisted that I wipe his dick off. I got the rag and cleaned him off. I laid in his arms as he held me. At that moment, I knew that I'd soon fall in love with him. It felt as if we were meant to be. His touch was soothing and comforting. I wasn't able to stop until I made him mine. His ole' lady was going to be manless.

Wake Up Call
Kay-Kay

Around six in the morning, according to the clock on my dresser, I was frightened outta my sleep by a loud pounding on the front door. Choppa jumped up, hurried into his pants, and grabbed the burner that he had put on the nightstand before we went to bed.

"Who the fuck is that?" he asked. "Why is somebody knocking on the door this time of morning?"

"Hell, yo' guess betta than mine. It's pro'bly somebody lookin' fo' Mama."

I could smell a dank scent comin' from outta Mama's room. I knew what that smell was, crack. I heard Mama's footsteps going to the door.

"Who is it?" she snapped.

I heard the squeaky door opening.

"Dayum, girl who whooped yo' ass?" I recognized Lacey's voice. "Your face is jacked the fuck up." She was talking real loud.

"Shhhh, girl, dayum. Stop talking so loud. My kids sleeping," Mama said.

"Oh, my fault."

"Come in my bedroom and we'll talk."

"What happened to you, last night? Why didn't you come back to the strip? I thought somebody had killed you or something."

"Didn't I say lower yo' voice? I got into it wit' a female that's all, over her sorry man. Now come on to my bedroom; I'll tell you 'bout it."

I heard them walking back to Mama's room.

"Ooh, I smell my shit burning. You gettin' high without me? That's dirty, Jean." Lacey still hadn't turned the volume down.

"Close yo' big mouth. Damn, why you acting like your ass is the only one up in here? I ain't gon tell you again to be quiet, I'ma let the door hit you in the ass," Mama said, talking almost as loud as Lacey. I heard her bedroom door close.

Choppa sat his burner back on the dresser, and we laid back down across the bed. He pulled me into his arms and held me like he intended to never let me go. I definitely didn't want him to. I decided that I was gon' be to him what the bitches before me couldn't, and what others hoping to take my place could never emulate.

Choppa had never had anyone on his team that would hold him down like I planned to. I would be the answer to his every dream, and he would be mine.

Two Days Later
Tammie

It was nine-ten at night and I had hit the strip again, walking and pacing, looking for a trick. The money I jacked the deacon for was spent. I gave both of my daughters one-hundred dollars apiece and the rest went up in smoke. So there I was again, doin' the same shit that almost cost me my life a couple of days ago.

Lacey was trick scoping too. Cars were rolling by picking up other ho's. A white ho named Becky walked up to the corner where we stood.

"Hey, you remember that trick who picked you up in that Impala the other night? White guy, in his forties?" she asked me.

"Girl, they're all the same unless they spend a grip. That's the only way one stands out from the other," I replied, feigning a nonchalant attitude that was in contrast to the nervousness that I suddenly begin to feel. Until this very moment, I had managed not to think about Bruce.

"He was shot and left for dead in his car," she continued, making my stomach bubble.

"Is he dead?" I asked.

"Nope. He survived the shooting. but I hear that he can't identify who did it."

I brushed her off. "Well, I don't kno' shit about all that."

"I just thought I'd let you kno'."

"Good looking out, but I don't kno' nothing about it, and I hope he's okay."

She gave me a grin. "You sure you didn't do it?" The ho's mouth was blank inside.

My blood started boiling. "Becky, I just told you. I don't kno' nothin' about that. Now get yo' bald mouth away from me. Kick rocks."

"Yeah, ain't nobody tryin' to hear that shit. People get robbed, shot, and killed around this piece all the time. So, what you saying?" Lacey chimed In.

"I was just saying. Y'all ain't gotta be all bitchy about it."

"Getcha anorexic ass outta my damn business, and stay outta it," I said.

She roamed off. I swear she looked like she hadn't eaten or slept in a whole week. Bags were grouped under her eyelids. Her pants weren't touching her anywhere, and that ass was flat as a pancake.

A coal-black Expedition pulled up to the curb, and the passenger window slowly slid down. From the driver's seat, a dark-complexioned guy flashed us a smile.

"Wassup? Come here, you in the short black dress." I knew he was talking to me, so I marched to his vehicle to see what he was talking 'bout.

"Wassup, daddy. Whatchu looking to get into?"

"I'm lookin' for a good time. Can you give me one?"

"Yeah, I can give you the time of your life."

"For how much?"

"Twenty for head, sixty for it all. But I don't do anal, sweetie."

"I want both. You give good head?"

"Honey, I'm well worth the price, you'll see," I promised.

"Okay. Get in," he said.
I told Lacey that I would be right back.
"Be careful," she said.
I jumped in his whip and off he drove. I put my seatbelt on and sat back.
"So what' your name, babe?" he asked me while he drove.
"Destiny. What's your name?"
"Thomas."
Thomas resembled Brian McKnight. He had skin the color of a Snickers candy bar, and he was fine. I examined him from head to toe. He wore a pair of jeans with a white tee. I also noticed a wedding band.
"So, you're married, sweetie?" It didn't matter. I was just making small talk.
He glanced over at me. "Yeah, I'm married. Is that goin' to be a problem?"
"Hell, no."
"Good. Because I'ma let you do everything that she won't. I'm tired of fuckin' in missionary positions. I'm ready for some kinkiness."
"How long you been married?" I asked more outta curiosity than concern.
"Too long. Fifteen years and some change and she still won't give a brother a blow job."
"Well, I ain't gon' stop 'til the job's done, baby. I promise you that."
"Good. It's been a long time since I've been able to enjoy sex."
"What's she; a nun or something?" I asked sarcastically.
"No. She's a teacher."
I added, "Well, maybe you can teach her to do what I'm about to do to you. Or if she still

won't, you can always come back and holla at me. I'll hook you up every time."

I directed him to park up the street in the alley. When we reached the destination, I said, "I'ma have to get paid before we do anything. I hope that's not a problem."

"No. It's not a problem at all."

He reached in his back pocket and handed me three twenty-dollar bills.

"Thank you," I said after taking his money and putting it in my purse. I then glanced over at his foot and his black casual shoes had to be a size twelve. *The wood has to be a big one,* I thought.

He stripped off his T-shirt and jeans. The only thing he had on was his boxers.

"Take off yo' dress and bra," he instructed.

I pulled off my dress and bra. He glimpsed my plump breast, and said, "Damn, I want to put my mouth on them pretty two you got right there."

I smiled but made no comment. There would be no lovemaking. My game was to get it over as quickly as possible so that I could turn the next trick.

He pulled his hard penis through the slit of his boxer shorts and I say that brother man was packing. That meant that when he entered me, I would keep my knees pressed against his sides to prevent him from going knee deep. The night was still young and there would be others after him. I didn't need no sure sore monkey to start the night off.

He reached in his wallet and covered himself with a Magnum. Then he closed his eyes, laid his head back, and allowed me to do my duty.

"Put all of it in your mouth," he ordered.

I stepped to a ho's business. Everybody knows that a smoker has a sick head game; it's what we do to get our next blast.

"Ooh, it feels so good. You a pro with this," he moaned. His hips rose up of the seat.

I bobbed my head up and down on his manhood. I stroked it, slurped it, and called it my baby. Thomas was moaning like a bitch. I could very well believe that he hadn't had his dick sucked in a long time. I decided to go all out so that he would keep coming back for more. I held my mouth an inch back from his dick and spat directly on the head. Then I licked the spit off it while simultaneously rubbing his balls.

I pulled back after awhile and asked, "You ready to go inside the warmest place on earth?"

"Oh, hell yeah," he said.

"Well, what you waiting on, Daddy? Come on and get it." I welcomed him to the sweetest pussy on a crackhead he would ever find.

"You like this pussy, daddy?" I asked as I grinded in rhythm with his movement.

"Hell yeah, I like it," he said.

My pussy got so good to him, he tried to kiss me. I slyly turned my cheek to him. He nibbled on my neck and put a hunch in his back. I started moaning The Lord's Prayer. And I was not putting on. Trick dick had made me come.

A minute later Thomas spilled his seeds inside the condom. We both dressed and he dropped me back off at the strip, where I stayed for another three hours. By the end of the night, I had made two hundred and forty dollars.

Lacey told me she made one hundred and sixty. Now it was time to get high.

We left the ho strip anxious to get with that pimp called crack. On our way to our destination, a pimp in a brand-new white Caddie yelled, "Y'all got the right plan you just need the right man. Holla at me." Then he called out his digits and crept off. We kept it movin' 'cause there was no way I'd give all of my money to nobody after I've sold pussy all night. That, in my book, was for weak bitches.

As usual, we copped from Choppa, but this time he allowed us to get high in the bathroom of his trap house. Kay-Kay must've given his ass some act right the other night, I figured.

Two hours later Lacey and I finally emerged from inside the bathroom. We were both geeked, broke as a joke, and looking for a quick come up. Four of Choppa's workers were sitting around the living room talking shit to each other. Choppa was laughing and twisting up a blunt. I crooked my finger and him.

"What's good, Tammie, whatchu need?" he asked walking towards where Lacey and I stood by the side door.

"Ask one of yo' boys if I can break 'em off with a head job or somethin'."

"Say what?" he blurted as if he didn't already know my get down.

"Stop acting surprised. I'm dead serious. I ain't playin' no games. I'm trying to make it do what it do."

"Which one of 'em you want?"

Lacey interceded, "It don't matter; just ask them if they wanna bone somethin'. I need me one of 'em too."

Choppa called to his boys, "Ay, any one of you niggaz want to bang these chicks real good or get some brain? They tryna make some money."

All of 'em said no. A guy with a gray shirt on yelled, "Hell naw," and threw a pillow off the couch at us like we weren't shit. I ducked and it flew over my head smashing into the wall. "Y'all got mo' miles on y'all garbage ass pussy's than a '78 Chevy. We ain't no trick off's. We don't dope date. All these fine ass young stallions walkin' these streets. We ain't gon' pay for y'all ancient pussys," he said.

They all burst out laughing, including Choppa. That's how young dope boys did fiends like us. They felt that we were one inch from being considered dirt. At times, we fiends could really embarrass ourselves. There seemed to rarely be any limits on what we'd do for the drug. Guess they felt invincible. Like they couldn't fall weak, ending up in the same predicament.

"Let's go," Lacey said and dropped her head.

We were on our way to the door when the guy wearing the gray offered, "Hold up. I got forty dollars to see y'all freak with one another."

"I ain't goin' out like that," I replied in disgust and stepped off.

"Fuck it then. Yo' ass won't get shit," he said and walked away. "Hold up," he hollered once more.

Once again, Lacey and I stopped in our tracks. We watched him go to the refrigerator and pull out a huge green cucumber. He walked over to where we were standing and pushed it towards Lacey.

"I'll give you forty dollars if you jab her asshole with this."

I'm thinking, *damn I'm tired of getting my butthole played in and shit stuck in it, but what the hell? I need the money for my next hit.*

Lacey looked at me. I nodded to let her kno' it was cool. I dropped to my knees on all fours, and gave Lacey consent to make it happen.

Lacey dropped to her knees as well. "Tammie, you ain't got to do this," she whispered.

"Shut up. Don't you want to smoke some more?"

"You know I do, but fuck this."

I ignored her. The humiliation meant nothing, I wanted another rock.

"Go 'head but put it in real slow," I instructed.

All the dudes in the room, including Choppa, laughed while they watched Lacey perform the humiliating sexual act. I gritted my teeth and endured the awful pain as Lacey pushed the cucumber up inside my bowels. I thought I was gon' die. It felt like I was being torn inside out.

A guy in a red hoodie yelled, "That right there is crazy. Get some lettuce and tomatoes out the fridge and make a salad out this bitch."

Another one yelled, "Look at them dimples in her ass."

I blocked out their insults and did what had to be done for another hit. I rocked my hips back and forth, grinding with the cucumber and at the same time fighting back the pressure, cramps, and pain.

I had to fake it, so I began moaning, "Yeeees, yeah, baby. Give it to me."

No Win Situation

Someone yelled, "Does that feel good to you?"

"Oh, yeah, it feels good. I love it," I hollered back. But inside I was in pain. Not only was my ass hurting, the little pride I had left was shattered. *It is what it is.*

"I'm coming," I spit out, faking my orgasm.

I dropped down to the floor. Lacey pulled the cucumber out. I thought for sure I'd shit all over myself when the cucumber came out. I slowly rose up off the floor and pulled my pants back on. Dude handed me two twenties and told me I took that like a champion.

My ass was killing me so bad, but I got my bags of rock and split it with Lacey. I left out the house making no eye contact with them.

Once we were outside, Lacey put an arm around me. "Girl, we have to leave that dope alone," she said.

"You're right," I didn't hasten to agree. But we were only fooling ourselves that we could quit. Crack had us both in a chokehold that was impossible to break.

I had surrendered all of my pride chasing that high that smoking the drug provided. Lacey wasn't any betta; we had stolen, robbed, lied and begged to get high. Me? I had done even worse, and I was still not ready to give it up. It was gonna have to take me way down before I would learn to just say no.

It Ain't Squashed Kay-Kay

Alize, my girls, and I were sitting on the stoop outside our apartments, profiling and watching all the fly whips, sitting on big rims, pass by. Niggas was rolling by in shiny new Escalades, NAVs, BMW's, tricked out old school whips, and other flavors of hood rich vehicles, letting their statuses be known. Music thumped from the window of the apartment right over where we sat laughing and discussing all of our favorite subject, which was niggaz.

"What y'all ho's do when Choppa and Nine fell through the other night?" Monique asked. This was the first time the four of us had kicked it since that night.

"You already kno' how it popped off," I boasted.

"You let him tap that ass?" she questioned with a smirk across her face.

"Duh. Do I gotta spell it out for you? Or are you just special?" I joked.

"Don't hold back, give me the scoop," she insisted.

"Well since you wanna be all up in mine, yeah I let him hit," I confessed.

"How was it? I heard that nigga got a big ass dick," said Monique.

Shay and Alize giggled.

"Yeah, it's big. And he know how to work that shit too. Nigga had me floating on a cloud. And he's a lot nicer than you would think," I said. I had to let them know that I wasn't dumb off the dick alone. "For real, I'm really feeling Choppa, and I know he's feeling me too."

"You know he got a girl, don't you?" asked Monique.

I told her what Choppa had told me about that little situation.

Shay sucked her teeth. "That sounds like game to me," she said, rolling her eyes towards the sky.

Monique just advised me to be careful, then she added, "I heard that that girl he fuck wit' is so gon' over that nigga she'll act a fool on a bitch over him."

"Do you know her?" I asked.

"Yeah, I kno' her ass. She's half ass cute, but she ain't got nothing on you."

That made me feel good.

"Is Choppa a ho?" I asked Monique.

"Girl, you know how these mutherfuckas carry it once they blow up. Choppa got the game on smash so you know what the deal is. These thirsty gold-diggers be sweatin' him and that fly whip he be rollin' through the hood in."

"They might want him, but I'ma be the one to get him. Choppa is about to be mine," I asserted. After the other day, I was really feeling myself.

"How you gon' make a dude yours that already got a woman? You just a booty call, that's it," said Shay.

If she wasn't my girl, I would've kimbo sliced her ass.

"Not necessarily. I got some lovin' for him that will make him forget all about her," I countered.

"I hope you ain't talkin' 'bout sex. He can get that from any chick in this hood. Pussy is somethin' small to a giant," Monique said.

"Ugh," I groaned. "Why y'all hatin' and talking so negative?"

Monique looked at me with the love and concern of a bestie. "Now you kno' I ain't throwin' salt. I just don't want you to get yo' feelings involved and end up getting hurt. I'm only lookin' out for you," she said.

My expression was dim because they were ruining my excitement.

Monique rose up, reached over, and gave me a hug. "I'm sorry if I made you think that I'm trying to knock you."

I hugged her back. "It's all good."

Monique sat back down and asked Alize, "What you and Nine do?"

"You kno' he made my bed rock," Alize said.

"I bet he did. You betta try to get wit' Nine. He drives a cool ass Beamer."

"Tell me something," Alize said, crossing her leg. "Do you kno' if Nine has a woman?" Her tone, and the look on her face, made it obvious to me that she was praying that the answer would be no.

"I ain't never heard about him having a main girl. I've seen him with different females in his ride, though," Monique reported.

Alize let out a sigh of relief. "Good. As long as he ain't got nobody full-time. I'm gucci. Those part-time rats don't count in my book."

"You trying to be full-time ain't you?" said Shay as one of her lame exes walked by. She turned her nose up at him.

"You kno' it," Alize remarked.

Shay and Alize high-fived each other.

"You and Kay-Kay done snagged some boss niggas. Don't get brand new on a bitch," said Shay.

"We would never do that." I spoke for the both of us. Shay and Monique were our girls. Wasn't no niggas ever gon' come between us.

The sound of music coming from the club up the street overtook the music coming from the apartment's window. I glanced at the watch on my wrist and saw that it was near midnight. I slapped a mosquito that had decided to feast on my arm. I thought about walking up the street and begging my cousin to let us in the club again, but I didn't think he would go for it.

I looked up and saw a small group of females heading our way, prob'ly on their way back from the club. One of the females was staggering like she was drunk. That was so not cool. As they drew closer, I recognized the chick who was staggering.

"Look, that's the girl we got into it with at Boo-Man's club, ain't it?" Alize asked me while she gazed in the direction of the females.

"Yep," said Shay standing up and kicking off her shoes.

"She betta keep it movin', and not say a word to me. I ain't up for that bull tonight," I said while watching the drunk bitch closely. I recognized one of the females with her. She lived in the apartments right down from us.

When they strolled past us, the female we stomped yelled, "What y'all all up in my face fo'? Y'all act like y'all ain't never seen a drunk woman before."

Alize stood up. Before she let out a word, I snatched her arm and yanked her back down. "Don't let her get in yo' head."

"Yeah, you betta sit down before I dig off in that ass," the fool snarled. I guess the beating we put on her a week ago had worn off.

She stopped and grilled us from across the street. I looked her chubby ass up and down. She was wearing a silver-fitted halter-top, some tight, skinny-legged blue jeans, and a pair of silver, strapped heels.

"I got an ass whoopin' on deck for you," Alize blurted to her.

"Y'all them mufuckas from the club that jumped me."

I wonder how she recognized us from that distance and in the intoxicated state that she was in. I guess she must not have been as drunk as I thought.

She charged across the street towards us like a bull that had seen red. I sprung to my feet, ready to give her another beat down, but her friends ran up behind her and pulled her away.

"Bitch, you didn't want none of this no way," screamed Alize.

The chick yelled back something unintelligible. Alize and Shay hurled back insult after insult while Monique and I just laughed. Most of the time I lived for this type of shit, but truth be told it was getting old. My thoughts were on Choppa and the things Monique and Shay had said about him. I didn't want to believe that I was just another jump-off to him, or that he had been running game when he said that he was about to break up with his girl. So while Alize and Shay was whooping and hollering back and forth with somebody that wasn't worth any of our time, I had Choppa on my mind.

A Month Later
Kay-Kay

I had been spending time with Choppa at his dope spot almost every day for the last month, and I'd been making dope runs for him. I couldn't believe how he had bubbled, and I was bubbling up right along with him. I was down for my man. He hadn't kicked his ole' lady to the curb, yet, but I knew it was just a matter of time before he did. He always looked out for me, and when I needed somethin' he made sho' I got it. From the passenger seat in his truck, I looked over at him with a smile on my face.

"Babe, where are we goin'?" I asked. He had called me an hour ago and told me to get dressed but he hadn't told me where we were going.

"I'm taking you shopping, shorty. Unless you don't wanna go," he said.

"You kno' I wanna go, baby. You're so sweet to me." I gently ran my nails up and down his arm.

"You betta stop, before I pull over and make that thang talk to me," said Choppa.

"What you waiting on?" I called his bluff.

Choppa laughed. "Girl, you's a fool wit' it."

"Naw, I'm just real 'wit mine. I thought you knew." He loved when I talked slick to him, but he knew I was being for real. This past month had shown him that I would represent for him.

"Yeah, I know how you carry it, baby girl. That's why I'm about to cop you your own whip."

"What did you just say?"

"You heard me. I'm 'bout to take you and buy you a whip. And I'm not talkin' about no punk ass shit. I'ma let you choose anything you want."

I screamed with excitement. "Baby, don't be playing with me," I said, tryin' to get my breathing back under control.

Choppa wasn't lying. He took me to three different car lots and waited patiently until I saw the car of my dreams. It was a black Dodge Magnum and I was in love at first sight.

"I want that one right there." I pointed.

The Dodge Magnum sat on the lot, off to itself, like it had been set aside for my eyes only.

"Are you sure? Or do you wanna check out a couple other lots?" Choppa asked.

"I'm sure, babe, unless you would rather I choose something else."

"Naw, it's up to you. How bad do you want that bad boy?"

"So bad, I'm about to pee on myself."

Choppa laughed at my humor, and then we walked up to the car and looked it over. Even before Choppa got with the car dealer and handled the business transaction, I was imagining myself pulling up in my apartments in my new whip. Monique and them were gonna freak out.

Choppa went to his truck and grabbed a shoe bag outta the back. I knew that the shoe bag was full of duckets because I had seen him stash money in shoe bags before. He bopped inside the dealer's office with the bag down by his side. I climbed behind the wheel of the Dodge Magnum and flossed. The leather seats smelled so lovely and felt so soft. I was gonna be *that bitch* on the block.

Since hooking up with Choppa, my life had done a fast one hundred and eighty degree turnaround. My girl, Monique, had upgraded her status too. She had been transporting weed for Choppa and was doing so good that she purchased a Chrysler 300. Life was good.

I no longer rocked Wal-Mart and knock off clothing. I stayed dipped in the dopest labels. Real bitches' rock real shit. Choppa and I had even discussed leasing me an apartment so I could move outta my mama's and up out the ghetto. Monique said she was gonna do the same thing, move once her money was properly stacked. We frequently went to Chi-town together where Choppa had a plug on weed and bricks, and we did his pickups. My baby was pushing er'thang from X pills, to green, and them blocks.

Choppa had two dope traps and they were both doing large numbers in excess of ten bands each a day. This, I saw with my own eyes when I helped him count his daily profits. Money was flowing like champagne on the set of a rap video, and my man was the star. I loved being on his team, making runs and drops for him, proving that I had his back.

Now that I had a nigga that kept me laced and happy, it seemed like 'er nigga in the city tried to push up on me. I wasn't trying to hear all that, I only wanted the man who made my life a fairytale come true.

Thirty minutes later, Choppa emerged from inside the dealer's office waving the title to the Dodge Magnum above his head. I hopped outta the car and ran and jumped in his arms, screaming, "Baby, I love you sooooo much." Tears of joy streamed down my face.

Choppa cupped my ass. "A nigga loves to see that big pretty smile you're wearing right now. Here's the paperwork to your new whip; everything is official so po po can't fuck with you. Gon' back to the hood and show mufuckas how I treat you. I gotta make a move; I'll hit you up later."

"Okay, babe. Thank you so much." I hugged and slipped my tongue in his mouth. We kissed passionately then Choppa passed me a red envelope that he had hidden under his shirt, and rushed off to make whatever move he had on deck. He didn't even give me time to ask him what the card was for. It wasn't my birthday or any special occasion. I seated myself in my new car, ripped open the envelope, and began reading the beautiful card with *To My Wife with Love* on the front.

Inside it read, *You're such a wonderful woman and I could never tell you in words how much you truly mean to me. You're the person who has changed me, and helped me to become the man that I am. Life is too short to wake up with regrets and there hasn't been one second when I've regretted having you as my other half. Nobody said that life would be easy, they just promised that it would be worth it, and baby you're truly worth a million to me. Love, Choppa.*

My heart dropped, and I had butterflies in my stomach, when I counted out ten one hundred dollar bills that he had placed inside. I screamed to the top of my voice, hurried up and called him. He answered on the first ring.

"Thank you, baby," I yelled. "You're so sweet."

"You're wifey, baby so I'm just showing you love. Keep ridin' with me and you'll see that there is more to come. Now, use that money to spoil yo' self."

"I love you, baby," I cried out.

"I love you, too."

When I pulled up in front of the apartments where I lived, Monique and Shay was just getting out Monique's ride. I honked the horn at them then slowly rolled my window down. "What y'all tired ass bitches about to get into?" I yelled out the window.

"Girl, who's whip you pushing?" inquired Monique.

"Who's driving it? My man just copped it for me, fresh off the lot," I boasted as I stepped out the car grinning from ear to ear.

"Ho, stop lying," Monique screamed with excitement.

I walked up, showed them the papers, and let them read my card with my dough inside. Monique's eyes watered after she read it aloud and she and Shay both replied, "Awl."

Yeah, I ain't gonna front, I was stuntin' hard. Then, I noticed an egg white Infiniti G35 pulling up. Alize jumped out screaming, "Y'all see what my man just copped me?" We all started jumping up and down like we had just won the lottery.

"These hatin' ass chicks ain't ready fo' us, li'l sis. Choppa just got me a car too," I broadcasted. Alize dashed over to where I was standing and bear hugged me. We were super excited and cheesing our asses off.

"Girl, we all gotta go out tonight and stunt on bitches," said Monique.

"I'm down with that as long as Choppa don't have a problem with me stepping out," I replied.

Later, when I talked to Choppa and asked him if it would be a problem if I hit the club with my girls, he said, "I don't want you out tonight."

"Why not?" I sulked.

"Damn, Shorty, do I have to give you an explanation every time I ask you to do something?" he said in a scolding tone.

"Dang, what's wrong with you?"

"Nothin, just chill at the crib for the night. I'll holla later, or if not tomorrow."

I said goodbye to my boo and took my butt to bed with a slight attitude. *Why did Choppa spazz on me?*

A popular club called Five Star, on Lover's Lane Road, was hosting its annual B.P.P. Party. Only ballers, playas, and pimps could attend the event. If you weren't over twenty-one with an invitation, then you were wasting your time if you tried to get in. Security would send you walking back to whatever you came there in.

Every chick in the hood fantasized about stepping in that party with a fine, thugged out, high roller standing up against her hip. Real street code dudes from every part of the USA would show up. There would be Midwest, East Coast, West Coast, and Dirty South peeps standing outside waiting to get in the club. They only wore the best money could buy, from the iced out jewelry to the suits and fly threads. The females all always looked like they'd been preparing for the event weeks in advance. Their hair would be perfect. The expensive outfits were gorgeous, with the open toe three-inch or betta stilettos. They were celebrities to us. Trophies and awards would be given to the attendants as if they were at the BET Awards.

The awards were given for things like Hustla of the Year, Playa of the Year, Baller of the Year, and Pimp of the Year. Then there were first, second, and third place winners and runner-ups.

Choppa had been invited, but I couldn't go because I wasn't old enough. He said that he and some of his homeboys would dip in there. He had sent me to the mall a couple of days ago and I got him a black Armani tuxedo, black Armani gators, and a pair of two and a half carat diamond earrings to wear.

It was one o'clock in the morning, and I was in my bedroom, dead to the world sleeping, when Alize tapped on my room door.

I turned over annoyed, asking, "Whatchu want?"

"Get up and come go with me. I need to make a run."

"I'm tryna sleep."

"Please," she said in a needy tone.

"No. Where you trying to go this time of night anyway?"

"To the BPP party Nine and Choppa went to."

I rolled over on my back, yawned and said, "You can't get in that party. You gotta be twenty-one to get in there, and you ain't been invited either."

"I'm not trying to get inside. I just wanna see Nine. I think he got a bitch wit' him."

"Why you say that?" I curiously asked.

"Cause I heard a female voice in the background when I called him earlier."

"You already kno' you gon' hear a ho talking in the background. He's at a party."

"I heard her ask him who he was on the phone wit' then he told me he'd holla at me later."

"Awww." I rose up out the bed and Alize was wearing a white tee with a pair of DKNY jeans with her white Nike Shox with her hair pulled back. I threw on a tee, a pair of True Religion jeans, and my white Air Max and told Alize to come on so we could see what Nine was up to.

We jumped in my ride, and I drove over to the club. Alize claimed that she was too nervous to drive her own shit. I could tell from all the whips outside that the club was super packed. It took us about fifteen minutes to finally park. We got outta the car and walked the entire parking lot until we scoped Nine and Choppa's rides. They were parked side by side. The back taillights of their vehicles were facing us. I noticed a light coming from the inside of Choppa's Escalade. I heard his radio, as I got closer.

"Let's get up a li'l' closer so I can see what's going on," I told Alize.

"It looks like I see a head in Nine's ride, too," Alize fumed.

We slithered to the vehicles like two detectives. Alize inched her way over to Nine's driver side door and I crept to Choppa's. I eased to the driver's side and pressed my face up against the tinted window. A bitch's head was bobbing up and down in his lap. I snatched open the door ready to lose my mind. At the sound of the door being jerked open, the unidentified female's head rose up and our eyes met in a fierce gaze. I was looking into the face of Monique.

"Bitch, is this how you carrying it?" I seethed. Tears instantly welled in my eyes. I could not believe these two would betray me like this.

"It is what it is," she responded, still gripping Choppa's pipe.

"Ho, this how you want it? You done fucked up."

I swung the door open, jumped over Choppa, and me and Monique locked up. I heard some commotion going on with Alize, too, but I couldn't stop swinging on Monique to even go check on her. I had Monique by the hair pummeling her snake ass.

Choppa pulled us apart and pushed me outta his truck. He hopped out behind me, and Monique followed behind him. Her nose was bleeding and her hair was flying all over her head. It looked like she'd been electrocuted.

"C'mon, bitch, you want some more of me? I'ma whoop that ass real good for creepin' with my man. I hope it was worth it." I was bouncing around like Floyd Mayweather Jr. as I challenged the heifer to another round of whoop ass.

Monique stepped towards me, but Choppa wouldn't get his ass out of the way. The black mufucka had the nerve to ask me, "What the fuck you doing here? Didn't I tell your hard-headed ass to stay home?"

"Nigga, get outta my face," I screamed then pummeled his face with my fists.

"Chill out, shorty. You causing a scene," he gritted in my ear, pinning my arms to my side.

When he let me go, I popped Monique in the nose again. She stumbled back, regained her balance, then tried to attack. Choppa roughly pushed her away from me. "Fall the fuck back," he barked.

"She just hit me and you think I ain't gon' be salty behind that shit?" she asked Choppa while he was holding her. She continued trying to get loose from him.

"Don't hold that slut back. Let her go," I gestured my fingers for her to come on so I could slaughter her like I wanted to.

"Move, Choppa. She busted my nose," she cried.

"C'mon, you ain't shit but a bust down. You's a sneaky one that'll fuck anybody," I shouted.

The next thing I saw was Choppa jack her up against his Escalade. "Stop wild'n out."

Monique spit in his face. "Suck a dick, Choppa. You ain't gon' throw me up against yo' truck doggin' on me like I ain't shit."

Bam. Bam. Bam. Choppa stuck his fist to her dome busting her across her head.

"Quit," she screamed and threw her hands up. That's when I ran up on her and landed a punch on her right eye.

"You bitch," she screamed.

She threw a quick lick at me that hit me on my ear 'causing a ringing noise like a bell was going off in my head.

Monique had some mad fighting game and I knew that I'd have to come on wit' my shit if I didn't want to get my ass tore up out the frame. I began boxing on her so fast she pro'bly thought she was getting stung by wasps. I grabbed her by her weave, pulled her down, and threw her against somebody's silver four-door Lexus on chrome wheels; causing the car alarm to go off. That's when I blessed her with a sock on the nose. Choppa grabbed her by her arm and started pulling her up off the ground.

"Fuck away from me," she hollered out at him, enraged.

"Naw, get yo' bitch ass in the truck so I can take you back to yo' car," he snapped.

That's when I saw a young female in a pink dress and a pair of stilettos take off running and limping. Next, I heard Alize shout, "Uh huh, you betta run." Alize must have already beat some skeezer up outta Nine's car.

I focused my attention back to Choppa. He drug Monique to the passenger side of his truck and made her get in.

"Oh hell, fuckin' naw," I yelled when she got in. I ran to the passenger side of the vehicle. I pushed Choppa back, grabbed her by her arm, and pulled her outta his truck. She fell on the grass; I kicked her in the grill so hard that she pro'bly wouldn't be able to suck nobody else off for two weeks.

A security guard shined a light over toward us from a distance and hollered, "What's goin' on over there?"

"Everythang's Gucci," Choppa yelled back.

"Come on, dawg, let's roll," Nine shouted out at Choppa from inside his car.

Choppa closed his passenger side door, walked around to his driver's side, and started his vehicle, and he and Nine drove off. Alize walked over to me. Monique scrambled to her feet and ran back inside the club. The security guard followed her.

On the way home, I glanced over and saw a tear fall from Alize's eye.

"Girl, don't be sitting over there crying over no nigga. You kno' how niggaz are; they ain't shit," I said.

"I trusted Nine, though. He told me he was being faithful to me and I believed him. I thought that he really liked me and I find that broad in his car." She sobbed.

"Girl, get yo'self together. At least you didn't catch yo' friend giving him some neck."

"Yeah, that was foul. I didn't know Monique got down like that."

"I see right now that I can't trust these ho's."

"You can't trust these ho's or your man," Alize corrected.

"I kno', right?"

I turned the radio on 98.3, Old School and R&B. Ironically, the radio jock was playing R. Kelly's oldie, "When A Woman's Fed Up", which was exactly what I was at the time. I was fed up with backstabbing bitches and no good niggaz.

I pulled up to our apartment complex and noticed Choppa's Escalade parked, and Nine's Beamer parked behind it. I parked my ride and turned my ignition off. "Ain't this some shit? Those niggas must want us to go postal on their asses. I got out the car, and I hit the lock button.

Choppa and Nine got outta their rides and walked toward us.

"What you think they want?" I asked Alize.

"They tryin' to beg they way back to us."

"I wanna kno' what kinda lie Choppa has thought of for the reason he had Monique's nasty ass slobbing all over his magic stick."

"Humph. I'm sure he done thought of a stupid excuse."

They got up to us, and Choppa said, "Baby, I need to holla at you in private."

"I ain't got shit to say to yo' ass. You wrong for that shit. That was just downright dirty, and yo' ass kno' it," I hissed.

"Yeah, I fucked up, baby. Can I at least talk to you one-on-one and we handle this shit like two mature adults? Let's be twenty-one about the shit."

"Yeah, I guess. But I can't think of a damn thing you can say to justify letting my best friend break you off."

Alize looked Nine up and down, popped her lips, crossed her arms, and asked, "What kinda sorry ass lines you 'bout to say for that shit you did?"

"Uh...I'm sorry is 'bout all I can say," he said with both hands in his tuxedo pockets.

"That's all the hell you gotta say after I caught yo' ass wit' that bitch in the pink dress lookin' like the pink panther," she snapped.

"I don't want that damn girl. I want you."

"Oh, really," she replied sarcastically.

"Yeah, I only went with that girl to the party on the strength of Monique. It was her friend. A matter of fact, watch this." He got on his cell, called a number, and stepped far off. I couldn't hear what he was saying no matter how hard I ear hustled. When he finished his discussion, he stepped back over to Alize.

I commented, "At least he wasn't getting his dick slobbed all over."

Choppa looked off for a second then right back at me. "Why we gotta be out here in the open discussing our personal shit? Why we can't holla at each other somewhere private?"

"You were getting yo' dick sucked in the open. You and that bitch didn't go in private and do that. So why can't we air our shit out here?" I responded, intending to flare up his flame.

"Man, I don't want to talk about that. That shit she was doin' to me just slipped up and happened."

"So what you sayin' to me is that yo' dick just slipped down her throat and got stuck?" I hurled.

He looked down at the ground and back up at me.

"Let's talk in yo' crib."

"Yeah, right. What . . . eva," I moaned.

Just then, Monique came screeching into the parking lot, parked, and got outta her vehicle. She strutted up the sidewalk looking straight ahead, avoiding eye contact.

"Fuckin' maggot," I shouted at her.

"Girl, shut the fuck up talking to me. I ain't trying to argue witchu. I'm on some grown woman shit. You wouldn't kno' nothin' about that," she shot back.

"You prob'ly give head like a grown woman, but you ain't on no grown woman shit. You should feel mighty stupid 'cause I still got him."

"His woman at home got him. You just somethin' to kill time."

Choppa interceded, "Gon' head and go in the crib, Monique, befo' I bury my foot in yo' ass fo' that spittin' you did earlier. Get at me in the morning 'cause I got some business fo' you to handle."

Monique stopped in her tracks and sighed. "Choppa, you done bust me 'cross tha head fo' her, and you think I'm gon' keep puttin' in work fo' you?"

Choppa walked up to her and grabbed her by the throat. His nostrils flared. "You gon' do whatever the fuck I tell you to do. Don't get outta order wit' me no mo.' You betta stop lettin' yo' lip pop."

"Get yo' hands from 'roun' my neck," she begged.

"Stop trying to act like you regulating. You don't run shit," Choppa checked her.

Monique's eyes waddled back in her head and she wiggled her body, trying to get loose.

Choppa finally let go of her neck and she coughed and wheezed, trying to catch her breath. When she finally got a gasp of air, she walked up to her apartment door.

"I'm gon' see you in the morning 'bout that business you gon' handle fo' me right?"

"Yeah, I'll see you in the morning," she reluctantly replied before running inside.

I grilled Choppa, getting all up on his chest. "I know you not gonna let that bitch continue working for you?"

"Hell, yeah, it's all about the money, baby. How you think a nigga is able to bless you so well? I was dead wrong for what I did but that don't stop business. Money talks and bullshit runs a marathon. I swear I'ma make it up to you." He tried to hug me but I pushed him away.

Next to us, Nine was tryin' to make up with Alize. A silver Buick LaSabre drove in the parking lot like a bat outta hell. The chick in the pink dress hopped out and Nine said, "Lacresha, tell my girl that me and you ain't been havin' no kind of dealings, and that I only took you to the party 'cause Monique kept naggin' me to." The female rolled her eyes, moved her bang outta her face with her hand, and replied, "Yeah. It was Monique's idea and I'm sorry for 'causing confusion in y'all relationship." Then she looked at Alize and said, "I would have explained that to you if you hadn't of hit me in my head. Honestly, he was talking about how much he likes you, and I was telling him about how me and my baby's daddy planning to get married. It's nothing between me and yo' man." The girl turned around, got in her ride, and went on about her business.

"See there, baby. I ain't scared to show you that I'm coming correct. I ain't on no bullshit," Nine said.

Choppa appeared to be uncomfortable with Nine's actions. "Nigga, you soft. It's just now starting to show," Choppa mumbled playfully although we all knew he was serious.

Nine went, "Tsk." He hugged Alize, grabbed her hand, and they went inside our apartment. At least Nine was man enough to prove to my sister that he really loved her. I stood outside talking to Choppa until the anger I felt withered with every word that my cheating ass man whispered in my ear.

"Baby, you kno' you can't be mad at me forever," he commented in my ear. I pushed him back. He grabbed me by the waist, pressed his lips against my neck, stamping a wet kiss on it, and started licking all over my neck, which was my hot spot. I had no control over my pussy, I hugged him back, and moans came from my mouth.

    We too went in our apartment. Choppa and I were going hard in my bed that night 'til five o'clock that morning. He licked all over my body and went down low. As he previously said, the moo-lah talks and bullshit can't even walk. There was no way I was lettin' the man of my dreams walk away from me. I had so much in store for us. Yeah, he cheated on me with Monique and I took him back. I'd deal with Monique down the road.

A Sleepy Sunday
Tammie

"Mama, you ain't gon' believe what went on last night," Kay-Kay said, playing with the breakfast on her plate more than eating it.

"What?" I asked as I stood at the stove and helped myself to some pancakes, scrambled eggs, and turkey sausages that she had cooked. The food looked and smelled delicious. It's aroma had awakened me and lured me into the kitchen. I fixed my plate, carried it over to the small kitchen table, and sat across from Kay-Kay. She said she needed to talk to me about her latest drama.

"I caught Monique suckin' Choppa's ding-a-ling."

My brows shot up. "What did you say?"

"I ran up on them at the B.P.P. party last night. She was in his truck, sucking his thing."

"Are you serious? I hope you whooped her ass." My mouth was a straight line.

"You kno' I wasn't gon' let that ride. I tore her up," said Kay-Kay twirling a turkey link on the end of her fork.

"I would've beat her into the middle of next year if I had caught her wit' my man," I said with a snarl, then picked up my fork and stabbed a sausage link with it.

"I put the beat down on her behind," she said.

"What did you do to Choppa?"

"Nothin' really."

"You shoulda tore a hole in his cheating behind, too. Outta all the females he coulda been creepin' on you wit', he went and got wit' yo' damn bestie. If that ain't trifling, the sky ain't blue."

"Exactly. And Monique is even worse. I thought we were betta than that. I ain't never tried to play her up outta none of her boyfriends."

"You gon' learn that you ain't got no friends. The only person you can trust is yourself. Don't put nothin' past nobody. People will do you an underhanded deal in a New York minute."

"I know. But, I never thought Monique would though. Dang, I'm kinda crushed over that." Her expression matched her words and her voice reflected pain. I tried to give her some sound advice.

"Just move on. Men gon' do stuff like that. Don't ever put trust in yo' man because he'll fail you. I learned that after years of dealing wit' y'alls daddy. I loved and trusted that man so much, I did whatever he asked of me, and I asked no questions. I would've robbed a bank with no damn gun, and no damn getaway car, had he told to. Loved his ass so much I started smoking crack to keep up with that fool. Now look at me. But I can't blame nobody but myself. I shouldna been weak-minded."

"Sho' shouldna." I turned my head to see Alize coming into the kitchen.

I shot her a dirty look. "Shut yo' behind up. I didn't ask you to throw yo' two cents in."

Alize rolled her eyes. "I'm just sayin'. I ain't gon' ever get messed up wit' crack."

"You don't kno' what you won't do in yo' life," I snapped.

Kay-Kay asked, "Mama, how you get hooked on drugs? My dad forced you to do it or you sampled it and got addicted?"

I sat my fork down on the plate and recounted my demise. "Your daddy was my high school sweetheart. After school, we both worked hard at our jobs. One day he came home and told me that he and a few others at his job had been laid off. About two weeks later he started slangin' and just kept doin' it. He never went back to a regular job. He started lacing his weed. One time he asked if I wanted to try it in a joint he rolled. I said yeah, like a fool, and here I am."

"So he tested his own product, and you two ended up on it?" asked Alize.

"Yep, he broke the hustler's number one rule: never get high on your own supply. And, like an idiot, I joined right on with him. But before we started using, we did it up big for a minute. Your daddy was making more money in an hour slanging crack than he made in a week working a nine to five. He had a brand new Caddie and jewels that blinged so bright they could blind you," I reminisced.

"Dag, Mama. Y'all were ballin'," Kay-Kay remarked.

"Those were the good old days. But me and your dad went from riches to rags. The same thing that blew us up brought us crashing down. Then your daddy got desperate and jacked that old white woman. When he went to prison nine years ago, shit went from bad to worse for me. . . and, well, I guess for y'all too. But I swear I'ma get off the pipe and get in the church because I've been doing things I'm too ashamed of to face when I'm not high."

Now I was thinking about all the degrading shit I had done while out there clucking. Selling my body to get high had almost gotten me killed, and had led to me almost killing that white man. Sometimes that night would come back and haunt me in my dreams. I quickly pushed it outta my mind and wiped the beads of sweat that had formed on my forehead.

"Hopefully, sooner than later, I'll be able to get outta this low-income apartment and find a nice house somewhere to live in, and have a normal, happy life for a change. I just need to get my mind right," I added.

After I finished eating and talking to my girls, I went back to bed to get some sleep. I'd been up half the night. I was tired and worn out. I rested across my bed and assumed that I'd get some shuteye, but things didn't go as planned.

Loose Lips Sink Ships
Choppa

It was almost unbelievable how much dough I was bringin' in every week. Me and Nine were out in the streets goin' hard. I didn't push weight for nobody as a flunky. I worked for my damn self. I was holdin' my own. I had runners, post-up boys, servers, and all that. I had two dope houses and I was livin' the life of a celebrity. Haters said that I was on some arrogant shit. The truth is, I was just confident about my hustle, and I was going all out for mine.

I was in my dope spot right around the corner from where Kay-Kay lived. Monique showed up like I told her and was baggin' my product up. I was watching a little TV when my cell phone rang. It was my ole' lady, Carla.

"Wassup, Choppa? Why you ain't been coming home at night?" she asked me.

"I'm tired of yo' arguing, fussing, and fighting, nah mean? I ain't trying to be arguing wit' you er' five minutes 'bout bogus, off the wall, kiddy type shit."

"That's a lame excuse. You tellin' anotha one of your lies," she accused.

Frustration and anger began to overwhelm me. "What's really good, Ma? Whatchu call me fo', to argue?"

"I didn't call you to argue. I called you to find out what woman you been boning 'cause you sho' ain't been givin' me none." I could picture her neck rolling and her arms moving back and forth.

"I ain't doin' none of what the fuck you claiming I'm doin'," I lured effortlessly.

"Well, break it down and tell me what's really goin' on wit' you?"

"I'm out here in these streets doin' what I do best, makin' money. I can't always come home. Sometimes I crash at one of my spots for the night. Shit, you kno' how I roll. So why you comin' at me crooked?" I leaned back on the couch in the living room and propped my shoe up on the glass table.

"I'm just sayin', the reason we don't get along ain't because I don't love you, it's because you don't spend time with me," whined Carla.

"Listen. Let me take care of what I need to do, and I'ma fuck wit' you sometime tonight. Don't keep callin' me though. I'm comin', and that's my word."

"Whatchu mean don't keep callin' you?" she sounded irritated.

"I'm sayin', baby girl, you ain't got to call me no more askin' me what time I'm comin'. I gave you my word so I'ma keep it one thousand wit' you and show up. Aight? We good?"

"I won't call you back after this," she screamed in my ear. "I ain't gon' call yo' sorry ass back none today. You talkin' to me like I'm a fuckin' child. I tell you what; fuck you and that raggedy ass phone."

"Fuck you, too." I hung up the phone. *Lil mama throwed off for real.*

Ten seconds later, she was blowin' my phone up again. I answered on the second ring.

"What's up, Carla?" I asked in a hostile manner.

"I kno' you been fuckin' around. Don't keep telling me it's no one 'cause I ain't stupid. I know there's some other bitch in the picture 'cause all of a sudden you're acting funny-style."

"I ain't dealin' wit' nobody else," I maintained. "I'm a street nigga. I can lie well enough to pass a polygraph.

"Come on now, Choppa. You kno' you been fuckin' around. Just keep it real." Her voice softened. She was tryin' to game me into admitting some shit. Ha! Imagine that!

"No, I ain't. Tell me what you talkin' bout."

"You kno' exactly what I'm talkin' bout. Stop playin' stupid." Now she was screaming again.

"I don't kno' where you gettin' ya info from, but you got me fucked all the way up." I sat the phone down on the couch, put it on loudspeaker, and twisted up a blunt. I needed to blow one to the sky to have this conversation.

"I already kno' 'bout you and that young chick around the corner from yo' trap. She lives on Wells Street. That's prob'ly the same one who answered yo' phone that time."

"Man, I don't know what you talkin' about. You need to find something else to do with your tongue besides yap about some stupid mess some jealous mufucka told you." I was frontin' hard.

Carla definitely had her facts right. Somebody had been scoping me out, ran back, and told that. Shorty had me dead to the right with her accusations so there was only one thing left to do. I flipped that shit on her, and put her on the defensive.

"You know what? You make me wonder what the fuck you doing. Because when a person can't trust, usually they can't be trusted." I slung the underhanded accusation at her in a tone that was chastising.

"Don't try to reverse your shit on me because it's getting hot."

"Naw, for real, people been telling me you got a little friend. Let me find out. Don't make me have to come down there and hurt nothin'." I hung up the phone, feigning anger.

Carla called right back, bitching, and making threats.

"Ay, check this out, I'ma see you later on. I got some business to handle right now, and it can't wait," I said, tryin' to end her tirade. But she wasn't having any of that.

"Yes, the hell it *can* wait. Fuck trying to handle some business. I'm yo' business," she hollered. "So whateva you got goin' on over there just gonna have to wait."

"Aight," I said, switching tactics yet again.

"Okay. So whatchu gon' do? You gon' stop fuckin' that red bitch and giving my dick away?"

I let out a heavy sigh because my patience was thinning out. Obviously, she wasn't gonna stop barkin' about this shit til' I gave her a comforting answer to ease her mind.

"Aight, listen, I'ma be blunt witchu, and I'ma keep it on the up and up," I said, carefully choosing my words. "There is a broad that's been trying to get at me who lives out this way, but we just cool, that's it. Ain't nothin' shakin' between us."

"Have y'all had sex?" she inquired.

"Naw. I ain't neva touched her."

"You falsing."

"What am I lying about? Tell me?"

"Not fucking her. I kno' y'all been fuckin'. I just wanted you to be honest and tell me the damn truth, but nooo you can't even do that. Now as far as this young bitch is concerned, I already got the low down on y'all two. As a matter of fact, I even kno' about her clowning you and another one of yo' ho's at the B.P.P. party."

I got silent for a second before asking, "Who tellin' you all this?"

"Yeah, you didn't think I knew about that, huh?" She chuckled. "The security guard that shined the light on y'all outside the club is my sister's baby daddy. He recognized yo' truck from when you dropped me of at my nephew's birthday party a few months ago."

Damn, dude did look familiar. I thought.

"Yeah, I was posted up with a bitch who was rocking a red dress that night, but she didn't go to the club with me. So tell that snitch ass, corny nigga to get his facts right before he come running to you on some tattle-tell, ho shit. Fuck around and get bodied."

"Well, let me say this, startin' today I betta not find out about you and no more of yo' flippers. And I kno' you been seein' Kay-Kay on a regular basis. That's why you ain't been comin' home or givin' me no attention, but that is goin' to end right here and right now," she stated on a no nonsense tone.

When I heard her say Kay-Kay's name, my heartbeat sped up. All I could think was, Monique must have run back in the club that night and spilled her guts to the security guard.

"Don't get mute now." Carla raised her voice, interrupting my thoughts as I hit the blunt that I had unconsciously allowed to burn down without hitting. "I kno' you hear me loud and clear," she said.

"Yeah, I hear you," I said blowing smoke towards the ceiling.

"Well, hear this, too because I won't be repeating it to you. If I find out you still screwing Kay-Kay, I'm gon' go to her house and me and her gon' have to have a talk. Woman to woman."

Now she was way pass the speed limit and it was time that I slowed that ass down.

"Shorty, you betta check yaself. You ain't regulatin' nothin'. Don't forget you posted up in my crib. Er'thing up in there belongs to me. So, you can pack up and step. I don't need you. You don't do shit, but give me a headache. You lazy on top of that. You don't do nothin' but sit at home all day and get on my fuckin' nerves. If you bounce right now, it wouldn't hurt me. I'ma boss. I'll replace you on the snap of a finger." I spat it to her uncut.

"So, is this how you want it?"

"Fuck, yeah. Just like this."

"How would you feel if I had the po-po's to give you a visit at yo' dope spots?" she threatened.

"Shorty, you don't wanna go there. By all right I ought to crush you for even uttering some foul shit like that. Real talk, you betta be glad I care about your son and don't wanna make li'l man an orphan. But if you ever threaten to drop dime on me again . . . bitch I'ma make you famous." That was *realtalk.com*.

"Fuck you, Choppa," she said and hung the phone up.

Bitch gon' make me go up top on that ass. After I got off with Carla, I turned and looked at Monique who was at the table, on the adjoining living room, bagging up my work.

"Ay, what you smiling fo'?" I barked.

"Nothin'," she said and wiped the smirk off her face.

"Did you talk to that security guard at the B.P.P. party?"

"Yeah. Why?"

"You told my business to that nigga? Is you stupid or just dumb as fuck? That clown ass nigga got a baby by my girl's sister. Everything you told him, he ran and told my bitch."

"Oops. My bad." Monique offered as an apology.

I grilled her with intensity hot enough to melt her whole freakin' face. "Loose lips will get you cut off," I warned as I smashed the blunt out in the ashtray, on the glass table, in front of the couch. Monique could not handle the intense gaze that shot from my eyes. She dropped her head and pretended to be concentrating on sacking up the product.

In a child's voice she uttered, "I'm sorry. I was mad. I didn't kno' that he knew you. I wasn't trying to get you in trouble."

"Dumb ass girl, it ain't even about that. I could care less what get back to my bitch. If you don't know what the real problem is, then you're definitely not fit to be down with the hustle." I left the rest unsaid.

The more I thought things over; I knew I had to kick Monique to the side. I couldn't have

her around because she let her lips pop too much.
"Ay, you gotta go. I ain't feelin' this right here. You doin' too much, and I don't trust you from my fist to my wrist. Step." I hit flip mode and went from zero to a hundred in point zero two seconds. The vein in my neck was pulsating as I rose up from the couch and stalked over to where Monique was working.
"Why? I'm sorry. I wasn't trying to start no drama between you and yo' girl."
She still didn't get it. Now I was heated. "Just gon' on before I bust you in yo' shit," I growled.
"Well can you pay me fo' what I just bagged?"
"Fuck, naw."
I grabbed her by the arm, jerked her up outta her chair, and threw her outta the door.
"You hurt my arm," she griped.
"I'ma put a hurtin' on yo' ass if you don't get away from here." My hand went to my waist and I was not bluffing. The scowl on my face was deep, and steam rose off my head. Monique peeped that I was ready to make her a front-page story in the newspaper so she hurried to her car and floored the gas pedal.
I watched the bitch bend the corner; there was no regret in me. I was through dealing with her in any way, shape, or form. Chicks like her was a nigga's downfall waiting to happen.

Expect the Unexpected
Kay-Kay

Alize and I were sitting In the living room watching "The Color Purple" on DVD when I heard loud knocks on our door. I rose up off the sofa, walked to the front door and peered through the peephole. It was Lacey on the other side with a head full of pink rollers in her hair, some red shorts on, and a white spaghetti strapped shirt. She was lookin' a hot, ugly mess.

"Who is it?" I asked outta habit.

"Lacey. Where Tammie at?"

"She's asleep."

"Well, go wake her up. I need to talk to her about something." It sounded like Miss Lacey had herself a little attitude. I could guess what it was about.

"Whatchu need to talk to her about? I can tell her when she wakes up."

"Just open the door up." She spoke to me as if I was her child.

I opened the door. "How can I help you?" I asked with one hand on my hip.

"Go and tell your mama I need to speak with her." She had both hands on her hips. I could tell that she had come for verbal combat.

"Alright, since you insist on me waking her up." I marched into Mama's room and delivered the message, knowing that she wouldn't be too happy about being awakened for some BS.

"What is so damn urgent?" Mama huffed. Then she covered her mouth as she yawned.

"I don't kno'." *But I bet I have a good idea.*

"Aight, tell that heifer I'll be out in a minute. Let me at least rinse my mouth out. Damn, can't get no sleep around this place. Ugh!" She complained.

I went back into the living room to report what Mama had said.

Five minutes later, Mama came into the living room wearing a long T-shirt that served as her nightgown. On her feet was a new pair of house shoes that I had bought her two weeks ago. Her hair was in a messy ponytail, and toothpaste was smeared on the corner of her mouth. Her eyes were red and her body language was warning Miss Lacey that she had betta had a good reason for rousing her outta her sleep.

I scooted back further on the couch, folded my legs up under me, and looked at Alize as if to say, *this is about to be good.* The only thing we were missing was some buttered popcorn.

"What's up, Lacey?" Mama asked.

"I wanted to bring my problem to you about your daughter," replied Miss Lacey, cutting her eyes at me.

"Which one of my daughters do you have a problem with?"

"Kay-Kay." She slung my name like it tasted foul in her mouth. "She ain't nothin' but a hatin' female. She's jealous of Monique. She accused Monique of trying to get wit' Choppa, but Monique and Choppa just friends. Yo' daughter needs to get her mind right. Her and Monique supposed to be best friends, now they're fighting each other over Kay-Kay's jealousy."

My mouth flew open. I could not believe how Monique had distorted the truth so that her two-timing behind came outta it looking innocent. *Lying, backstabbing whore.*

Mama let Miss Lacey go on and on until her tongue got tired. Then Mama set the record straight.

"Monique told you a lie. Kay-Kay caught her sucking Choppa's dick last night, and that's why Kay-Kay whooped her tail. If she gon' tell it, she need to tell it right," said Mama who was being much more civil than I had expected because although she had fell off, when it came to me and Alize, she didn't play.

With a look of shock on her face, Lacey looked at me and asked, "Kay-Kay, is that true?"

"Yep. I'm mad and hurt behind it, too. I thought me and her were s'posed to be ace coon-boons. I would've never did that to her," I started with sincerity. Because real bitches don't do their bestie dirty like that. Tears tried to form in my eyes but I was done crying over it. I had already made up with Choppa and I planned to get the last laugh.

Miss Lacey told us that Monique had told her something altogether different from the truth. "Umph...umph...umph," she sighed.

"She gave you the wrong information, Miss Lacey. She's trying to make me look like the villain."

Lacey walked toward the door and said, "Hold on. I'll be right back." Then she walked out.

When she returned about three minutes later, Shay was with her. "Tell me the truth, Shay. Do you kno' anything about your sister fooling around with Choppa behind Kay-Kay's back?" She questioned her youngest daughter in front of us.

Shay dropped her head. "Yeah," she mumbled. I could tell that she didn't want to get involved in the matter.

"What? Why didn't you tell me, baby? That's some low-down dirty shit that Monique pulled."

"I didn't want to get in it, and I love my sister so I just kept quiet about it."

"Girl, don't uphold her in her wrongdoing. Next time, let her kno' that's not cool." Miss Lacey sounded livid.

"Like I said, Mama, I didn't want to get in it and I knew how much Kay-Kay liked Choppa. I didn't want her to be hurt," Shay explained.

She raised her head up and looked at me. I smiled at Shay and she smiled back. It wasn't her fault that her sister was a slut.

We heard a car door shut. I peeped out the blinds. It was Monique getting outta her car, and she was walking up the sidewalk. I opened the blinds.

Miss Lacey looked over my shoulder. "That's her ratchet ass right there. Tell her to come here," she instructed. It was sometimes funny how our ghetto slang rubbed off on our parents. Mama said stuff that she'd hear us say around the house all the time.

Shay walked away, headed to get her sister.

"For what?" I heard Monique ask as she and Shay were approaching the door.

"I don't kno', just come in," Shay retorted.

Monique slowly came in looking all around like she was confused. "What's the deal, Mama? Whatchu want?" The look on her face told me that she knew that the truth had come out and now it was reckoning time.

Miss Lacey stepped right up in her daughter's lying face. "Why you lie to me like you wasn't sneakin' around with Kay-Kay's man? Was you doin' him last night?"

Monique got defensive. "Why would I do that?"

"You nasty heifer, you lying because yo' sister done already dropped a dime on you. At least she was able to tell the truth even if it hurt her. I didn't raise you to be like this. You and Kay-Kay grew up together and you gon' stoop this low? What's wrong witchu?"

"Ain't nothin' wrong wit' me?"

Before the last syllable could get outta Monique's mouth, Miss Lacey slapped the taste out her mouth. "Don't you ever do that shit again, and you gettin' up outta my house today. Mufucka's been singin' in my ear that you 'roun' here pushin' dope and doin' it big now. You gotta be doin' something from the way you been splurging lately. You ain't gave me no money or paid not one bill. Not only are you a liar, you selfish. Go live wit' yo' daddy. You'll try to fuck a man I been wit' if you did yo' childhood friend like that."

"Why you taking sides against me?" Monique yelled at her mother then ran out the door.

Everybody, including her mother had turned on her. Some things were just outta order, especially for a woman. Niggaz got called playas, but when a female did it she was looked down upon. This was one of those instances. Revenge came back around, and I didn't have to lay one finger on her.

Not Forgotten
Tammie

Lacey and I were walking up the street talking on our way to the ho stroll. I wore a blue mini jean skirt, a black halter-top, and a pair of black pumps that I had borrowed from Alize's closet. The two they dated kept them looking flawless in some of the best clothes and shoes. I polished my toenails red, and I knew I was lookin' good. My hair was shoulder length and wavy. I was really gettin' my sexy on. Although I was a bonified crack ho, I had managed to keep my looks up. After all, my looks were my only source of income, sort of speaking.

As we walked I asked, "Girl, what went on wit' you and Monique after you left my place?"

"I put that ass outta my apartment. You already kno' I don't play."

"You serious?"

"Hell, yeah. We been neighbors fifteen years. Our girls grew up together. I don't condone stuff like that. Besides, she lied to my face then had the nerve to holler at me like she carried me in her womb for nine months."

"Yeah, you right. I wouldn't ever do you like that. I wouldn't even try to play you outta one of yo' tricks."

"That's love."

"Hell, yeah that's love." I agreed.

We made it to Wells Street in 'bout ten minutes. Same old, same old. Gator hollering and acting a fool with his ho's, trying to get them to make him some dollars. Cars passing by picking up ho's; women strutting up and down the strip like Clydesdales. Lacey and I posted up on our usual corner and waited to break luck.

A two-thousand and six olive green Cadillac Catera drove up alongside me.

"Ay, girl. C'mere," a handsome black man, 'bout in his mid-thirties, said to me.

I walked up to the car. "What's good, baby?"

"I'm out here trying to play with some titties, and I wanna watch you play wit yo' self."

"Oh, yeah." I smiled, thinking, *Damn, this is easy money. No fuckin', no suckin', just play wit my titties and he watch me play wit' myself.*

"How much is that gonna cost?"

"Thirty," I answered, leaning down and sticking my ta ta's out.

"Jump in. Let's get this party started," he said smiling. His hair was low cut and I could see his waves swimming. Dude was fine. An experienced ho never really posts attention to how a trick look, they were all one and the same. But I still liked to size mine up in case I came across a keeper. Slanging pussy was not going to be my hustle forever.

I opened the door and got in. I heard Lacey holler, "Be careful."

I nodded. "Okay," I hollered out the window.

Dude pulled off and looked over at me for a second, "What's yo name, baby?" he asked while driving.

"Destiny. And yours?"

"Samantha, but er'body just calls me Sam."

My jaw dropped so low somebody coulda stuck a fist in it. "What you say yo' name is?"

"Sam," the person calmly responded.

I put my finger up and waved it from side to side. "Oh, uh-uh. You said Samantha at first, didn't you?"

"Yeah, I did."

"You a lady?" I'm sure that shock was written over my face.

"Yes, love," she admitted. "I'm a woman, but I live the life of a man. I'ma stud. But don't knock it until you try it."

"Oh, baby, I'm the last to try to judge somebody, but I don't do women." *Even though I let female stick a cucumber up my ass for get-high money.*

"What if I paid you two hundred dollars?" My eyes got big. Two hundred dollars could buy a nice amount of rocks.

"Never say never, right?" I quickly changed my tune. We smiled at each other, and I directed Sam to the motel around the corner where I often took my dates. The rooms were only ten dollars an hour at this fleabag.

Once we were inside the room, Sam didn't waste any time. She told me, "Take off your clothes, and lick your nipples."

I gave the customer what she wanted.

She licked her lips as she watched me run my tongue around my areolas, then my nipples. "Now lay back on the bed and massage your clit. I wanna see it pop out the hood." Her voice became husky with desire.

I opened my pussy lips wide enough for her to see pink. Then I made circles around my clit with my finger. I moved my finger slowly, then faster. "Yes, just like that," she moaned. Her hand was inside her pants moving in a slow, circular motion.

"I want you to come for me," she urged.

"I'm on the verge already," I panted. I was lying, of course, but with two hundred dollars on the line, I would've lied to Jesus.

"Come for, daddy."

This butch bitch is sick, I thought to myself.

"Ooh . . . Ooh . . . Ohhh, here it comes, daddy," I faked it.

Before I could protest, she had her face on my coochie, munching away. I closed my eyes and tried to think about anything but what was going on. That's what I did with most of the time when I was with a trick. However, this time I was unable to drift off into a place I called nowhere. I was appalled by what the fuck I was doing. *Tammie, don't you have any shame?* I admonished myself.

When I had given Sam her money's worth, I dressed silently. No words were passed between us as she drove me back to the strip and dropped me off where she had picked me up. I got outta her car and posted up at my usual spot.

I scoped out Lacey still trying to serve a trick up. Something hit me and I thought to myself, *I gotta stop this shit right here.* Selling my body and posting up on a strip all night in order to make money to buy crack. And I just let a woman eat my pussy. How far down was I gonna sink?

I stopped in my tracks and just looked at my surroundings. Gator was walking around in a red, linen pants suit set, looking country as hell with a pair of shades on, rings on every finger, including his thumb, a chain reaching mid way his chest, and a huge cross dangling from it. *A pimp wearing a cross.* I guess even pimps have a li'l religion. I laughed at the irony of that.

Gator had six hookers. Delicious, Honey, Caramel, Chocolate, Strawberry, and Vanilla. He had all six of 'em out on the strip tonight. All of them were beautiful. I don't kno' why they thought they needed him. He didn't do nothin' but holler at 'em, call 'em names, and take all their money. Yeah, he would protect them, and put 'em up, but that's it. He had an alley where all his ho's' tricks would have to park in and be serviced so they wouldn't be outta his sight. Or, in case something popped off, he'd be able to protect them because the tricks could get very demanding and wacky at times. That was the main reason I always packed my burner.

I continued observing the negative scenery that I had placed myself in. Seven transsexuals were walking around. Four looked like pretty women, while the other three couldn't cover up their manly features; with the big Adam's apple and huge men hands and long feet.

My eyes wandered further up the strip. I saw a group of about ten gay male prostitutes huddled over in the far right section, in front of an old, red-bricked, vacant building that was formally a restaurant called Ms. Joanne's Soulfood. Two of the gay prostitutes were holding their thumbs up at the cars passing by, desperately wanting a customer to stop. The others stood laughing, drinking, and carrying on. I shook my head in disbelief at how far I had fallen. A tear ran down my honey, weathered cheek.

I decided at that moment that tonight would be my last night prostituting. Hell, I was betta than that. My plan was to make as much money as I could tonight, leave the pipe alone, find a descent paying job, and live for my kids; they needed me.

I shook my head and began walking toward Lacey. "I'm changing my life," I mumbled to myself.

I took three more steps and saw a drag queen a couple of feet from Lacey, squatting by some bushes, with his miniskirt pulled up, pissing like a chick. I walked closer toward Lacey who was waiting for the next man to pull up. I ignored the sound of urine being let out behind me.

"You broke luck yet?" I asked as I stopped in front of Lacey.

"Not yet. How did your date go?"

"I made two hundred dollars," I shared.

"Damn, I need a quick score like that."

"You know if I got it, you got it."

The drag queen behind us said, "Excuse me."

I swiveled around and faced him, "Whatchu need?"

He was still squatting on the ground. He farted twice and said, "You got some tissue?"

The smell of feces hit my nose. I covered my nose with both hands. Talking from behind my hands, I said, "I got some baby wipes in my purse." I waved my hand back and forth pass my nose to make the shit odor go in a different direction.

"Girl, give me one so I can wipe my crack."

I reached over inside my purse, got my wipes out, and held my hand out with the wipe.

"Here."

"Girl, you gotta bring it to me. I'm still boo-booing," he said.

"Eww!" Lacey and I both responded in disgust.

I reluctantly stepped toward the guy and handed him a baby wipe.

He smiled. "Thank you, girlfriend. I gotta start keepin' some of these things in my purse. They really come in handy. I don't kno' why I only keep douche and condoms."

"I try to keep plenty of condoms handy, too. Normally, I wait to see if they already got some on them before I screw them so I don't have to use all mine up." I replied in a sister-girl tone that I used when talking to the homos and transvestites.

"No ma'am, fuck that. That is not the business. You betta use yo' own condoms. You don't kno' if a hole been stuck in it or what on the condoms they bring. I use my own." He hissed and wiped his butt and pitched the wipe behind him on the ground. He stood up and his big ole' wiener was exposed. He hurried up and yanked his skirt down with the quickness.

"Oops, I didn't mean for you to see all that, honey," he cackled.

I turned and walked away so he could finish. "No problem," I called back over my shoulder. This shit was really getting to me.

"Hold up," he called back.

I turned around. "What's up?"

"Thanks for the wipes, sweetie."

"Oh, you're welcome," I replied and went back over and stood by Lacey. The dude eventually straightened his clothes up on him and pranced down the street in his blue jean shirt and skirt. He wore a pair of red high-heeled pumps and he was steppin' in them betta than a female would've been able to.

Lacey and I both watched him maneuver down the street.

Lacey laughed. "He's got a shape on him like a woman, and he can walk perfect in those high heels."

"Tell me about it. Shiid. I'm almost damn jealous," I remarked.

"Me too. That's some weird ass shit, you can hardly tell the difference between a man and a woman these days."

"Don't nothin' I see on this block surprise me."

Only a couple of minutes had passed when a familiar looking black vehicle pulled up to the curb. The driver rolled his window down, and I bent at the waist to peer inside. It was Thomas, one of my former customers. I stepped up to the truck.

"What's happenin', stranger? Where you been hiding?" I asked.

He flashed a smile and replied, "I've been outta town on business. But I've been back for two days. I came on the strip looking for you as soon as I got back, but I didn't see you around."

"Yeah, honey, I needed to take a few days off and tend to some business myself. Anyway, what's up?"

"I'm trying to spend a little time with you," he said.

I wasn't up to it, in fact I was taking my ass home. Straight up, I was tired of this shit. "I'm sorry, honey, but I was just about to turn it in for tonight. I'm not feeling to swell. Maybe my friend can entertain you." I waved Lacey over and introduced them.

Thomas was pleased with Lacey's appearance, and we both assured him that she was a pro. "I want both of you," he smiled. "A friend of mine will meet us at the lake. We would like to spend a quiet time with you ladies just watching the waves bounce off the rocks and having good conversation."

"That sounds nice, but I don't feel up to it." I declined his offer even though it wasn't often that men wanted to spend more time with us than it took to suck them off. Any other time, I wouldn't have hesitated to jump on the offer, but I was so not feeling this lifestyle anymore.

Thomas must have sensed my hesitation. He said, "My friend and I just want the company of two women who don't have any hang-ups. We'll promise you each a thousand dollars for your company the rest of the night."

Lacey kicked my foot and gave me a look that pleaded with me not to fuck up her come up. "Okay, I'm down," I agreed. To Lacey I turned and mouthed, "This is the last time."

I slid up front with Thomas while Lacey climbed into the back.

The smell of alcohol emanated off Thomas now that I was seated next to him in the truck, but his speech wasn't slurred, nor did he appear to be intoxicated. "Where did you say we were headed, honey?" I asked.

"To the lakefront. I want to spend some time with you, make love to you on the shore."

I got all mushy on the inside. "How sweet. What's wrong? Wifey ain't treating you right?" I kidded.

"No, she's not. That's why I came and found you. You kno' how to sex me down, and make me feel like a man."

"Yeah, you came to the right place. Miss Destiny gonna make you feel real good, baby." I placed my hand on his thigh and started rubbing his leg up and down, slowly. *Maybe he will turn out to be much more than a trick to me.*

"Thomas, I'm really looking forward to getting to know you tonight. And I mean beyond the business aspect of this," I chanced telling him. I did not know how he would take it. Perhaps he would think I was talking to make conversation but I wasn't. I needed a stay friend in my life when I walked away from the strip for good tonight.

Thomas didn't respond so I shut my stupid mouth. Why was I dreaming about a trick rescuing me from my hell, anyway?

Lacey cut in, "So yo' friend gon' meet us at the lake?"

"Yeah, I told him I was gon' pick him up a companion for the night."

"I normally don't go far off to meet a man that I don't really kno'," Lacey explained obviously starting to feel uneasy.

"You're in good hands, don't worry. We're good people. I would never hurt either one of you, or allow somebody else to hurt you while you're in my presence, okay," said Thomas, smiling reassuring me while he replied to Lacey.

"Okay. I'ma trust you," Lacey said.

We arrived at the lakefront, which was actually Lake Michigan. Thomas parked his vehicle and we all got out. The sounds of the waves splashing against the huge rocks were soothing to my ears. I relaxed a bit. The three of us sat outside on the big rocks and talked. It was turning chilly and I began to shiver.

Thomas took his jacket off and offered it to me. "Here, baby. Take my jacket and put it around your arms so you'll stop shaking," he instructed.

"Thanks, baby."

Lacey was gazing at the water in a daze.

*

The wait for Lacey was over when a dark blue, four-door, two thousand and ten Lincoln MKZ pulled up alongside Thomas' car.

"Nice car," Lacey remarked.

The dude parked his car, turned off the ignition, and stepped outta the ride. It was Bruce, the deacon that I shot a couple of months ago. My heart began racing uncontrollably. Bruce walked toward me with a gun in his hand. "So, we meet again." He smiled maniacally and raised the gun so that it was aimed at my chest.

My heart pounded faster than congo drums. I looked down beside me and realized that I had left my purse in Thomas' car, which left me unarmed.

"What's going on?" My words came out on a plaintive cry.

"Don't say a word, bitch," Bruce snarled. He kept the gun trained on me as he stalked closer. The sound of gravel crunching beneath his feet was frightening. I looked at Lacey. When I saw how confused and terrified she appeared, I felt helpless and definitely afraid.

"Bruce, I'm sorry about what I–"

"Didn't he tell you not to speak?" Thomas said. He was no longer the nice Thomas I thought I knew, so I got quiet.

Bruce spoke in a low, taunting tone. "You got your friend here in a lot of trouble," he said to me, and looked over at Lacey. "Tie these street walkers up," he told Thomas.

Thomas went to his Expedition and returned with some rope. He walked over to Lacey first and tied her hands behind her back. He threw her down on the ground and Lacey almost lost it.

"What the hell is going on? Why are you doing this?" she screamed and kicked.

Bruce looked at me. "You thought I would die the night you shot me, huh? Well, you thought wrong. I had my good friend and longtime church member, Thomas, to have sex with you and make you feel comfortable around him. It was all a set-up, you stupid whore."

"I'm sorry," I cried.

"I don't have sympathy for you," Bruce gritted, then slapped me to my knees.

The side of my face felt like someone had pressed a hot iron to it. I bolted to my feet and tried to run, but Thomas threw his body in my path like an NFL linebacker protecting the goal line. I landed on my back with a crunching thud.

"Ahhh!" I winced.

"Thomas, tie that whore up too," commanded Bruce.

Thomas tied me up and dragged me back over beside Lacey.

"Damn, Destiny, you lookin' like you've lost your best friend," Thomas said.

"Look, Bruce, me and you can talk this over. It ain't got to go down like this." I made a feeble plea to a man with no conscience.

"I don't have one sentence to talk over with you. Bitch, you made a big mistake when you didn't make sure that I was dead. Now I'ma do to you what you failed to do to me." He looked down at me with no mercy in his eyes.

My life was now in Bruce's hands and I could only hope that maybe he'd have mercy on me and let me go. I kept thinking about Kay-Kay and Alize, and how they'd feel once they were told I was dead. Then, I heard the gun clap three times. I jumped each time it exploded, expecting to feel a bullet rip into my head. Thomas collapsed to the ground.

"No witnesses. He was just a stupid pawn," said our abductor.

My eyes bulged with heightened fear. Bruce had just killed his partner with no remorse, so how could I expect to be spared?

Bruce aimed his gun at Lacey's head and shot twice. Lacey's head exploded in a sickening spray of blood and brain matter. A shower of blood splattered across my face.

"Nooooooo," I screamed but my shrilling voice was muffled by the sound of the huge waves splashing against the gigantic boulders. And there was no one around to answer my frantic cry.

Bruce calmly walked over to Thomas' body and took his cell phone outta his back pocket.

"I'm glad text messages can't be traced," he said and turned the gun on me. "I was saving the best for last," he said without emotion.

He hit me with three slugs. One to the head and two to my chest. A pain shot through my body. My head felt like it was being cracked open with an axe.

I moaned, "Uggghhhh." Next, I felt a hard kick to my stomach.

"See you in hell," Bruce told me.

I felt the life seeping outta me. I knew that this was the end. My entire life played before me in unbelievable clarity. I closed my eyes and prayed. *Dear Father in heaven, blessed be thy name . . .*

Three Days Later
Kay-Kay

I answered my new, hot pink, Blackberry cell phone that Choppa had surprised me with the day before. It was him calling me.

"What's good, Ma?" Choppa asked.

"Not much, Boo."

"You heard from yo' Mama or Lacey yet?" he asked. I had told him earlier that day that nobody had seen or heard from Mama or Miss Lacey in three days.

"Naw. It's almost noon. She's usually here by now," I explained to him.

"Turn yo' television to channel four."

"Why? Wassup?"

"Just turn it on."

"I'm trying. But, I can't find the remote. Alize makes me sick when she don't put the remote where it's s'pose to go," I fussed while I looked around the living room.

"Hurry up, Kay-Kay before it goes off."

"Forget the damn remote," I said. I pressed the ON button until I made it to channel four.

A young white female news broadcaster was on the lakefront speaking into the camera. "Once again, Dan, I'm here at the scene of a grisly triple homicide. Early this morning the bodies of a black male appearing to be in his early fifties, and the bodies of two black females, both believed to be in their late thirties, were found by boaters. Police say that all three of the deceased were shot multiple times. Unfortunately that's all I have right now, Dan."

"Sad, Rebecca. Sad," exclaimed the newscaster. "Anyone who has information that can lead to the identity of these victims, we urge you to contact your local police department. Someone out there might be able to help the authorities solve this crime. Next up, the mayor visits an elementary school."

I froze. My heart felt like it was about to pound outta my chest. I held my cell phone up to my ear. I had forgotten that Choppa was even on the phone.

"Hello. You okay, Kay-Kay?" Choppa questioned with a deep concern, but I couldn't respond. Instead of speaking, I dropped my cell phone to the floor and hurried over to Miss Lacey's.

"Shay, is yo' mama at home yet?" I asked as soon as she opened the door.

"Naw. She didn't come home again last night. Why? What's wrong?" She looked worried.

"Shay, I think somebody mighta killed my mama and Miss Lacey. Choppa called me and told me to turn on my TV. They were talking about three people shot at the lakefront. I think it may be Mama and Miss Lacey."

"Noooo," Shay started screaming.

Alize ran out in the hallway. "What's wrong?" she cried. "Why Shay screaming like that?" she asked me.

"Alize, I think Mama and Miss Lacey are dead."

Alize started screaming too. I started crying. I didn't want to believe that my mama was dead, but somehow, I knew it was true. Nothing was said on the news to substantiate my fears, but inside I just knew. Still, I held out hope that I was wrong.

My hands shook as I drove to the police station in search of some answers. Alize and Shay accompanied me; the three of us uttered silent prayers that our mothers weren't the victims described in the news report.

At the police station, my worst fears were confirmed when the police described the bodies. It was my mama. I lost it after that. I couldn't hold back my tears any longer.

An autopsy revealed that Mama and Lacey died from gunshot wounds to the head. The police had no leads. There were no eyewitnesses and without eyewitnesses, there was no suspect. The days leading up to Mama's funeral were dreadful days for me and Alize. I kept myself drunk off vodka and orange juice every day. It was the only way I knew to cope.

I was in so much pain that I wanted to die. I knew that one-day Mama's lifestyle would get her in trouble, but dayum, not dead. Yeah, Mama's mouth could get very breezy at times, especially when she drank or wanted to "touchdown" as she called smoking crack.

What was strange was how all three of them were murdered. Police said robbery wasn't the motive. And because all three of them were shot up close, the police believed that Mama 'em musta been known by the murderer. They thought the dead man mighta been a John, especially when they discovered he was a deacon and a husband. But who did Mama, Lacey, and the trick upset to the point where the person just straight up murdered them?

At the funeral, Choppa and Nine sat with me and Alize on the front pew. Choppa tried his best to comfort me, but extreme grief overpowered me, and it was obvious in my loud cries and outburst in the church. I had to see my mother lay in a casket and wasn't a damn thing I could do to bring her back.

The church was crowded with Mama's associates from the neighborhood, along with some crackheads, and some of Mama's hooker friends. I even saw Gator at the funeral. He stood out in his country, purple suit with the jewelry blinging everywhere. Gator's flavored ho's were with him.

I listened to a preacher read passages from the Bible. Neighbors, and some of Mama's friends, got up and said many nice things. The preacher actually did a good sermon due to the fact that he didn't kno' Mama, and she hadn't been to nobody's church in over ten years.

I was inconsolable as I listened to all the nice things the speakers said about my mother. No, she hadn't been perfect, but I had loved her to no end. I was in a grief stricken daze as we rode to her final resting place. There, the preacher offered one last viewing of her body before she was lowered into the ground. Alize tried to jump on top of Mama's casket, but Nine caringly held her back.

I left the cemetery as soon as Mama's body was placed in the ground. I didn't want to be around anybody. I needed time to myself, so I asked Choppa and Nine to see after Alize. They both told me that they would.

I headed to the lake. I needed to see the exact spot where Mama's murder occurred. I needed to see the place where she took her last breath. I needed some closure.

I got outta my ride and right away, the sound of the waves hitting the shore did something to my soul, and calmed my body down. The birds chirping and flying over my head, along with the slight blowing of the wind, rejuvenated my hurting spirit. At least Mama laid outside in peace after she was murdered.

I remembered the lake being her favorite spot when we were younger. She always said that the sound of the water melted her soul and made her forget about her worries. I sat down on a nearby rock.

With eyes full of tears I said, "I don't understand why someone would've wanted to hurt you, Mama."

I looked up at the sky to talk to the main man upstairs. "God, I kno' that Mama could've lived a betta life, and she could've been a betta mother. Despite all of that, I loved her and I'll always love her. Nobody has the right to take somebody's life, nobody. That's your job. You give, Lord and you're the only one who should take away. I hope whoever killed Mama, Lacey, and that dude rot in hell. Why did the person have to shoot them?" I sobbed.

I began reminiscing about my mother, how happy we were back in the days, the laughs we shared, the good times, the bad times, and each event we experienced together. The hurt of losing her was intense and overwhelming.

After a half hour or so, I stood up, walked over to my ride, then opened my car door, grabbed my purse and took out my bottle of Tylenol's. I opened the bottle, poured out at least twelve or more caplets, and popped them in my mouth.

"Don't do it," I heard someone say. My head snapped around in search of the voice that sounded exactly like Mama's, but nobody was there. Deep down inside I felt her spirit. I spit the pills out on the ground and began sobbing again.

In Trip Mode
Choppa

Summer was on its last leg, but the slow change in temperatures had no effect on my grind. A month had passed since Kay-Kay's mother got murdered. A few weeks after the funeral, I kicked Carla to the side and elevated Kay-Kay to wifey status. She proved her loyalty. She was a down ass chick. She helped me push weight, serve hypes, and all that. She was exactly what I needed in my corner.

Kay-Kay mighta been young, but she carried herself like a Boss Bitch. That right there was trill. Er'thing about her was on point, from the way she looked at me while making love, to the cute smile she gave me er'time I walked through the door. She was ready and down for whatever.

Kay-Kay and Alize had to move outta the apartment after their mother was murdered. They were underage so the manager wouldn't allow them to stay without an adult guardian. Neither of them had a place to go. Kay-Kay had the funds for an apartment but her age stopped anyone from lettin' her lease.

We copped a spot in Pearly Gates Condo's downtown on Jackson Street. The condominium was real nice, and had three bedrooms, a spacious living room, hardwood floors throughout, plus two bathrooms for eleven hundred a month. I especially 'preciated the fact that the condos were gated in a quiet, laid back, drama-free environment.

Alize moved in with Nine and my mama over on the North side. Nine stayed with Mama because of her poor health. She was a sickle cell patient and made lots of trips to the doctor and hospital.

I hopped up outta our king-size bed at seven o'clock in the morning. I had a shipment of work comin' in and I needed to get it distributed. I had sent Kay-Kay off early that morning to Chicago to pick up my ten blocks and bring 'em back to Mil-Town. I sent her cause the po-po's ain't quick to start harassing a female like they do dudes. A female looks less suspicious. Kay-Kay had called me thirty minutes ago and told me that she was back on Milwaukee soil and would be at my spot around the corner in less than twenty minutes.

I showered, handled my hygiene, and put on a Coogi shirt with some Coogi jeans, splashed some cologne on, and dipped out the apartment, and jumped in my ride. I made it up the street when I detected I wasn't holdin' no iron. So, I turned my whip around, got out, unlocked my apartment door, and headed to my bedroom. I reached under my bed, pulled my chrome out, and tucked it by my waistline. I hopped in my ride again and peeled off to the spot to meet up with Kay-Kay when my cell went off, I answered on the first ring, it was Kay-Kay.

"What's up, baby? Where you at?" I quizzed.

"At the spot waiting for you. Whatchu doing?"

"I had forgot my heat so I had to go back to the crib for a second, that's all."

"Aight, I'll see you when you get here," she said.

"Aight, fa sho."

We hung up.

*

I rolled up to the spot and noticed Kay-Kay's car parked on the side of the street. I parked directly behind her. I got outta my ride, unlocked my dope spot's door, and greeted Kay-Kay with a big hug.

"What's up, my boo?" I asked.

"Nothin', I missed you, baby. Did you miss me?"

"You kno' I did, baby. I had to sleep in that big ass bed by myself when you left. I was lonely."

"Well, I'm back now," she said.

We kissed for a minute then she let go, taking her arms from around me.

I locked the door behind me and noticed that Kay-Kay had my blocks on a small table, stacked.

I looked at her. "Damn, baby, you got 'em out the car and stacked for yo' man, huh?"

"Yep."

"Come on, help me. I need to cut and bag one brick, and I'ma sell the other nine. A dude gon' swing by later and get the rest."

She raced to the kitchen and came back with bags and a knife.

"Let's do this," she announced.

We sat down at the table. I cut it up, and she bagged it.

Three hours later, the table was full of rock sacks. We were almost done, when I heard a car door slam. A few seconds later, I heard what sounded like glass being broken.

Me and Kay-Kay jumped up and pulled out our heat. Kay-Kay had a nine milli that I had got her three days ago for protection for when she was making dope runs. We ran over to the window and peeped out. I saw Carla outside busting the windows out my ride with a silver colored bat. She was on some Jazmine Sullivan, busting windows outta my car shit.

"Come on up outta there, Choppa," she yelled from outside.

"Goddamn. This crazy motha. That's my ex outside," I yelled at Kay-Kay.

I unlocked the door and ran out. "I kno' mufuckin' well you ain't out here busting out my windows."

"Oh, yes I am, nigga." She yelled at the top of her voice.

We stood several feet from each other. I didn't get up close to her 'cause she was in a mental state.

"Bitch, if you don't put that bat down I'ma be on yo' ass like stank on shit. Haul off and bust anotha one of my mufuckin' windows and watch and see what I'm gon' do to yo' ass," I warned her.

She made three backward steps and "Bam" she hit my whip wit that silver bat again.

My eyes grew wide. "Stop hittin' my goddamn truck, befo' I murk you."

"I'm gon' keep hitting it," she screamed. "You left me for that jump off that's inside that do'way right there." Her finger was jabbing towards the house.

I turned my neck to the door and Kay-Kay was standin' in it, lookin'.

Carla yelled at Kay-Kay with her bat in hand, "Me and Choppa just fucked two days ago. So, I kno' you don' think he's being true to you, do you?"

Damn, she just put me on blast.

"You ought to have yo' big grown ass at home this time of morning, trick. You too old to be actin' so childish," Kay-Kay stated sensibly.

"You need to leave my man alone and getcha own. Me and Choppa been together too long for me to just let it go."

"You might as well let it go. We stay together, and I'm who he kisses all over every night, so if he's laid up in bed wit' me, er' night, how does that make him yo' man?"

"What? Choppa, you told me that you been living wit' yo' mama. How you gon' keep runnin' to my house and you kno' you living wit' that stanky, project raised, gutter rat?" she yelled, then pointed her finger at Kay-Kay.

"If you smell somethin' stanky, you must smell yo' fish that's in the seat of yo' panties, 'cause mine smell like red roses don't it, Choppa?" Kay-Kay replied.

Observing their verbal volley was like watching a tennis match.

"Yeah, some *dead* roses," Carla cracked back.

I had heard enough of their childish insults.

"Both of y'all on some pre-k shit," I interjected.

"Choppa don't talk to me," Carla shouted. Spittle ran out the side of her mouth. "Monique told me all about y'all two when I saw her at the grocery store."

Kay-Kay made several steps toward Carla, but stopped when Carla began swingin' the bat from side to side, threatening, "If you come any closer I'm gon' hammer you til' you flat as this street we standin' on. If you think you bad, then come on."

Kay-Kay yelled, "You makin' yo' self look bad out here this time of the damn morning, goin' ham over a nigga that ain't even yours no more."

"He *is* mine."

"You just as wrong as two left shoes if you think Choppa's gon' leave me for yo' mentally disturbed ass," Kay-Kay taunted her.

"Child, please. You only a temporary thing. What me and Choppa got is permanent," said Carla.

She was talking out the side of her neck. I set the record straight, because I was fed up with the drama. A nigga can't get his weight up with a lot of bullshit poppin' off.

I snatched Carla by the blouse and pulled her face close to mine. "Bitch, don't front like you got it like that. I told you, I don't fuck with your retarded ass no more. You over here clowning, and think that's gon' get a nigga back? Push on." I shoved her away from me.

The next thing I knew, Carla rushed up to my whip and shattered my front glass. *This fool done went too far.* I stepped towards her, ready to tap that head, but she managed to crack me across the shoulder with the bat before I could wrestle it away. I fell back a few steps, ran up on her again, and grabbed the bat. At the same time, Kay-Kay came running down the stairs towards us. She pulled her steel outta her pants and rapped Carla over the wig wit' it, knocking her down to the pavement.

"That's gangsta, boo," I told Kay-Kay. "That's how you ride for your nigga."

Carla was on the ground, knocked out.

Kay-Kay said, "I ain't through wit' her yet."

She grabbed the bat off the ground and swung off on Carla's blue, two-thousand and ten, Chevy Trailblazer, knocking glass out. She knocked out the front, side, and back windows.

Then I saw her go to the back of the Trailblazer and bust out the taillights. Right before she finished, she kicked two dents in the passenger side door.

"Now what," she screamed at Carla who had finally come back to life, and slowly stood up.

I shook my head in disbelief at how hard Kay-Kay had gone in for me. "Yeah, shorty a rider," I said to myself.

Carla trampled back to her Chevy Trailblazer and Kay-Kay walked past me in the house breathing heavily.

Carla looked at the damage done to her ride and yelled, "She done fucked up my shit."

She got in, and burned rubber driving down the street.

We gathered up all my dope, and took it to another spot, just in case a neighbor called the po-po's. We didn't want no problems outta them son-of-a-bitches.

Noon
Kay-Kay

I was sitting in the Chevrolet dealership waiting for them to finish replacing Choppa's windows. Since he needed to get rid of some work, and take care of his business, I volunteered to take his ride and get the windows replaced.

I picked up an Ebony magazine, with President Barack Obama and his family on the front, and began reading it. Seconds later, two handsome black males came and sat down beside me.

The darker-skinned guy asked me, "How you doin' today?"

I looked up from the magazine. "Oh, I'm aight. How you doin'?"

"Oh, er thang's bliss on my end," he replied rubbing his neatly trimmed goatee.

"Good," I responded and directed my attention back to the news article about the President and his family.

"Whatchu reading that has all of yo' attention?" he questioned.

I raised my head up once again. "I'm reading about the President and his family."

"Yeah, I like him. Barack is a good one. What's yo' name, mah?"

"Uh...Kay-Kay," I said after hesitating.

"Where yo' man at, Kay-Kay?"

"He's handling his business right now," I said closing the magazine for a second.

It had become clear that he was pussy footing around wit' me for a conversation.

"What kinda business he handling?"

"Boo, you're asking too many questions, don't you think?"

"Damn, my bad, baby." His smile reached his light brown eyes. Still I wrinkled my nose up at him.

"I don't kno' you from a can of paint, and you up in here questioning me like the Feds," I admonished. He chuckled in that way that street niggas do . . . always wearing their game face.

"You're right. So, again, my bad. You gotta excuse me if I'm losing cool points, but straight up, you're so beautiful my words won't come out right," he rapped. His baritone was soft yet deep. Then his eyes ran over my body like one of those hand-held metal detectors.

"Whatchu lookin' at?" I asked. Then I pointed to my face. "My face up here."

"My bad. For a minute your body had me hypnotized."

"Why are you so rude?"

"Nah, I'm not rude, baby doll. Let me start all over. How you doing? My name is Deon." He held his hand out like he thought I would shake it. *Not hardly.*

"Everybody calls me Young King, though," he added.

Young King? Young King?

I rolled my eyes up at the ceiling trying to recall where I'd heard that name.

I glanced over at him. "Damn. Yo' name sounds familiar."

He leaned back in his chair and began patting his foot. "I'm a rapper. You ever heard that song, Can You Drop?"

"Oh. Yeah it goes, Can you drop it down low/ All the way to the flo…?" I recited, probably sounding like a groupie.

He grinned. "Hell, yeah, that's me, boo."

"You kno' I use to hear that song on the radio all the time. But I never knew what you looked like."

"Well, here I am in the flesh. What you think?"

"I wanna have your babies," I joked.

Young King chuckled.

"On a serious note," I went on. "You got talent. That song was one of my favorites. Just about er'body in my neighborhood jammed off that song at our block party."

Young King reached out and took my hand in his. "Yo' shorty, how 'bout you and a couple of yo' homegirls come to the club tonight and get yo' party on. I'ma be performing."

"Which club you performing at?" I asked, removing my hand from his but not in a rejecting manner.

"Chocolate City," he said, obviously not offended.

"I kno' exactly where that is."

"The club's owner, "A," is having his thirtieth birthday celebration tonight. He asked me to perform."

"You get paid when you perform?"

"Now you're asking too many questions," he replied with laughter in his tone.

"You got me back," I acknowledged with a smile.

"Yeah, I'm quick with my shit, so try to keep up."

"No, you betta try to keep up." I flashed him a sweet smile and stuck my finger in my mouth.

"Is that right? You swift like that for real?" Young King replied, as he glanced down at his icy Rolodex.

"Gon' handle ya business, playa. Don't let me stop nothing," I remarked.

"Damn, I wish I could stand here and talk to you all day, but I need to make a run. Are you gonna fall through the club tonight so I can look in yo' pretty face when I'm through performing?"

I hesitated for a minute before speaking and thought… *I could go 'cause on the weekends Choppa usually made it in at four and five in the morning, that's when the workin' dopeheads gave him almost their entire paycheck. So he'd be on his grind til' the sun came up.*

"Yeah, I'll be there."

My Blackberry began ringing singing, "Number One," by R. Kelly and Keri Hilson.

I got my cell outta my Louis Vuitton bag and my caller I.D. read Choppa. I walked off to get a little privacy. "Hello."

"So what they say about my ride? How much is it gonna be to fix my windows?" asked Choppa.

"Dude hasn't come and told me, yet. I told them to just fix it and however much it cost I'd pay it."

" I gave you two g's, but if it's more than that which it shouldn't be, call me and I'll jump in yo' car and head over there wit' some mo' money."

"Aight. I'll let you know."

"Fa sho'."

I pressed the END button on my Blackberry and put it back in my purse. I glanced up and noticed Young King and his friend heading back in my direction.

"Aight, boo. I'm 'bout to jet. Should I look forward to seeing you tonight or what?" asked Young King.

"I'll be there," I promised.

"That's wassup. Put my cell number in yo' phone and let me kno' when you get outside the club so I can make sho' you get in free. All yo' drinks gon' be on me."

"Alright," I told him and then programmed his number in my cell as Ms. King. Just in case Choppa happened to snoop through it, he wouldn't find anything. I had to keep my game strong at all times dealing with a dude like mine. Young King and I said our goodbyes and he went out the door. Excited, I called Alize.

Lyfe Jennings "Must Be Nice" came on. I was movin' my head to the music enjoying the hell outta that song while I waited for Alize to answer.

"Hello."

"Dag, girl, I almost hated for you to answer. I was enjoying the music."

"Well, damn. You want me to hang up so you can call back and hear the song?"

I laughed but otherwise ignored her sarcasm. "Whatchu got up for tonight?" I sure asked.

"Nothin', really. I'm just gon' chill. Why? Whatchu trying to get into?"

"I just met the dude, Young King that raps that song, "Can You Drop."

"Straight up?"

"Yeah. He wants me to come to Chocolate City tonight on Water Street to see him perform. I wanna kno' if you'll roll out with me. I'm inviting Shay to come, too."

I didn't hear a response. It was like she was still thinking on whether she'd go or not. That's when I told her, "He said we can get in free and the drinks are on him."

"I'll go then. Where you tellin' Choppa you goin', are you telling him you going to a party?"

"Hell, no. I'ma just tell him that me, you, and Shay havin' girls' night and we goin' out to eat and to the movies."

"Good. That's what I'll tell Nine, too. I wanted us to be on the same page and not tell two different stories. Them fools will fuck us up quick. You know they're both insecure as hell . . . quiet as it's kept."

"You ain't lying. So whatchu gonna wear? Get some money from Nine and let's hit Southridge Mall."

"Please. Nine keeps money in my hands. I ain't gotta go begging him," she bragged.

"Well, excuse me."

"Oh, baby you excused. You betta get it right."

"I see you got your boyfriend doin' you right over there, huh?"

"Yes, ma'am. I do."

I was proud of Alize 'cause she had grown up and had taken Mama's death way betta than me, plus she made sure Nine took care of her.

"Check this out, I'ma come scoop you up in an hour. We can find us some fly fits to turn some heads tonight," I told her.

"You kno' it. It's goin' down."

"By the way, are you goin' back to school in September and finish yo' last year up?"

"Nope. I might get my G.E.D. later on."

That answer disappointed me badly.

"Come on, Alize. You kno' Mama wanted you to finish school and go to college."

"Excuse me?" she said and faked a cough. "You ain't in college. I told you, I might get my G.E.D. later, but not right now. I got too much on my mind at this time to be trying to be up in somebody's school. 'Specially with er'thang that happened wit' Mama. I can't do it right now," she sadly explained. I felt her pain and knew exactly where she was comin' from.

"I feel you. Just try to go back later on and get that G.E.D., okay?"

"I will. Where you at?"

"I'm trying to get windows put back in Choppa's truck. His crazy ass ex came to the spot this morning and knocked all four windows out with a baseball bat. She wants him back, but I got him."

"What?"

"Yep, but I bet that bitch regrets it, ' cause I put a designer ass whooping on that ass." I recounted the whole incident for Alize.

"I missed all that damn action. Why you didn't call me?" she exclaimed.

"I'm good. I handled that like a real woman."

"Kay-Kay don't let that thirsty skank steal yo' man from you."

"Oh, naw. I ain't even worried about that. Choppa ain't goin' nowhere. I hold him down. I'm one of the few people he can depend on. When it's all said and done, Carla gonna be history and I'ma be the last one standing."

"I hope so."

"Don't hope so, Alize. You betta kno' so."

We spoke a few more minutes and I ended the conversation.

A tall, slim white employee of the dealership stepped to me. "Your truck is ready," he said. "It'll be fifteen hundred."

"Okay, that's good," I replied. I went up front, paid, and left.

As I drove away, I was excited about the party we'd be attending. I remembered that I needed to call Shay, who lived with her crackhead auntie, who was on drugs worse than Miss Lacey had been.

I rang Shay up and invited her on an excursion to the mall with me and li'l sis. The three of us were about to hit the stores hard, and come outta the mall with outfits that would surely have us lookin' good when we stepped into the club tonight. I just had to make sure I played my hand right with Choppa.

What A Damn Night
Kay-Kay

My girls and I pulled up in Chocolate City's parking lot straight stuntin' and ready to give the haters something to frown their faces up about. The parking lot was filled with all flavors of whips, from old school rides sitting on new school chrome, to the latest model trucks and whatnot.

I was feeling at ease because the lie I'd told Choppa had went over without him even trippin' on me.

Choppa said that he'd be handling business all night and Nine would prob'ly ride to Chi-Town with him to pick up a few bricks. That was good 'cause then I'd get to stay out even later.

All three of us stepped outta my ride with our hoochie mama gear on. I wore a silver Ralph Lauren dress that was so tight you would've sworn I glued it to me. Alize wore a white Michael Kors fitted dress with gold stilettos, while my girl Shay sported a Dolce & Gabbana, sky blue fitted mini-dress that I bought for her with a pair of Dolce & Gabbana silver strapped, six-inch heels.

I hit Young King up on his cell phone, and he sent a bouncer out to escort us right on in. We caught the hard stares from those who had been standing in line, prob'ly hours, waiting to get in.

We walked in the club, switching our asses like we were in competition to become the next Miss America. The club was packed from wall to wall. Females were standing around looking with their fresh nails, outfits, and weaves. Some of the hairstyles looked good, like they had been in the hair shop all day to obtain that perfect hairdo. I silently gave props to the true divas, while shaking my head at those with cheap weaves and K-mart attire. Chocolate City was not the place for that.

"We're going up to the second level, to VIP," shouted the bouncer over the loud music. We stayed on his heels.

The crowd was so thick I thought we'd never make it up. We walked up all thirty-five steps until we got to the top. He told us to sit at a table reserved for us with three chairs. This section had plenty of local rappers and high rollers who were sitting at their reserved tables rolling up phat blunts, smoking blacks, and sippin' on the best liquor. I saw Grey Goose, Moet, and Cristal on the tables surrounding us. I could see the stage perfectly from our view where Young King would perform.

"What y'all wanna drink?" the muscular framed bouncer asked. "Young King says you entitled to whatever you like. It's all on him."

"Can you bring me a bottle of Grey Goose?" I answered.

"Yep," he replied.

"Thank you."

"I'll be back. Just give me a minute," he said and disappeared downstairs and into the crowd.

The club owner came upstairs and started walking around welcoming everyone to his club, nodding, and shaking hands with the guest. He seemed happy, prob'ly because it was his birthday and a huge crowd was at the club to celebrate. He was really taking in bank. He introduced himself as Mr. Chocolate City.

When he came to our table, he leaned over and whispered in my ear, "Where yo' man at, Sweet Thing?"

"Why?"

"Cause if that nigga don't kno' how to treat you, I'm here to tell you, I do."

"Thanks, but no thanks."

"If you ever change yo' mind you kno' where you can find me."

"I'll keep that in mind," I said wishing he'd hurry up, move along, and stop whispering his beer smelling breath in my ear.

The bodyguard made it back with our bottle of Grey Goose, and sat it on the table, along with three cups of ice. "If y'all need anything else, just let me know," he said politely.

"That's wassup and I appreciate the love," I replied sincerely. He appeared to be a real sweetheart. "Tell Young King thanks."

"It's nothin', Ma."

He turned and went on about his business.

The club owner who was still standing beside me bent over again. "I didn't kno' you belonged to Young King. My bad, that's my partna."

"We just friends," I corrected him. He favored Martin Lawrence. He nodded and went over to the table behind me where some chicks were sitting lookin' ghetto fabulous with the different colored hair weaves laid, and they were dressed to impress. "They can have his short Martin Lawrence looking butt," I said in a low tone so that only Alize and Shay could hear me.

All three of us reached for our cups. I broke the seal on the Grey Goose bottle and poured some into our cups. We began sippin' and peepin' out the club scene. The dance floor downstairs, which we viewed through the clear glass, was flooded wit' dudes and females dancing, sippin' their drinks, and having a good time.

I looked down toward the door and saw Monique walking in, twisting her hips through the crowd. I ain't gon' hate, she was jazzed up from her head to her toes. She wore a red fitted shirt, a pair of dark blue skinny jeans, and red pumps. She had a tall, slender, butterscotch complexioned female accompanying her.

Alize chuckled, then sat back with her cup in hand. "Look at what the damn wind just blew in."

"Yeah, I see her."

I hollered to Shay, "Did you tell Monique that you were goin' to be up in here tonight?"

"I haven't talked to her since Mama's funeral."

I nodded.

Alize leaned in toward me and said, "Don't let that spoil our night."

"I won't."

Mariah Carey's song "H.A.T.E. U" came on. I sang to the music, taking sips in between singing. My head was loose off the Goose. And when I got right off of alcohol, I got freaky. I stood up with my cup in hand and started rolling my firm body slowly. I could see a group of people to my left watching my every movement. I was entertaining the hell outta them. Shay stood and slow grinded while Alize sat back laughing at us.

"Y'all sick wit' it," she stated.

When the song was over, we sat back down. The weed smoke from the dudes to our left was smacking me in the nose. Not only was I tipsy from the alcohol, I think I was high off contact. Suddenly, the lights were dimmed lower and the stage lights were turned on. A guy got on stage and announced that Young King was about to perform. Several groupies dashed over to the stage for a close-up view.

Young King's hype men came out then Young King came out rappin' off the beat of his song, "Can You Drop?" Females were shaking what they'd been blessed with. The club was crunk. Young King took his shirt off and threw it into the crowd. I simply smiled to myself while watching him show off his chocolate, sexy chest.

I danced to the music along with Shay who was rolling her torso like a wave in the water. When the song was over Young King left the stage. Shay and I sat back down in our seats. Three outta the five dudes from the table behind us came over with their chairs and started talking to us.

One of them looked like he was five nine, maybe a hundred ninety, or so pounds. He had a muscular build and golden brown skin. He was wearing Calvin Klein jeans, a striped blue and white polo, and a pair of fresh Jordans. "What's good, cutie?" he asked and sat by me.

"Not a lot. I'm just trying to enjoy my night. What's up with you?"

"I'm out to chill and hang out wit' my boys. That Goose got you right, don't it? You shakin' that ass tonight," he smirked.

I giggled. "It's got me feeling good."

"You lookin' sexy in that fit you got on. You fine as fuck."

"Thank you," I blushed.

"Is that yo' real hair? It's so waved up and curly."

"Hell, yeah it's mine. I got lucky. My grandmother was bi-racial. I guess I got it from the white side of the family. I don't really kno', I'm guessing."

"I love to see some long hair," he said and reached for my hair and felt it.

I smiled and pulled my head back a little. "Are yo' hands clean?"

"I haven't washed them since I got outta the shower earlier. Why?"

"I don't want my hair to fall out," I kidded.

He gave me a smirk. "I ain't gonn' make yo' hair fall out. I ain't contagious."

I laughed.

"I'm Donnell, and you are?"

"Kay-Kay."

Donnell pulled a pack of Newport shorts outta his shirt pocket. He placed his cup of liquor on my table. I took two more sips of my drink, and placed my cup on the table. I was feeling buzzed. My head had gotten right, and I felt like I could dance the night away.

Donnell lit his cigarette and took a long drag off it so hard the tip lit up. "You don't mind me smoking do you, pretty lady?"

"No. I don't mind."

"You want a cigarette? If you smoke while drinking, it'll really make you feel good. You'll get a little higher without drinkin' as much."

"Let me try it. Pass me one. I ain't never smoked before." I was feeling frisky for sure.

He passed the cigarette to me. I put it in my mouth and let him light it for me. I took a short drag off it. Before long, I was feeling a little higher. I passed the remainder of it over to Shay who finished it off while sippin' and talkin' with the dude that was all up in her ear causing her to cheese hard.

My bladder was beginning to feel like it would bust any second, so I told Alize and Shay that I needed to use the restroom. They both nodded *okay* and we stood.

I leaned down in Donnell's ear. "I'm 'bout to go to the ladies' room. I'll be back in a second."

"Don't let anotha dude stop you from comin' back, cause I'm trying to get to kno' you."

With a smile, I responded, "I'ma be back." My girls stood up to follow me to the ladies room.

Inside the restroom were five stalls. Three were taken and the other two were available. A Puerto Rican female was sitting at a table with tampons, maxi-pads, perfume, lotion, paper towels, and hand sanitizer. She was reading a small magazine that looked to be the Jet. I went into one stall and Shay went into the other one. After I handled my pee problem, I came outta the stall, walked over to the mirror, and pulled my lip-gloss outta my bra. I spread gloss across my cute, tiny lips. Two females washed their hands, and the club's courtesy girl gave them paper towels, and offered them lotion and perfume. One chick used a little of the lotion she had and they went out. I had never seen a club that had someone in the bathroom handing out personal items before.

I washed my hands and the Puerto Rican chick handed me a paper towel and offered me the items on the table. I refused 'em, but told her, "Thank you." Alize and I waited for Shay to come outta the stall.

The bathroom door opened. Monique and her friend whisked in.

She looked at me and asked, "Where my sister at?"

I turned my nose up. "I kno' you ain't askin' me a question."

"I didn't come up in here to argue or fight witchu, Kay-Kay. I want to holla at my li'l' sis. I saw y'all walk through."

"Hold on, Monique. I'ma be out in a minute," Shay's voice came from inside a stall.

I stepped up in Monique's face. "You ran back and told Choppa's ex all about me, huh?" Monique unlocked her lips to voice something, but I quickly shut her down and began speaking again. "You kno' you was outta order for that shit, but I ain't gon' trip about it, 'cause I dealt with that bitch when she brought the drama."

"I don't kno' what the hell you talking 'bout."

"Bitch. You kno' what you did."

"No, I don't," Monique lied again with a stern look.

"You just gon' keep lying, huh? Carla already gave me and Choppa the scoop. She said that yo' ass told her about me. I'm glad you did 'cause she needed to kno' that I'm who's new in Choppa's life."

"You may be new, but trust me, you just one outta the many. That boy ain't gon' settle down wit' you."

"You let me worry 'bout all that," I quickly said gettin' heated by her jazzy words.

"Oh, you gonna see. If you really wanna kno', I just saw yo' man riding a girl around in his truck," she mentioned with a huge smile, tryin' to push my button.

"I don't even believe you. All you do is damn lie. If you told me it was raining outside, I'd have to go look for myself 'cause the sun might be out. You just lie to hear yourself talking," I stated and Alize laughed.

Shay came outta the bathroom. "Damn, y'all two still at each other's throats."

Shay and Monique hugged.

"What's been goin' on, big sister?" Shay asked Monique, happy to see her sibling.

"A whole lot of nothin'. I had to come speak to you. I don't have yo' house number or nothin'. I heard you moved in with Aunt Rita."

"That's where I'm staying. I'm gon' graduate, go to college, and then find my own place."

"That's wassup. I'm so proud of you."

Shay rubbed her head. "I'm tipsy."

"Whatchu been drinkin' on?"

"We had been sippin' on some Grey Goose. Whatchu been sippin' on tonight?" Shay asked Monique then stepped over and washed her hands off. The Puerto Rican girl gave Shay a paper towel.

Monique popped her lips. "I ain't sippin' on shit, but a beer. You kno' I don't sip no heavy liquor."

"That beer ain't gon' do nothin' but go right through you," said Shay.

Aggravated, I said, "Shay, we gon' be waiting outside the door for you while you talk to yo' sister."

"Thanks, hun," Shay said.

I opened the bathroom door, stepped out, and waited for her. Trey Songz' hit, "Say Aahh" was blasting. I moved my head with the beat determined not to allow Monique's childish attitude to spoil my night. Alize stood beside me dancing while we patiently waited for Shay.

Monique, Shay, and Monique's friend soon came outta the restroom. Shay stood beside us while Monique and her friend moved past us.

Monique turned around to me. "When you see who Choppa was riding around with earlier wearing a pink halter-top, tell her that I said, 'Hi.'"

"Whatever, hater. Choppa's outta town handling his mufuckin' business. He ain't with nobody," I screamed.

"Believe that if you want to," she yelled and kept it movin' through the crowd.

Shay hollered in my ear, "I'll be glad when y'all quit beefing and we kick it together like we use to."

"Never. She had my man's dick touching her tonsils. I ain't fuckin' wit' her like that no more. She betrayed me and I ain't forgiving her for that," I scoffed. "Some things can't ever be forgotten." I pushed my way through the crowd to get back upstairs in the VIP section. Shay and Alize followed behind me.

I made it through the crowd of people , and was walking up the stairs, on my way to my seat, when I locked eyes with a familiar face, Choppa. He was posted up in a booth with a redbone who was wearing a soft-pink halter.

So, Monique wasn't lying. This nigga never went outta town. He was just playin' me sideways so he could hang out with this tramp ass ho.

The dude, Donnell, stood up and let my chair out, trying to be a gentleman, but I walked right past him, and was making my way over to Choppa, when I saw Young King comin' toward me. I ignored him, and walked over to Choppa.

"Why is this ghetto lookin' hoodrat all up on you?" I yelled, and got a betta look at her, and from what I saw, she wasn't even all that.

Stunned by the whole situation, they both were looking all crazy and caught off guard. Choppa just sat there then said, "Who told you to come to this club? I thought you said you and yo' girls were gon' be chillin' tonight, not clubbin'."

"Choppa, who is she?" asked his little side ho.

"I'm his woman and who the fuck is you?" I spat.

The female got silent, rose up outta his lap, and stood with her arms folded, like she was his female bodyguard or savior. Alize and Shay stood beside me, lettin' her kno' they had my back. The female quickly bowed down when she saw that I wasn't alone, and stepped to the side.

"Choppa, you need to handle this," she said.

"I'm 'bout to give you the business if you don't shut the fuck up. I ain't the problem, yo' ass is." I checked her and she zipped her little thin ass lips.

I redirected my attention back to Choppa. "So explain yo'self. Who is this and why was she all up on you?"

Before he could respond, I popped him square in the mouth.

"You ain't shit but a dog," I screamed.

Choppa jumped up from his seat and said, "What's your goddamn problem? Why you flippin' out?"

"Nigga, don't play stupid. We stay together, and you out messing up on me." I continued to strike him as tears leaked from my eyes.

He grabbed my arms, but I snatched a loose and continued wailing on his no good ass.

Bop! He punched me in the eye.

I cried out in pain and tried to claw his mufuckin' face off, but he shoved me back. Then his high-yellow bitch popped me upside the head.

I stormed into her like a wild horse. The only thing on my mind was to whoop her ass and kick Choppa in his nuts. Me and the high-yellow broad were going head up when Alize and Shay jumped in and started swinging, too.

Right when we were gettin' the best of her, Choppa, along with several bodyguards, stepped in to break us up. One huge bodyguard swung me like I was a lifeless doll. I didn't kno' what happened, when I was suddenly thrown to the floor. I bruised my knees and elbow up, but that didn't stop a trooper like me from hoppin' back on my feet. I came back throwing blows even harder, until the big bouncer stopped me again. I kicked and screamed the entire time he held me.

Finally, the club's owner came over.

"Ay, y'all take this shit up outta here. Today's my mufuckin' birthday. I ain't got time for this right here. What just went on?" he asked me.

Trying to get myself together, I took a deep breath and rubbed my eye.

"My supposed to be man hit me in the eye because he got caught creeping with his side ho." I was tired as hell, and huffing like I had just fought a ten round fight.

The club's owner turned to Choppa. "You ain't got no business hittin' on a female."

"Man, I ain't lettin' no bitch punk me. Bitch betta stay in her place," Choppa said as if I was some bitch off the streets, and not wifey.

"Dude, we don't hit or disrespect women up in here. I'ma have to ask you to bounce," said the owner, tersely.

I stuck my tongue out, mocking Choppa. He turned around and got ghost, followed by his whore.

The club's owner turned to me, "Look, Miss Lady. I kno' you're upset, but we can't have this commotion goin' on in my club."

"My bad. When I saw my nigga in the club with some random skeezer posted up on his lap, I snapped. I mean, it was like she was his all and he straight up forgot or didn't give a fuck about me."

"I feel you, but as much as I feel yo' pain, I'ma have to ask you to leave too. No hard feelings, but if I let you stay, every person in here may wanna start some shit and think nothin' of it 'cause I allowed you to stay. So, I gotta treat you like I treat er'body else that fights in here. I ask 'em to bounce."

"I understand. No problem." My bubble had been busted quickly.

"I can have one of my bouncers escort you and yo' girls to your car if you want me to," he offered.

"Please do. I don't trust that nigga. If he hit me once, he'll hit me again. And he's prob'ly mad as all outdoors right about now."

"Okay then. I told you if yo' man don't kno' how to treat you, to holla at a real nigga like me."

I nodded.

We were going downstairs when Young King and the bouncer came, took me by the arm, and escorted me to my car. I was embarrassed about the situation that occurred between my man and me.

Once outside, the bouncer made sure we made it to my car safely then he proceeded back into the club. I started my ignition and got outta my ride.

Young King explained that it wasn't good for me to go home because of what had just gone down between Choppa and me. He suggested that I chill at his place for the night and sleep in peace. At first, I hesitated, but he was right. Once I made it home, we would've been arguing and fighting like cats and dogs. But was his concern genuine or did he have something slick on his mind?

"Are you just trying to get in my panties or are you really concerned?" I questioned.

"I'm not just trying to fuck you. I'm trying to get to kno' you, Ma. If I just wanted to bone, I could easily take somebody up in the club home wit' me. But I'm not looking for no whack ass, groupie love. That ain't what I'm about." He sounded sincere.

"I'm just checkin', that's all." 'Cause, I'm not no jump." I made myself clear.

"If you want one of yo' homegirls to stay over with you, that's aight wit' me. I want you to feel comfortable. I ain't tryin' nothin' stupid wit' you."

"I'll see if Shay will stay with me."

"That's what's up."

Shay and Alize were already in the car and waiting for me to finish talking with Young King. I went around to the passenger side backdoor and motioned for Shay to let her window down.

"What's crackin'?" she asked.

"Young King wants me to stay the night at his crib, and I would feel more comfortable if you stay with me. Can you stay?"

"Let me see. I'll call and tell my auntie I'm gon' be at yo' crib for the night. But why you don't want Alize to stay wit' you?"

Alize cut in, "Girl, Nine would have a fit on me if I stayed out all night."

Shay held her hand outta the window. "Lemme use yo' phone so I can call my aunt."

Shay talked to her aunt and then passed me the phone. "She say it's fine if I spend the night wit' you."

I walked back over to where Young King was standing. "My friend said that she would chill at your house with me," I informed him of Shay's decision.

"Good. Stay right here. Get in yo' car and hold tight. I'ma bring my ride back 'roun' here." He sounded pleased that we had accepted his offer.

"Hold up —," I got silent and went into deep thought — "I gotta drop my sister off first."

"K. I'll follow you then. After you drop her off you can trail me back to my place."

Young King went and brought his ride back over to where I was parked and followed me to Nine and Choppa's mother's house, where Alize got out. My heart raced before I got there, because I wasn't sure where Nine was. If he had seen Young King pull up behind me he would have went back and reported it to Choppa, quick fast. It was kinda disrespectful for me to have had another dude follow me to Choppa's mother's place of residence, but I was so hurt that night that I really didn't care. I was sick and tired of his bullshit.

On my way to Young King's house, I called Choppa. I wanted him to at least tell me why he did me the way he did. I felt like I deserved some type of explanation and an apology. He owed me that much. To my disliking, the butthole didn't pick up his cell. I held on until his voicemail came on and then I started goin' in on him.

"Bastard. You make me fuckin' sick and I'm tired of you and all of yo' bitches. I kno' you see me callin', and you ain't got the decency to answer when you see me my number. You wanna face off with me in the club, and pop me in my shit like I'm yo' punching bag. But that's okay. I got yo' ass," I roared into the phone before hanging up.

Shay said, "Stop stressing over him. He ain't gonna answer that phone 'cause for number one, he got busted and number two, if that thing is still with him then he ain't gon' answer fo' sho'."

"I won't call him no more tonight," I promised.

Shay chuckled. "Kay-Kay, pretty soon we gon' be banned from every night club in Miltown. Every time we step up in a club, we duking it out."

"It does kinda seem like that," I laughed. "People be underestimating me, and I have to let 'em kno' they ain't 'bout this."

"True."

"I kno', right?"

"Uh, huh."

Young King's two-bedroom apartment was nice, to be a bachelor pad. It looked like it had a female's touch added to it by the way it was decorated. When we walked in, there was a huge fish tank in his living room with piranhas swimming around in it. It was beautiful. Shay and I walked over to the sofa and sat down.

"I'm goin' to go take a shower," Young King said and left outta the room.

"It's nice up in here, ain't it?" Shay asked, taking in the decor of the crib.

"It's super clean, too. He has it lookin' good in here. I ain't gon' lie."

I reached over on the small table, grabbed the remote, and turned on the plasma television, that took up half of the living room wall. "Next Friday," starring Ice Cube, popped on. It had been a while since I'd seen it, so I watched it and got a coupla good laughs off of it.

Thirty minutes later Young King showed back up in a white t-shirt with some short pants on. He sat with me and Shay, and the three of us were laughing at the movie, until Shay fell asleep on the sofa and started snoring.

Young King was sittin' in his recliner. We both looked at Shay, then back at each other. It was obvious my girl was tired.

"Tell yo' girl she can go lay down in my extra bedroom. The sheets are clean and er'thang."

I shook Shay. She bucked her eyes then musta realized where she was.

I giggled. "Get up and go lay yo' butt down."

"The guest room is back there," Young King said.

"Good. I'm tired," she said, yawning and rubbing her eyes.

"Don't be blowin' yo' dragon breath ova here on me," I teased.

With a smile she said, "Fuck you, girl."

We both giggled. Shay got up, and went in the back, leaving me alone with Young King.

He got up from his seat, swaggered over to where I was seated and flopped down by me.

He looked directly into my eyes. "You wanna talk about it?"

"Not really."

"We can if you want to."

"Yeah, I guess venting would be a good thing. It was hard for me to see my man cheating on me. He crushed my heart with that move."

"You gon' be aight. He's losing out on a good thing right now."

"He wouldn't even pick up the phone for me when I tried to call him earlier."

"You shouldn't call him. Let that nigga pick up the phone and call *you*. He was being foul. He gon' start wondering what you up to, and if you doin' the same thing he doin'. If he really care 'bout you, he'll call."

I nodded in agreement. I really needed to hear things from a man's point of view.

He tugged my arm and told me to lay in his arms. While I laid on him, he played with my hair and assured me that I'd be okay. He leaned down and started passionately kissing me. His hands made their way to my rear, and he began massaging my ass cheeks. As much I enjoyed it, I moved his hands off me and pulled my head back so we could stop kissing.

"What's wrong?" he asked.

"I'm too upset right now. I keep thinking about my man. I can't get him off my mind."

"Well, just let me hold you."

I rested in his arms for hours, until he woke me up and escorted me to his bedroom. I laid on top of his covers on his bed. I didn't want him to think that because I was mad at Choppa that he could try to play me outta some pussy. Wasn't happenin'. Well, at least not that night.

I saw him go into the top of his closet and pull out some extra cover. He placed the quilt on top of me, kissed me softly on my cheek, and laid beside me until the next morning.

I half slept after that, tossing and turning trying to keep thoughts of Choppa out of my head. I shook my head, thinking of how he would prob'ly fuck me up on contact when he saw me.

Spazzin' Choppa

I went to the crib the next afternoon to shower and change clothes so I could hit the streets again. I unlocked the front door, opened it, and went in. Kay-Kay was standing on the other side. She looked like she'd been up all night. Bags, and a dark blue bruise, decorated her face.

"Where you been?" she had the nerve to ask.

"Out," I replied, purposely being short.

"Out where? Don't you feel that you owe me some kind of explanation?"

"Hell, naw," I growled.

"Why not? You been wit' yo' boo thang all night?" she seethed with both fist balled.

"I ain't been wit' nobody all night. Gon' head on wit' that bullshit."

Kay-Kay came up on me and pushed me with all her might, causing me to fall back on the living room sofa. I was already tired, and had just crawled outta ole' girl from last night's pussy. She started popping me in the face. I grabbed her arms and restrained her before she got another chance to swing off on me. I flipped her on her back and held her down.

"Shorty, the next time you swing at me, I'ma straight up crush yo' ass. You understand?" I warned her. She was on some extra shit.

She started screaming, crying, and kicking. "You ain't shit. I hate you."

I drew back and pimp smacked her. That shit echoed throughout the room. I snatched her by the collar and stuck my balled fist against her nose. "You think you can handle these mufuckaz right here? C'mon, and I'ma show you that you got me fucked up. I ain't no pussy who gon' let you hit on me. You got me twisted, homegirl." I released her collar and stared her down, thinking she would now get that behind in check. But Kay-Kay fooled me.

She ran over to a small table, grabbing a vase full of artificial flowers. "Mufucka, you bossing up on me, but I'm a boss bitch, and I'll go up side yo' goddamn head with this glass vase, if you put yo' dick beaters on me again," she threatened.

I stepped to her, tryin' her. She struck me over the head with the glass vase. I touched the back of my neck and looked at my hand. My fuckin' hand was covered in blood.

"You want some more? Bring yo' monkey ass on 'cause I got it fo' you," she barked with the vase still in hand.

I wasn't going out like that. I stormed up to her again, grabbed her by the hand, snatched the object from her, and threw it into the wall, shattering it into tiny pieces. I snatched her up and carried her in the bathroom.

Once in the bathroom, I wrestled with her until I had her in a chokehold, then I forced her head down into the commode. "This what you want, bitch?" I gritted, as I listened to her cough and gag.

After a few more seconds, I mercifully brought her head up. She coughed up water all over the floor. I ignored her, and was about to dunk her head in the toilet a second time.

"Choppa, I'm sorry. Please stop," she begged.

"I ought to drown you up in this mufucka," I raged. She had fronted me bad last night; death was what she deserved.

I gazed at her for a second before realizing that I'd betta dip out the bathroom and leave her alone, before my temper amped me up to kill her stupid ass. I calmed myself down and bounced before I slipped up and caught a body over some domestic stupidity.

Expect the Unexpected
Kay-Kay

Here I was, kneeling down on the bathroom floor reaching for tissue to blow my damn nose, and get all of the water outta my nostrils. I couldn't believe how Choppa had treated me, when he was the one in the wrong.

Once I had my tissue, I rolled off a handful and blew my nose so hard it hurt. I had a major headache and my body was shaking with both anger and fear. I saw in Choppa's eyes that he was actually capable of killing me. *What type of love is that?*

I mean, was I really in the wrong for catching my man cuddled up with some tramp at a club? How could he push my head into a shitty toilet bowl? I wiped my face with the tissue, stood up, and strutted into the bedroom where my purse was. I got my cell phone from my purse and noticed that I had two text messages.

The first message was from Alize. *Hey, just wanted to see what you was up to.*

I texted her back. *Choppa just had my head under toilet water.* I pressed the SEND key.

My second message was from Young King. *What's good?*

I bounced down on the bed and began texting back. I was excited and happy that he thought about me.

My text read, *Not doing good. Choppa and I just got into it real bad.*

I leaned back against the headboard and tried to gather my thoughts. All of a sudden, I began to sob. *That lowdown nigga tried to drown me*. The ringing of my cell phone ended my sobs. I quickly got myself together and answered the call. My sister's voice sounded alarmed.

"What's the deal? Why the hell is Choppa over there puttin' yo head in the damn toilet?"

I let out a sigh. "Girl, he's just trippin' out cause I checked him 'bout that bitch he was wit' at the club. The nigga got all bent outta shape 'bout it and started flexin'. Its whatever with us. I'm so tired of all his bullshit, and I'm really tired of checkin' all these girls over him. This don't make no sense."

"Nine be trying to show his ass sometimes too, and I have to get ignorant. Anyway, let's stop talking about Choppa. What's up with you and Young King? What y'all do at his crib?"

I turned over on my stomach, cupped my hand under my chin, and smiled.

"We just kind of cuddled until we both ended up falling asleep. He just sent me a text message. I text him back before you called. He's cool. I like him, but I don't want to run behind him sweatin' him or nothin'. I'm really feeling his swag."

Alize giggled. "Sounds like you really like his ass."

"Yeah, I do. But we need to hang out and chill some more, and just remain friends. Choppa would blow both of our heads off if he even thought we were fuckin' around. And, I'm not trying to have Young King caught up in a stupid situation with me and Choppa. I don't want him to get hurt or nothin'."

"You right. I believe if Choppa saw y'all two up in each other's face, he'd fuck y'all up," said Alize.

"You already kno'," I agreed. That's why I'm not trying to take it there with Young. This fool I got for a man is too damn crazy to be cheatin' on," I said, examining the bruise on my arm where Choppa held my arm behind my back.

"Have you heard anything from Shay, today?" Alize asked switching subjects.

"Nope. She s'posed to be trying to get a prepaid cell soon. I'll call her then, but I don't like calling over to her aunt's house. Her auntie stays drunk and be acting stupid and if she gets wrong with me I'ma let her ass have it, straight up."

"I kno' that's right." I heard a beeping sound coming from my cell notifying me that I had received a new text message. "Hold on, I got a text."

My phone read new text from Ms. King. I pressed the key to retrieve Young King's message.

It read, *Sorry that you dealing wit' all that. Let's meet up somewhere and talk.*

I texted back, *Where?*

Young King replied, *Wherever you want to is cool wit' me.*

My response was, *Meet me at the lake in an hour.*

He agreed. I wrapped up my conversation with my li'l' sis and told her that I'd chat with her later.

In a matter of forty-five minutes I had showered, dressed, and was on my way outta the door sporting a white, Ralph Lauren Polo, cotton mini dress with a pink Polo logo on my left breast. I had on my white Ralph Lauren flip-flops, and pranced to my car, and got in.

Right when I had started the ignition, my cell phone rang. I hurried and grabbed my purse on the passenger seat, fumbling and searching for my cell.

The caller I.D. read Choppa. I rolled my eyes, my nose flared, and I let out a hard sigh. I mumbled to myself, "Now, just what the hell does he want?"

I started not to answer at all and let it go to voicemail, but decided to handle his ass a different way. "What is it, Choppa?" I answered with an irritated, hostile tone.

"This ain't Choppa. Choppa's in my bed sleeping, after the super head job I served him earlier," some chick said.

"Who the fuck is this?" I asked, blood boiling, and ready to get stupid.

"This is Carla. I told you it wasn't over between me and Choppa. He paid to have my truck fixed, and still fucks and sucks me, Boo-boo." she triumphed to annoy me.

"You gon' make me find you and whoop yo' mufuckin' ass."

"Oh, I ain't hard to find. I want you to step yo' foot over here on my property. I guarantee you the paramedics gon' be coming to pick you up."

"I ain't wit' all this jaw-jappin'. Tell me where you live at and I betcha I fuck you up on contact."

She replied, "I'm over here on 40th and Burleigh."

"You betta make sho' you got some damn good life insurance when I make it. You just don't kno', you a dead bitch walking." I was gonna deal with her once and for all.

I hit the red button and terminated the call. I had a million and one thoughts prancing through my head at that moment. I wanted to meet with Young King, but I had to go and blow that Carla chick's spot up. I couldn't go out like a punk. I had to let her kno' that I could back up whatever I said. Not only that, but Choppa definitely needed to be checked for the foul shit he was doing to me once again.

I dialed Young King's number.

"Hey, boo," I said when he answered. "Look, I'm not going to be able to meet with you right now. I just had an emergency come up, and I gotta go take care of it."

"Handle that and holla back at me later on so I won't be worried 'bout cha," he said.

"I certainly will and thanks."

"It's nothin'. Is there anything I can do?"

"Naw. I will contact you as soon as I take care of this situation. I promise."

"Aight," he replied. "But don't make a promise that you can't keep."

"Oh, trust me. I'm going to keep it. Holla at cha later, okay?"

"Aight, that's wassup."

I put my car in reverse backed outta the driveway, and made a beeline to my destination.

I drove on 40th and Burleigh and spotted Choppa's Escalade, parked alongside the street, in front of a beige and brown house. I parked directly behind his truck. I looked around at the ghettofied scenery. Small kids were walking the street with no parental supervision. Young dudes wearing sagging pants were hugging the block. I leaned over and opened my glove box to make sure my strap was where it was supposed to be. I grabbed my nine milli out and stuffed it in my Louis Vuitton handbag. I was hyped, and ready to pull both of their cards.

I murdered my ignition, grabbed my handbag, and opened my car door. I got out ready to approach the house. I barely missed stepping on a shattered Hennessey bottle and slicing up my foot. This was in fact the hood. I sauntered up the sidewalk, seething inside. A child with her hair all over her head, appearing to be at least four, ran past me. The minor stopped running and turned around staring at me. I felt like taking my brush outta my purse and brushing the hell outta her little nappy head.

Just pitiful, I thought walking toward the house. Cute as the little girl was, her mammy should have combed her head, but that's how no-good mammy's roll with their scandalous asses.

"Are you going to Carla's house?" the cute little girl asked. She was standing barefoot with her beautiful caramel skin.

"Yes. That's where I'm going."

The little girl smiled at me. "You're pretty."

"Awl, that's sweet of you. You're pretty, too."

"My mama lives in that house right there," the girl announced pointing to the house directly beside Carla's.

"Oh, okay. That's nice."

"My mama in her room with my brother daddy. They got my mama's room door locked."

I just smiled. I was anxious to get to Carla's door to knock so she could come out and face me.

"My brotha daddy spent the night last night, but my daddy gon' stay at our house tonight. I'ma call him today and tell him to. My mama don't care if he stays." Then she hesitated before saying, "My daddy and mama be locking the door, too."

I shook my head at the fact that the Mama had exposed her child to all of her business.

The little girl's front door swung open. A fair-skinned thin young woman in her early twenties peeped out.

"Daija, get yo' hard head in this house right now. I told you to stay yo' black ass in here," the mother screamed at her child. *Damn hoodrat.*

"Bye-bye," the child said waving at me and ran home.

I gave her a grin back. I was supposed to be kicking ass, instead I was outside with a four year old and her ghetto mama, which I was happy that the woman had called the girl inside. I didn't want her to see me beat the black off of Carla. I had a weakness for kids, and one day wanted my own.

I flew back into alley cat mode, walked up to Carla's door, and knocked twice.

Carla opened the front door. "What, bitch?"

"You were just talking cash money shit on the phone. C'mon outside and let's handle this shit." We were nose to nose. Only the screen door was between us.

"Like I told you, it's whatever. You came to my house, and I told you I was gon' be ready to get down," Carla screamed before unlocking the screen door and stepping outside.

I stood, fist balled, and ready. Carla stood in front of me for a minute before she swung off. The lick hit me dead in my face.

"Oh, it's on now," I hollered and threw my purse down and started giving her the business.

I socked her four times in her face, and had an advantage over her with my height. Carla was throwing her fists right back at me, quickly. I clutched her weave ponytail and snatched it out. The ponytail fell to the ground, and we were steady going at it. I reached for her shirt, grabbed it, and shoved her with all of my might.

"Boom." Her body made that noise when it crashed into the house. Her body slid down on the ground, but she instantly jumped up.

I looked down at my French manicure. One of my acrylic nails had been ripped off. Blood was flowing from it, causing an agonizing pain to shoot through my fingertip. I ran over to my purse, lying on the ground, to retrieve my weapon, when Carla jumped on my back.

I wiggled from side to side, attempting to sling her off me. "Get off me skank," I managed to yell, wiggling all around.

She was holding on to me with her legs wrapped around my body. Her hands were around my neck, she was choking me out.

I fell backward on my back and she was underneath me moaning and groaning, pro'bly from the hard impact. It sounded like every bone in her body cracked. I was able to pry her hands from my throat. I hopped up, and dove on top of her, punching her in her face. Blood oozed down her eye. She started pleading for me to stop.

I rapped her two more times before I was unexpectedly being pulled off her.

"Get your hands off me," I told the strange person holding me from the back. I couldn't see their face.

"Ay, slow yo' roll, girl," the voice urged and let me go.

I turned around to see Choppa standing shirtless in a pair of jeans.

"What you doin' over here?" he had the nerve to ask me. "You got all these people out here watching you show yo' ass. Calm this shit down."

I glanced up and observed at least ten neighbors, including the youngsters on the corner, gawking, but that was my least worry.

I stepped to Choppa. "Whatchu mean, what I'm doin' over here? I should be asking you that same question, nigga." I had my finger inches from his face.

"It's nothin'. I was just over here chillin' 'cause you on some mo' shit," he lied.

"Chillin'?" I asked, panting.

"Yep. How you kno' I was over here?"

"This crab bitch right here called my phone and told me."

I stared down at Carla, who had just got up on her knees. After a few seconds, she managed to stand, staggering from the hurting I had put on her.

I looked at my flip-flops and decided to take my right one off. I bent over, slid the shoe off and struck Carla's head.

Smack. Smack. Smack.

She used her arms to protect her head. She was too wobbly and unsteady to fight back. Instead of retaliating, she walked to her backyard and disappeared.

I redirected my attention to Choppa. "How you gon' be over here with this busted up, ugly chick? You just dumb, and I'm tired of wasting my time with you. Every time I look around you screwing something."

"But, baby, you kno' I love you more than anything. Don't even trip on this broad. I ain't tryin' to fuck up what we got, for her. Be easy, Ma," Choppa said and reached for my arm.

I jerked away from him. He'd just dumped my head in the toilet, then wanted to play Mister Nice Guy after being busted.

I was walking over to my purse when I saw the little girl from earlier standing in the doorway.

"You beat up Carla," the child cheered.

"Shut yo' damn mouth," the child's mother barked, and covered the little girl's mouth with her hand.

"Yes, I sho' did, baby girl," I bragged.

I bent over, retrieved my purse, and observed a doghouse in the back, along the side of the house. I told myself that, that was exactly what Choppa should have been living in with his dog ass. A damn doghouse.

I was becoming a little alarmed that Carla had gone into the backyard and never returned. My first initial thought was to go to the back and see if she had collapsed and died from the beating I had given her, but instead, I slung my purse strap on my shoulder ,and had walked off to dip out and go home.

"Hold up, baby. Let me run in the house, grab my keys and come home and holla at you," Choppa insisted.

"Choppa, fuck you," I snapped, and never stopped walking to my ride.

I got to my car and was about to open my car door when er'body in the streets, suddenly dispersed. *What's wrong with them?* I thought. I turned around to see why everyone bounced out running and screaming..

What I saw caused me to tremble and panic.

If It Ain't One Thing It's Another Choppa

I dipped in Carla's crib to grab my keys, when I heard screams. "What the fuck goin' on now," I muttered to myself.

I quickly ran to the bedroom, got my keys off the dresser, and sprinted outside to see what the deal was. Carla was holding her pit bull, Psycho, by his leash. Everybody in the neighborhood knew that Psycho's bark was as vicious as his bite. The red-nosed pit began barking and drooling, like he was ready to chew a hole in somebody's ass.

"Don't do that shit, Carla," I roared, knowing what she was about to do. But she ignored my command.

"Get her, Psycho," Carla ordered and let go of the dog's leash. The canine charged toward Kay-Kay with his deadly fangs showing. Kay-Kay was fumbling around in her purse. I could hear Carla laughing hysterically at the dog dashing towards Kay-Kay.

I grimaced as Psycho leaped.

Kay-Kay whipped her steel outta her purse and pulled the trigger just in time. Three rapid shots rang out in succession. Psycho collapsed on the ground immediately and started wheezing hard. He had bullet holes in him, and cherry red blood was leaking out.

"You just killed my dog," Carla hollered and ran over to Psycho.

I walked over to the dog and frowned. The animal's tongue was hangin' outta his mouth, and his eyes were burstin' outta his head.

Carla fell to the ground, crying on him. I shook my head, and kept it movin', on my way to my whip. I was ready to get the hell outta dodge before somebody hit the po-po's up.

"Kay-Kay, gon' hit the pavement and roll out before the po-po's come," I advised.

"You betta try to find you a new bread snatcher cause that one has gon' to dog heaven, "Kay-Kay told Carla and opened her car door to get in.

Carla jumped up off the ground and scampered toward Kay-Kay swinging her arms like she was deranged. "You killed Psycho," she screamed.

Kay-Kay bust in the air. Pow. Pow.

Carla stalled and just stood there in shock, Kay-Kay aimed at her.

"If you want me to blow yo' head off step to this nine and I'ma injure you for life. You gon' get dropped like yo' dog. Now try me," Kay-Kay urged.

Carla turned around and went in her house. Kay-Kay got in her car and disappeared, I did the same. I had witnessed enough craziness to last me a whole century, on the real.

I bust a move and headed to my trap spot to see what was poppin' off before heading home and listening to Kay-Kay cuss me about being at Carla's.

My partna, Gully, who ran one of my trap spots, told me that my product was out. There was a drought in Mil-Town. Didn't nobody have work. Junkies and smokers were scurrying around the city in desperate search of drugs. Whoever got straight first was gonna rape the game.

I put a call in to my connect, Dirty Red, from Chi-Town. But I didn't get an answer. I figured he'd see my number and hit me back like he usually did. I wasn't 'bout to leave a voicemail, that wasn't my style. He was good people, but still I knew that I couldn't trust nobody in the game. In my life I had learned to trust only a few, and that was only to a certain extent.

I never doubted Gully's loyalty. That boy was a straight fool, too. He would scatter lead with no hesitation when he had beef. And, he liked feeding his pockets just as much as I liked to feed mine. We were like family, and he was like a brother to both me and Nine. Whenever I needed Gully he was there for me, whether I needed him to bust his gun or make paper.

I pulled up to the trap and fired up a Newport. I glanced in my rearview mirror and saw that Nine was driving up behind me. I deadened my engine.

Nine and I got out our whips and approached each other.

"What's the word, soldier?" I asked and we dapped fist.

"Shit. Just rollin' through to see what's happenin'."

Nine tucked one hand in the side pocket of his jeans, and held his cell phone in his other hand.

"That's wassup. I'm ready to blow. You got some green on you?" I asked, ready to get high to calm my nerves after dealing with Carla and Kay-Kay.

"You kno' it, dawg. Let's go in the crib and roll up. I ain't smoked shit all day."

I chuckled. Nine normally smoked morning, noon, and night. If he could find a way to smoke while he slept, he would. That's how serious it was with him.

Once inside my trap we sat in the small living room in two lawn chairs. That's how we got down. Trap houses looked inside just like the name of 'em, trap, which was old and raggedy and only served the purpose of hustling outta 'em.

Nine removed a Philly from his shirt pocket, unwrapped it, and split it down the middle. He reached down into his sock and pulled out a sack. I watched Nine take out the tobacco and insert a healthy portion of that green in the cigar. I listened to Gully tell 'bout what happened at a strip club called The Gentlemen's Castle. He and a few of my runners went there the night before.

"Ay, you listening to me? What's good? You acting like something wrong," he questioned me.

I sighed. "Just got a lot of bullshit goin' on. My bitch's gon' have to get right before they get left. I got two who stressin' me the fuck out."

"Goddamn. You lettin' 'em stress you like that? You betta put 'em in check or either stop fuckin' wit 'em." Gully laughed. "I don't let mine stress me. If any of mine stress me I'ma be knockin' that ass out. You got to let 'em kno' that you run shit and bust 'em in they shit every now and then," Gully said as he sat on the worn out black leather sofa.

Gully was a hustler by day and a pimp by night. He had about five different baby mama's who all knew each other. He didn't lie when he said he'd knock his bitches out. If one of his females got outta pocket he'd check her quick, but lately he had been on chill with hammering them because Milwaukee's a woman's state. He'd recently gotten outta prison after serving a one-year bid for domestic violence. You couldn't be putting your hands on the females without going to jail if the law was called. The boys in blue had no mercy on a woman beater. You would get jammed fo' that and if the woman tried to drop the charges it still wouldn't matter because the state took over the case.

Nine finished rolling the blunt and licked the cigar from its beginning to end then got up and put it in the microwave for ten seconds to make it stick betta. He got his lighter from his jeans pants pocket and fired it up.

"I'ma hit this bitch first," he said with the cigar in his hand and took a puff. Smoke from the blunt crept through the air.

"Pass it here." Gully reached for the blunt. Nine passed it to him. Gully inhaled the smoke through his lips and held it. Then, after a few minutes, he slowly exhaled. He coughed two times then beat his chest.

"That's what that potent shit does to you," I blurted.

Nine burst out laughing.

"This that killa weed right here, bruh." Nine reached for the blunt and Gully passed it.

"If you can't hang with the big dog's gon' get off the porch, nigga," Nine teased.

"Fuck you," Gully joked back.

Right after the third puff Nine was choking like he'd swallowed a handful of watermelon seeds. Me and Gully were laughing hard at him.

"You the mufucka that can't hang. Get off the porch li'l' puppy," I teased.

Nine was coughing so hard that a long trail of spit was hanging from his mouth. He leaned over trying to catch his breath.

I raised up from my chair. "You good, bruh?" I wanted to kno'. I was becoming worried.

Nine didn't respond he continued coughing 'til he finally caught his breath. He slowly sat up in the chair. His eyes were watery, red, and dazed. He appeared to be in another world. I was satisfied that he was breathing normal, again, but something just wasn't right with him, he wasn't himself.

Gully stood and paced over to Nine with a caring, attentive expression. "Nine, you aight, man?" he asked tapping him on the arm.

Nine didn't reply. He just sat there zoned out.

Gully had a seat in his chair. "Damn, bro, I feel light-headed." He blinked several times then touched his forehead with the back of his hand.

I took the blunt outta Nine's hand and then reached over on the small table and put it out in the small ashtray on the table.

"That blunt smell funny as hell. I think y'all got a hold of some bad shit," I uttered.

I scooted down in my chair. My eyes were going back and forth observing Gully and Nine's reactions. Gully hopped outta his seat; he was sweating as if he had just ran a marathon. He unbuttoned his jeans and dropped 'em on the floor.

Nine stood up and pulled his red t-shirt over his head. He bent over, removed his

Jordan's from his feet, and eased the jeans off and left them on the floor. He was standing in front of me in nothin', but boxers.

"Nigga, what's wrong wit' chu? Why you acting homo? Put yo' mufuckin' clothes back on, boy," I said.

Nine snatched his boxers off and was breakdancing across the floor. It was obvious that whoever they copped the weed from "wet it" with some type of chemical. Sweat was gushing down Nine's forehead. Meanwhile, Gully was bugging.

"I'm Jesus. I know my enemies will crucify me today but I'll rise again in three days," he claimed.

These fools are straight trippin. My baby bro' breakdancing and sweating like a racehorse to my left. I had Gully, to my right singing a church hymn thinking he's Jesus. I grabbed my cell outta my pocket and dialed Mama up.

"Hey, baby," Mama answered.

"What's goin' on, Ma?"

"I'm doin' pretty good. What's up with you and who is that in the background singing, Amazing Grace?" Mama asked.

"That's Gully, and Nine just stopped breakdancing and now he's doin' the moonwalk."

"Damn. What's gotten into them?"

"I don't kno', Mama. They smoked a li'l' weed that had to be wet. Now they actin' weird. Tell me what I need to do. I'm half-scared to take 'em to a doctor 'cause them folks might be lookin' upside my head like I messed them up," I explained.

I was checkin' out Nine who was sliding backward across the across the floor moonwalking.

"Choppa," Mama called redirecting my attention to our conversation.

"Yeah, Mama, what's good?"

"Get my baby some help. Call an ambulance or something and get him to a hospital. Don't let him stay there in that type of condition."

"Mama just tell Alize to come to my spot. She's been here before with Nine she knows how to get here."

"You sure?"

"Yeah, Mama, just send her to my spot," I repeated.

"Okay. And you betta not let nothing happen to my baby," she said.

Nine and I were Mama's only kids, and I always felt that she showed favoritism when it came to him. He was her baby and no matter what he did. In her eyes, he was perfect. My li'l' bro always looked up to me. Whatever I did, he always wanted to do it, too. Mama never blamed him for his actions. She would say that I should look out for him and tell him to do the right things. Hell, I couldn't tell a grown man what to do. I couldn't lecture him on doing right when I did fucked up shit myself.

"Don't holler at me, boy. Who did he buy that bullshit from?"

"I don't kno' but when I find out it's over for 'em."

Mama went ahead and delivered my message to Alize letting her kno' what was up. When Mama got Alize out the door she started, "Choppa, you need to watch out for Nine. You gon' have to start making sho' he don't fuck with crazy ass people. He had no business buying no wet weed from nowhere. Then, instead of you calling my baby some medical help, you call me. Do you think with your pea-brain?"

"Hold on Mama. Now, I didn't call you so you could be downing me. You trying to make me feel fucked up for some shit I had nothin' to do wit'."

"You started him to smoking weed. My baby was supposed to go to college. He was making A's and B's. He started hangin' out with you his twelfth grade year and dropped out to hustle."

"I didn't put no gun up to this nigga head and make him do nothin'."

"You might as well have. You introduced him to the streets and those thugs you hang out with. Especially, Gully's half-raised ass."

"Mama, I ain't got time to argue back and forth with you," I finally said to end our phone call.

"Let me kno' how my baby's doin'. And, I want to kno' what hospital y'all taking him to."

"I will let you kno' how yo' damn baby is doin' later," I said being sarcastic.

"Alright now. Don't slick talk me. You kno' I love you, too. You got to look out for Nine. You put him in the streets so you gon' have to take care of him while he's in them," she preached. I could tell through her speech that she was having shortness of breath.

"I'ma holla at chu later. Go ahead and catch yo' breath. Bye."

"Don't say bye. Say see you later. I don't like goodbyes," she slowly admitted word for word.

Nine sang out, "Amazing grace/ how sweet/ the sound…"

"Ay, chill out. I'm on the phone with Mama," I told Nine.

Mama managed to chuckle. "Oh, so he's singing spirituals now?"

"He's trying to."

"Get that boy some help before he ends up in a mental institution."

"Aight, see you later, Mama."

"See you later, baby."

I hung the cell up and sat back watching how stupid they were acting. It was half-funny and half sad. "Boy, sit yo' ass down somewhere," I ordered Nine, but he kept dancing.

Gully had hidden behind the sofa claiming that the dead people he heard earlier were after him. He was claiming they wanted to snatch his eyes out and leave him blind.

"Don't fuck wit' my eye. Get from 'roun' me mufuckas," he yelped swinging his arms to keep the ghost away.

I thought, *Dayum, I'm happy as hell I didn't smoke that shit.*

I was being entertained when I heard two hard knocks on the front door. I hopped up, peeped out the window, and saw Alize.

"Damn, I'm glad to see you, baby girl," I said. I unlocked and opened the front door.

Alize gave me a slight smile. "Where's Nine at? Yo' Mama said he's over here acting a fool. What the hell wrong wit' 'em?"

Before I could speak, she witnessed the shit for herself when Nine dropped to his knees crying.

She ran over to him. "Baby, you need to go to the hospital."

With a confused, worried expression, Alize grabbed him by the arm and sat him down on the sofa. She was unaware that Gully was hiding behind it fighting invisible people. She sat beside Nine rubbing his back trying her best to comfort him. Placing his head on her shoulder, she rubbed his back asking him what his problem was.

"Baby, you got sweat pouring from you head. Try to stay calm and relax, boo. I'm goin' to take you to the emergency room. You gonna be alright," Alize comforted.

I stepped over to where they were sitting with my bro's clothes in hand and was prepared to help her dress him and get him some help.

"Let's put his shirt and pants on him. I'll help you," I offered.

I got on the left side of Nine while Alize stood on his right side and we were successful with standing him up.

Gully suddenly stood up from behind the sofa. He was swinging off at the air, steady going to war wit' the ghost. Alize jumped and took off running toward the door. I guess it must have startled her when she heard all the commotion come from behind her.

"Y'all betta tell these mufuckas to leave me the hell alone," Gully cried hysterically.

From observing him boxing the air , it looked like he was going head up with a real live person, except there was nobody swinging off but him. The shit was funny as hell, but that wasn't the time to be laughing at that clown.

"Cut that out," I barked at Gully. "We up here trying to put Nine's clothes on so we can take y'all to the ER. So kill that."

"Fuck it. I'ma just let these bitches kill me. I'm giving up. Tell my mama, my B.M. and my daughter that I love 'em. I'm out this bitch, I'm surrendering," he spoke. He dropped down to the floor on his back stretched out gazing up at the ceiling. Meanwhile, Alize paced back over to where I was standing, I had to hold my bro' up with both of my arms 'cause she ran off.

We were lucky enough to get him dressed. I shipped both of them off to the ER with Alize. She asked me if I was goin'. I told her "hell naw." I didn't do hospitals and I wasn't gon' risk getting interrogated by nobody at the hospital. On top of it all, I had to be sho' I got in touch with my plug to cop a few birds.

Gully usually rode wit' me to meet whoever Dirty Red would send to meet me with the work.

Gully wouldn't be able to go with me. I'd have to ride solo, and strap up if I was able to catch up wit' my connect that day. Dirty Red had never crossed me. He was always solid and kept it one hunnid, but I had to remember what his name was and that said enough.

Dirty Red was about six foot seven with a facial resemblance to the late Malcolm X. He was born and raised in the "Sipp," Mississippi, but now resided in Chicago.

I was chillaxin' in a chair just thinking about the events that occurred in my life. My dad was a sorry ass nigga that I never had much to do with. He was married to my mama for sixteen years. He decided to up and leave my mama when I turned fifteen for a younger female that he had two kids with. I heard that he and his ole' lady had a girl and a boy.

My mama had never worked a day in her life and struggled to pay bills. She prayed day and night for employment and finally got a job at a convenience store, part-time. I did what I had to do and hit the streets hustlin' hard for an older cat named Big Hughe. He was like the dad I never had. When I started slangin' for Big Hughe he was whippin' a pearly white Benz on wheels. He stayed iced out with flashy jewelry that a young nig' like me only dreamed of wearing. And, that's where my life as a hustler began. When I had stacked up enough bread I got my own bricks and flipped 'em. When I had Mil-Town on lock I took Nine under my wings and schooled him to the game, and we been running shit er' since.

My mama was able to quit her job workin' part-time for a white dude who tried to work his workers like plantation slaves. I wasn't havin' that. Soon after Mama's sickle cell started acting up causing her to wear oxygen twenty-four seven. Six months later, she qualified for disability and started receiving a monthly check. I still kept her pockets right with what I pulled in off the streets. She disagreed wit' how I made my dough, but I wasn't trying to take heed to her objections. I had to step up to the plate and man up 'cause my dad decided that he wanted some young pussy and bailed out on us.

To me, Nine was not only my li'l' bro, he was like my son. I raised him after our pops vanished. Shid, I didn't have no talk fo' him. He did my mama dirty and I didn't have no understandin' for that. I felt like he was the reason I was forced to man up and make sho' money was comin' in the house. I was tired of seeing my mama crying and wonderin' how the bills would be paid. Seeing her shedding tears hurt me. Even so, Nine was and will always be her baby. She always blamed me for his actions 'cause she saw how he idolized and looked at me as a father figure throughout the years.

My cell rang, breakin' my thoughts. I reached in my front pants pocket and saw that it was my boy Dirty Red returning my call. "Whad's crackin', homey?" I asked.

"Aw, same thing, different day. What's poppin' off on yo' end?"

"It's a drought over here, man. I need you to send a couple of birds over my way," I told him. "You think you can look out for me?"

"How 'bout I get my people to meet up wit' you at the usual spot in 'bout twenty minutes?"

"Good lookin' out and I'll holla."

"You kno' I gotchu," Dirty Red responded before hanging up.

I tossed my phone on the passenger seat, grabbed my car keys, and bounced. As I headed to my whip, an unclean, bald mouth and straight up funky dope fiend approached me.

"Excuse me, man. You got some hard?" the fiend questioned.

"Shit dead round here fo' now. Get back at me later."

"I sho' will, buddy," the fiend said before wandering off on his crack prowl.

Next thing I heard was, "Aye, buddy."

I looked over my shoulder at the fiend re-approaching me. "What's up, man?" I wanted to kno'. I was irritated with him for interrupting me while I was trying to get to my meeting location.

"I ain't trying to sweat you hard, but can I hold somethin'?" he asked.

"I ain't no fool. You trying to game me?" I angrily asked.

"Man, it ain't like that, I swear. I just asked a simple question, don't get all fucked up 'bout it."

He backed away while trying to lie his way outta the situation that he'd created.

I jumped at him almost causing him to jump outta his damn skin.

"My bad, playa. I'm gone. I didn't mean to upset you, bruh. Just thought you could look out fo' a brotha. That's all, dude."

He took off down the street goin' a hundred glancing back every few steps to make sho' I wasn't comin' behind him.

I hopped in my ride, heading to the pickup spot. I had a thought to cross my mind 'bout the situation that had occurred. Smokers had the nerve to ask any and er'body fo' somethin'. Shid, dude, had me bent. I think I had heard every lie in the book come from a crackhead to get some smoke. I'd seen bitches do somma er'thang for a rock.

I splurged off the money I made hustlin' in the streets, but real story I wasn't happy For one, I had to constantly watch my back for po-po's or either hatin' ass salvages who would be willing to take me out the game over my dough. Two, I never slept peacefully. Whenever I got late night calls, I jumped to answer. I didn't kno' whether one of my spots got run up in and my workers got wet up or either the law decided to bust the doors of my trap houses down and threw my peeps in the county. And, if one of my crew members got jammed I had to worry 'bout whether I had a pure-bred on my team that wouldn't rat me out to the Feds. So, don't get me wrong my money was good, pockets never starving, but I had much shit to worry 'bout. And three, I always had trouble resting my head peacefully at night cause of the event that happened wit' me and Nine years ago that got us our nicknames Choppa and Nine.

Big Hughe had major problems with another cat who owned him money named, Loco. He offered Nine twenty-five stacks and me a piece to run up in Loco's spot and chalk line him and two days later we made sure we took care of it.

I pressed the eject button on my CD player and took out the Yo Gotti disk, and exchanged it for the Plies CD. I was hoping that the sound of music would fade out every memory I had of that day when Big Hughe named us. I did my best to dismiss that dreary day, but that shit didn't work. No matter how hard I bobbed my head to the beat of Plies' song, "She Got It Made," the events rolled through my head so fresh and clear like it had just happened.

I sat in my truck and waited for Dirty Red's people to come through. We met several times at this location. He owned the building that was a barbershop run by his brother. The street was in a rough area in the city. Dopeheads were plentiful. Every time I glanced up there was a different one roaming and trotting around fiending. They were half-dead and it was so many, I wondered if they were coming up out of the ground and shit.

I was tooled up and ready wit' my glock on my waistline, ready to take a body shot if somebody got crooked. I needed three whole slabs from Dirty to get me back right. I'm talking slabs as in kilos, nothin' less would do. Keys were goin' fo' twenty-five bands each. I had seventy-five bands in a Nike shoe bag on deck under my seat where I placed it earlier in the day.

I tilted my head back and was eyeing down some young foot soldiers in my rearview who popped up on the scene. One of the youngsters appeared to be about nineteen. He had just served a smoker wit' the ole' handshake but I knew that crack was being passed. The other three were standing there, choppin' it up, while their partna got his grind on.

All at once, the conversation must have drifted to my ride. All of their eyes landed on my whip, mouths moving. I couldn't interpret a damn thing that they were saying, though. A dark-skinned bony male stepped in front of my truck, waving his ass off and cheesing. Every rotten tooth was showing. He resembled that skeleton from, "Tales from the Crypt."

I felt my phone vibrating. A text came through. I got my cell out my pocket and pressed the button to read it.

It was from Carla. *Fuck you. You let Psycho get killed and didn't do shit to try to stop it.*

I shook my head and tossed the phone on the passenger seat.

I glimpsed up and noticed the same skinny dopehead that was waving earlier was at my driver's side window.

I'm thinking, *This mufucka gon' make me snap.*
I barely cracked my window to see what he wanted. "What's shakin'?" I asked, perturbed.
"I can wash yo' ride fo' you fo' only twenty bucks, player," he cackled.
"What! Nigga if you don't push on!"
The smoker looked nervous and uneasy. Guess it was from the way I was mean mugging him. His eyes started blinking fast and that rotten grin was wiped away.
"I wanted to kno' if you wanted me to shine this thing up fo' you man, that's all," his voice quivered. "My sister lives up the street and she'll let me use her soap and water."
"Fuck away from my shit, bitch ass mufucka. Do it look like I want my shit washed?" I snapped.
"I'm sorry, bruh, my bad," he said backing away from me.
The youngster who was serving the fiends stepped closer to my whip admiring it. The other trap boys did the same. "Yo, Alvin? Why you got your ugly face pressed up against partna's window? Fuck around and catch a hot one in the face," one of them warned the fiend who was soliciting me for a car wash.
"I was just offering him my services, J-Roc, I didn't mean to offend him," Alvin explained.
J-Roc was coming toward us. "Al, step off man. This dude shit already blingin'. These twenty-sixes lookin' good. You doin' it big," he complimented.
J-Roc came to my window. "Yo' shit pimped out."
"Preciate it, li'l' homey," I responded.

"Who you waiting fo', bruh? You lookin' fo' somebody?" J-Roc asked.

"Naw, I'm straight. I kno' who I'm over here fo'. Preciate you though."

"No problem," he said and walked away, Al went his separate way, too.

J-Roc and his boys posted up a few feet behind my truck but eventually they vanished one by one. I took a deep breath, relieved that the young cats wandered off. I had a very uncomfortable, eerie feeling wit' them lingering in my vicinity. I didn't kno' whether they were plotting to gank me or what. I was in the heart of the ghetto where anything could go down. One thing about it though I wasn't gon' freeze up if anybody got outta order. I wouldn't stall on showin' 'em how I earned the name, Choppa. When I turned back around, I noticed two chocolate breezy's strutting by. One had a big apple ass wit' honey-blonde, and red kinky twist. The other girl was sportin' a long jet-black curly ponytail. They both were geared in Roca Wear tube tops, tight grippin' Capri's, and lace-up scandals. The head of my joint was thumpin' like a heartbeat.

For a moment, they distracted me. I kept thinking about all the fun I could have with those two. I stared at them 'til they were outta sight. Dayum.

Time was moving along. I had been waiting for Dirty's folk's for a while. I was growing impatient. A loud, crackling noise made me ready to reach for my tool. Out of nowhere, a red object quickly flew past my face, landing on my passenger's seat.

"What the--?" I yelled out, unsure of what had just taken place. A brick was laying on the seat. To my left I saw that a brick was thrown at my driver's side window.

"Yeah, mufucka, you kno' what time it is," a voice roared. "Get right, befo' I paint ya windows red."

I saw three niggas with toolies pointed at me. They had caught a nigga slippin'. *Is this how it's gonna end for me?* I wondered.

Karma's A Bitch
Kay-Kay

I had Young King on the phone listening to me vent about er'thang Choppa had put me through, 'specially 'bout what went on with me and Carla.

"I'm just sick of this shit," I told Young King. "Every single time I look around I got to catch him cheating. Then he had me and that pigeon fighting over him."

"Look, baby girl, you either gon' stop fuckin' wit' that nigga or you gon' keep lettin' him cheat on you. You only got two choices. So, what you gon' do?"

I parked my car. There was a silence. All I could do was think. Unsure of what my decision or answer would be, I sat quietly, before turning the ignition off.

"Whatchu gon' do?" Young King asked again.

"I'm not sure. All I kno' is that I can't keep goin' through this right here," I sighed. "I'm not gon' lie to you, I love him. He was by my side when my mama was killed and he looked out for me. I didn't have nothin' before we hooked up."

"Tell me this, do you feel like you obligated to him on the strength that he was there when you needed somebody?"

With one hand holding my cell, I used my free hand to throw my car keys in my purse. I leaned my head back on the headrest, and stared up at the sky through my driver's side glass. I felt like Mama was up there in the sky as my guardian angel, smiling down on me. I could only pray that she would guide me and help her daughter make the right decision. Suddenly I remembered that I had Young King on the phone and stopped daydreaming.

"Yes, I guess I do feel that I owe him something. I can't give him his money back. I'm not working. I can only repay him with my love and affection."

He cleared his throat before speaking. "Listen, Ma, in life we meet people who are there for us when we need 'em. That's 'cause God places those people there to help us when we can't help ourselves. Then, you help yourself when you're able, thank them and move on, but that doesn't mean that you owe them yo' life or have to take bullshit off them because they did you a favor. That's how we get our blessings by helping others. If you do a good deed that deed comes back to you later. I feel like you making up excuses to stay there."

I threw my hand up in the air. "What other choice do I have? I don't have nowhere else to go. I'm not workin' and I ain't got no family that will take me in. You just don't get it…it's not that damn simple and easy for me to just up and peel out like that."

"Kay-Kay, it's not that hard, you making it hard by stalling on making a move. Now if you ain't ready to leave him and you feel like you can't live without him then you gon' always have drama. Unless, he changes, which he ain't gon' hardly do right now 'cause he's addicted to the streets, homegirl."

"Tssssk…you're right. I'ma work all of this out pretty soon. If he'd only stop fuckin' wit' these rats in the streets he'd be the perfect boyfriend," I stated lamely.

"That's the point, he ain't changing no time soon," Young King spat. I could tell from his tone that my cluelessness was beginning to irritate him.

He took a long deep breath. "Li'l' Mama, if you want to post up outta town wit' me you can. I got a show to do on Indiana tomorrow night. You down?"

The offer sounded good. I needed time to figure out what I wanted to do with my life. Not only that, I wanted to show Choppa that two could play at his li'l' game. More than a few times, he didn't come home. Now, he could worry 'bout where I was 'cause the shoe would be on the other foot.

"If you let me run off with you and chill that will help me out. I need to get away," I answered Young King.

"Fa sho'. When you comin' to my crib? I'm leavin' out in a few hours."

"Let me pack a few things and I'll be over in a minute. Look, I really don't kno' you like this to be poppin' up on your doorstep, but I like you and you cool and you've been a good friend and listener," I rambled on.

"It's all love, li'l' mama. Holla at me when you get outside, aight?"

"Will do," I assured him.

I jumped out my car, headed to the front door, and went to work packing all that I would need for my two nights stay.

As I went into the bathroom to get my Vicki Secrets mist and lotion, all kinds of thoughts raced through my mind. On one hand, I was afraid of what Choppa would do if I went through with this. On the other hand, it felt exciting to have met someone who really seemed to care about me.

I opened the bathroom closet and pulled out two body lotions along with the matching mist. Glancing into the long mirror in front of me, I began dancing and cheesing. I bent over and wiggled my ass slowly from side to side imagining Young King behind me rubbing his dick against me.

"Whoa, am I really having sexual thoughts of Young King?" I asked myself.

Putting an end to my own immature shenanigans, I decided to hurry up and get packed so I could roll out. And I had it done in a jiffy. The large pink and white Nike sleepover bag I carried out the door had all that I needed. I locked up and left out.

I made my way from the front door to the car, tossed the bag on my backseat, inserted my key in the switch, and sat for a minute. I needed to be sure that I wasn't forgetting anything that I may have been in need for later.

I was sitting for a second; callin' out things off the top of my head, makin' sure I had what I needed. Certain that I was straight, I put my ride in reverse. Looking over my shoulder to be sure my coast was clear, I backed up, put the gear in drive, and drove off.

I started having sexual thoughts of Young King again. I wondered if he was gentle or was he a rough neck who liked to make his girls head bang up against the headboard and beat it up.

"Guess I'll just have to wait and see," I spoke in a whisper.

Oh shit. Did I just say that? I thought. I was acting like a horny freak. I was talkin' to myself, and havin' all these ideas runnin' through my head about him, when my life was in shambles. I needed to get a grip, but I couldn't help it if he turned me on.

I got to Young King's crib and sat in the parking lot debating on whether or not I should get outta my car or put my key back in my ignition and bail. I finger tapped my steering wheel, nervous as hell. Seconds later, my cell was blowing up. I snatched my purse, and grabbed my phone from deep down at the bottom, along with all the junk I kept in it.

"What, Choppa?" I said with a bad temper.

"Ay, check this...I need you to come get me."

"Come get you from where?" I clenched and unclenched my fist.

"Over here on Vliet. I just got jacked."

"And? Why do you need me to come get you?"

"Look, bitch. I ain't in the mood for yo' attitude and all these dumb ass questions. My ride just got stolen, now come get me."

"Fuck you, nigga. Call that Carla ho to come get yo' stupid ass. 'Cause I ain't comin' to get shit. Matter of fact, I'm done wit' yo' lying, cheating, no good ass. Call another one of yo' bitches to come scoop you up 'cause this bitch right here, ain't. Then you got the nerve to call me out my goddamn name, like I stole yo' shit—"

"Ho, I said come get me. You betta be on this street in a few minutes," he ordered.

"Boy, you got one foot named Ike and the other named Mike, use 'em," I snapped on him, and hung my phone up.

I grabbed my luggage and got out my car, stopping to take a deep breath, before getting the courage to actually follow through with what I was about to do. I hit Young King up and said, "Boo, I'm at your doorstep." I thought to myself, *Yeah, Choppa. I'ma see how you like this right here.*

Unleashing The Fury
Choppa

I couldn't believe that Kay-Kay came at me wit' that left-handed shit. After all the shit I'd done fo' that rat ass bitch, then she played me like that.

Three mufuckaz stuck they burners in my face, robbed me, and she ghost? *It's all good. Bitch gonna feel my pain.*

It's bad business when you strapped and still get jacked, but those niggas had caught me slippin'. They made me get up out my shit, patted me down, and took the fo-fifth off my waist. Wasn't shit I could do. Next thing I knew, they was driving off wit' my ride, and the bands I had in a shoe bag under my driver's seat.

All I could do was pace back and forth down the street, waitin' fo' Dirty Red's people to show up. It had taken them so long to show up that I had all kinds of thoughts. Shid, I was kinda feelin' like my boy had set me up. The fact that the young cats robbed me in broad daylight stunned me. I noticed that the fiend from earlier was a few houses down. I motioned fo' him to come to me. The dude slowly made it up to me. It was apparent that he was scared, from the way he was lookin' at me. He was givin' me a look like, nigga what the hell could you want wit' me after you cussed me out earlier.

"What's happenin', man?" he asked. He glanced around alot. I guess he was scared to be standin' there wit' me. Folks walkin' round could've easily accused him of bein' a rat. I understood all that.

"Yo, my man. I just need to kno' the name of each one of those niggaz that just jacked me," I explained serious as a heart attack.

"On the serious tip, I hate that shit just went down wit' you, bruh, but I ain't gettin' involved in that shit, dude. No sirrr," he said with fear.

"I feel you." I nodded wit' understanding. "But they robbed me in broad fuckin' daylight. I'm heated, and real salty behind that. All I need is the names. Ain't nobody gon' kno' that you told me shit, and that's on my mama," I told him making it plain and clear.

"Aight, playboy. Give me three hunnid, and I'll tell you every last one of they names."

I realized that I didn't have no money on me.

"I tell you what…be over here in two hours and I'ma come back wit' yo dough. Don't leave and go nowhere now. I'ma get somebody to come pick me up and believe me, I gotchu when I get back."

"Okay, I'ma be waitin' fo' you at my sister house," he stated, turned, and sauntered away.

I hit Dirty Red up on his cell and told him what happened. He swore that he didn't kno' nothin' bout what had gon' on. Whoever they was, I was gon' do all of 'em the minute I found out their identities. *Bitch muthafuckas. Y'all about to find out why they call me Choppa.*

As I was conversing wit' Dirty Red, two high-yellow chicks in a new-modeled black Corvette drove up. They was bumpin' Ludacris' song, "My Chic Bad."

"Ay, Dirty, I'ma holla at you. I need to call somebody to come pick me up, so I can get outta this spot. These niggaz may come back, and I ain't even strapped," I said.

"Damn, boy. You fucked up, bad. You want me to have my people drop you off somewhere when they get there?"

"Naw, I'm straight," I replied, never taking my eyes off the badass bitchez that had pulled up.

"Cool. My girls should be pullin' up in a black Corvette soon."

I chuckled. "Yeah, they here now. They just pulled up."

"Don't laugh. Yeah, I kno' they two fine ass bitchez, but don't get it twisted. Looks can be deceiving. They may be dymes and look harmless, but they stay strapped, and they go hard. They some beasts."

"I feel you."

"I'ma call them now and let 'em kno' what just went down wit' you, and send 'em back where they came from . If I hear anything 'bout them niggaz who crossed you, I'ma let you kno' what's up. I'ma find out though, cause they fuckin' wit' my business. Mufuckaz I deal wit' that way trust that location. That's bad business if these thirsty cats over there robbin' who I deal wit. This shit got me pissed."

"Just holla at me and let me kno' something," I quickly said so we could get off the damn phone.

I wasn't gon' tell him shit that I found out, 'cause now I didn't trust him. This could've all been a set up. The chicken on the driver's side had parked directly in front of the house where it was s'pose to go down. I saw her place her cell to her ear. I figured it was Dirty Red who'd called her and gave the 4-1-1 on what had gon' down. I didn't have no money to cop the work they were s'pose to be droppin' off. I'd charge it to the game. She hung her phone up and crept off.

I got on the phone, callin' numbers. I had to get the fuck outta dodge. I dialed Kay-Kay's punk ass phone five times and that bitch wouldn't answer. Instead, she let me go to voicemail. That fifth time, I was fuming. When the voicemail came on that time, I went in.

"Pick up yo' phone. I told yo' punk ass that I just got robbed, and you don't even give a fuck. I made you, ho. When yo' mama got slumped, I took you in and took care of you. You didn't have shit. When I see you, I'ma knock yo' teeth down yo' throat and make you swallow 'em. Ole' grimey ass bitch," I roared and pressed END.

Finally, I got Carla to come through and get me. Not even all that had gon' on could stop her from havin' love fo' me. My game was stupid tight, and the ho's couldn't get enough of it.

The second I sat on the seat of her Trailblazer, she came at me wit' that bullshit. "I don't know why I still fuck with your grimy ass."

I just let her spazz. The only damn thing on my mind was makin' sho' that my bro' ,Nine, and my homey, Gully, were aight, 'cause we had to get at them boys that had caught me slippin'.

Carla dropped me off at my mama's and mashed out. Once outta her ride, it was on and poppin'. A few families needed to prepare fo' some slow singin' and flower bringin'.

My Great Getaway
Kay-Kay

Young King drove up to Holiday Inn Express. Two of his boys came along, trailing us. His guy, Trigger, was a tall, fair-skinned dude. He and Dee-Lo who was a dark-skinned stocky dude, who resembled LeBron James, were his hype men. The two men followed us in Trigger's black Chrysler 300 with chromed out twenty-two inch shoes on it.

Young King and Trigger went to get keys to our hotel rooms. I sighed with relief after he closed the car door. Now I could look at my cell and count how many times Choppa had called. My phone was on vibrate cause I didn't want it ringing too much. I checked it and Choppa had called me four times. Humph, he'd just have to see me when I got back 'cause I didn't have no talk for him. My phone began vibrating in my hand as I stared at the building to see Young King whenever he came out. I didn't want to have my phone in hand when he returned to the car. My cell had Alize's name as the caller. I answered.

"What's poppin', sis?"

"Girl, how 'bout Nine and his boy Gully got ahold of some bad weed. I had to go get both of 'em from Choppa trap spot and take 'em both to the 'mergency room."

"Who they bought it from?"

"I don't kno'. I was askin' Nine where he got it earlier, but he couldn't give me a straight answer. He thinks he's a gospel singer," she exclaimed.

"What the fuck?" I half laughed.

"Yeah, and Gully thinks that ghost are whoopin' his ass. They both were admitted. They gon' do blood work and run a few tests on 'em."

"Damn, you got a gospel singer and somebody who thinks ghost after him up at the hospital. That's messed up." I shook my head at the absurdity of it.

"Tell me 'bout it. Anyway, where you at? Choppa been lookin' fo' you."

"In Indiana with Young King. He's doing a show here tomorrow. We ain't comin' back there 'til prob'ly Sunday morning. I ain't thinkin' 'bout that fucka. You kno' I caught him over at Carla's."

"Are you serious?" Alize asked, sounding surprised, when we both knew how foul Choppa carried it.

"Sho' did. That's why I'm not goin' to hold a conversation with him right now. He's doin' too much," I expressed.

"Yeah, he really is, and I don't blame you not one bit for goin' outta town with Young King, but you kno' that Carla prob'ly still mad behind the fact that Choppa stopped foolin' with her for a minute and got with you. She's just a hating, miserable person. She wants him back completely; that's all that is. Don't even worry about that."

"You right. Right now I'm not thinkin' or worrying about either one of them."

I saw Young King comin' outta the hotel. "Well, I'ma let you go, girl. Just keep me posted on how Nine and his friend are doing. And don't tell Choppa that you talked to me."

"You kno' betta than that. I ain't telling. Blood's a whole lot thicker than water."

"That's what's up. I'll holla at you later."
"Aight, bye."
"Bye."

I dropped the phone in my lap and observed sprinkles of rain falling from the sky. All I could think about was how I'd love to bless Young King with some lovemaking while listening to the sound of rain.

On Paranoid Choppa

I had given up on hearing from Kay-Kay and pushed on. If she wasn't gon' fuck wit' me all the way instead of halfway, then I was done wit' her. I had so much shit goin' on at the time. Trust, a broad wouldn't be one of my problems. Naw, fuck that. Not me. I wasn't no weak, punk ass dude. I made that ho. She didn't make me. She was nothin' more than a broke, young, hood chick when I met her. All she had on her mind was catching a money makin' young cat like myself and ridin' him to get to where she was goin'. I had finally seen her true colors. I was good though; I wasn't gon' let no ho make nor break me. Fuck Kay-Kay.

My mama answered the door, lookin' crazy, when I popped on her doorsteps. Mama had her oxygen tank's tube connected to her nostrils. It always hurt me to see her wearing oxygen, yet I knew she needed it to survive. As long as she was blessed to see another day and breathe. I tried to overlook her health issues, and just be grateful to have her in my life. I hadn't been by to see her much lately because I had gotten caught up in the streets. She gave me a big hug, and I walked her back into her bedroom. Just before making it to her bedroom door, she paused and caught her breath.

"You aight, Mama?" I asked concerned.

"Yeah, baby. I'm good. Just give me a minute to catch my breath."

"Okay," I replied compassionately.

Then she made more slow steps with her oxygen cord draggin' behind us, 'til she made it to her bed. Her favorite television show, *Wheel of Fortune,* was blasting from the television in her bedroom.

I smiled. "Dag, Mama. I see you still watchin' yo' favorite TV show, huh?"

"You kno' I love Pat Sajak and Vanna White. They the only two white folks that I must have in my room wit' me Monday through Saturday." She chuckled a bit.

"As long as you enjoyin' it. That's all that matters," I stated as I helped her lie down on her queen-sized bed.

"Where's Kay-Kay?" she asked.

I sat down at the foot of the bed and steepled my hands under my chin. "Honestly, Mama, I don't know where Kay-Kay's at, and I don't care. Really, it's about over for me and her. She showed me today that she ain't official."

"Choppa, I'm not against Kay-Kay 'cause I don't kno' the full story. I will say this though, if a woman truly loves you as much as you love her she'll be there for you. Regardless, of being mad or not she'll be by your side. I kno' your half-ass tellin' me the story, though. Tell me what really happened."

"Naw, Ma. I didn't come here to talk about that. I came to see about you." I leaned over and placed a kiss on her cheek.

We watched *Wheel of Fortune* together, then I had to bounce.

I needed to get up wit' the dude from earlier, who was gon' drop dime on those punks who were wit' J-Roc. I called Alize and asked her if she would leave the hospital fo' a second and pick me up. Gettin' another vehicle wouldn't be nothin' fo' me, though. I had a two-thousand and ten, milky-white, Dodge Magnum on twenty-two inch chromes.

I wheeled up to the crackhead dude sister's crib. Lucky for me, he kept his promise, and was on point. Guess he was waitin' fo' me to show up. I pulled alongside the sidewalk and signaled fo' him to come holla at me. He quickly strutted to the car when he recognized who I was.

"Hey, playboy. What's happenin'?" he spoke standing at the window leaning in.

"Shit. I got yo' three hunnid, and I want those cats' names, and where they rest they heads at. So, what's the business?"

"One of 'em name is J-Roc." That I already knew. "His sister lives across the street, ova there in that light brown house," he pointed out. I nodded and let him continue. "Those two dudes who was wit' him was his guys Dip and Freddie. All three of 'em hang real tight. All of 'em do a li'l' hustlin' over this way," he informed me, then began glancing around, watching his back and surroundings. He acted paranoid.

He then held his hand out for his loot. I got his three hunnid outta my pocket, but before I handed it over, I had to make one more request.

Turning to him, I stated, "I need one mo' favor."

"What's up?" he anxiously wanted to kno,' ready to get his cash and get away from me, and prob'ly go smoke like a choo-choo train.

"Don't ever try to snitch me out. If you let that lip pop, I'ma make sho' my glock stop all yo' plots," I told him with a serious facial expression.

"I gotchu, and I ain't telling shit."

"I 'preciate that info. Good lookin' out, and here's yo' paper," I said, giving him what I owed him.

He balled the money up in his hand and said, "I got some more stuff I can tell you, too, if you really wanna kno'."

"Like what?"

"J-Roc's sister gon' have a big birthday barbeque at her house tomorrow for him. A DJ gon' be ova there and er'thang. The only reason I'm bustin' them young 'uns bubbles is 'cause Dip, J-Roc's homeboy, sold me two rocks that wasn't no dope. It wasn't rock, it was candle wax. I told J-Roc what he had done, but he just laughed 'bout that shit. He told me I should stop smoking dope if I didn't want that kind of shit to happen to me."

I didn't want to hear all the unnecessary talk. "So, what time the bar-b-q gon' start tomorrow over there?" I quizzed him, and changed subjects.

"Uh, my sister told me that it would start at five o'clock, and I'm sho' it won't end 'til 'bout nine or ten," he said and stood up straight.

"I gotchu, man. 'Preciate the love," I responded, and rolled the window up.

I put the car in gear and drove off. *Don't those fools know not to shit where they eat.*

Soakin' Wet
Kay-Kay

Young King and I were in the hotel parlaying. He was lying down in the bed, shirtless. I was laying beside him, rubbing his six-pack. He had his name tatted across his stomach. A bunch of other tats covered his chest, arms, and back. He was inked up.

The sound of rain began tapping against the windowpane, followed by roaring thunder. I snuggled even closer to him. This was baby making weather.

"Damn, it's raining hard as hell out there, huh?" Young King asked before placing my hand on the crotch of his pants.

"Umm-hmmmm," I cooed, rubbing his print. I could feel the hardness of it protruding through his jeans.

"Reach inside my boxers and feel it," he rasped, unzipping his jeans, making it easier for me to reach in and grab his python.

"I see you trying to make me wet up my panties," I cooed.

"I want 'em soakin' wet, boo" he replied.

I slid my hand in his boxers and gently massaged his dick, slowly. I rubbed my hand up and down it making it harder and longer. I eased it outta his boxers and watched it stand up. It was big and long as hell. His huge, chocolate dick almost scared the shit outta me. I liked a nice size, but I was afraid of the ones that looked like they would bust my kitty open and cause me to need stitches. My mouth dropped, and I let out a long sigh.

"What's wrong, baby girl? You don't think you'll be able to handle it?" He laughed.

"Uh . . . maybe not," I admitted. He was long and thick, and it looked like it would rip something apart once it got up in there.

"Don't panic, baby girl, I know how to be gentle," he said softly.

He climbed on top of me and kissed my neck. I placed my arms around his back enjoying the moment. "Kiss me," I moaned.

Our tongues explored each other's mouths. Passion began to build up in me like a rising tidal wave. I sucked his tongue hungrily. His hands caressed my body tenderly, as if he was a sculptor molding a precious art of work. He glided his hands underneath the waistband of my panties, and eased them down, revealing a neatly trimmed, sloppy wet pussy. My moistness seemed to excite him. His masculine breathing moistened me even more.

His finger traced my glistening wet folds as he whispered my name. I felt slow, delicate, circles being drawn around my clit. My back involuntarily arched off the bed. He widened my kitty lips open with his fingers and made it rain on my ass. His tongue slowly danced all over my clit. His licks were hot and wet. With one finger massaging my pussy hole, while his mouth did tricks on my pearl tongue, he worked his magic.

I relaxed my entire body and enjoyed every second of what he was doing to me. I slowly grinded back and forth moaning and groaning.

"You like this shit, huh?" His voice became deep and sexy.

"Uh-huh," I managed to murmur in between my oohing and aahing.

The things he was doing felt so good that I reached over and clenched on to a pillow. I concealed my face with it.

"Oh, shit," I screamed into the pillow, after exploding an orgasm all over Young King's mouth. All I could do was lay there panting and shaking from the impact of coming so hard.

I thought, *Now this nigga is the truth wit' his mouth. Goddamn.*

He raised his head up from between my legs, stood up, and stripped down to nothing but dark chocolate bliss. Young King grabbed my legs, sliding me to the edge of the bed and requested that I lay right where I was and not move. After removing a condom from his pants, he tore the rubber out, and rolled it upward on his dick, tossing the wrapper on the floor.

"You ready for this right here?" He shook ten hard inches at me.

"Yeah, I guess," I uttered, unsure. He raised my legs in the air, placed them on his shoulder, and slowly entered his dick halfway inside of me.

"I can't take this shit," I grumbled.

"Wait. Let me go slow, baby. I'll take my time," he promised, tryin' his best to be easy on me.

Once he had gotten all the way inside of me, he took his time. The more he moved inward and outward, the betta it felt, after he allowed me to remove my legs from his shoulders. Instead, I wrapped them around his waist. The sound of thunder rumbled throughout the air causing the windows to shake. Mother Nature was shaking up the outside and he was shaking up my insides.

Sweat poured down from his forehead and chest like tiny raindrops.

"Shit, this pussy so wet and tight," he whispered and began pumpin' faster and faster, until he came.

*

An hour had passed since we sexed each other down. I was lying next to him in a daze. He ran his fingers through my hair as I rested my head on his chest.

"You kno' you got some good wet-wet," he said. His words may not have been very poetic, but I grasped their meaning, and his intent, just the same.

"Yeah, but I try not to brag," I teased. My stuff was still throbbing from being stretched open by his mammoth pole.

"I don't see why that dude you wit' let you even leave the house. I wouldn't want you goin' nowhere. I'd be scared you might try to give that good coochie away," he kidded.

"My man don't care 'bout nobody but himself," I complained.

"I care 'bout you. I got mad respect for you, and I wouldn't ever treat you the way he does. Baby, if you want to spend a week or two at my crib 'til you find a job, and get on yo' feet, you're welcome to," he offered.

"I don't kno' about that. I appreciate the offer, though. I care about Choppa a lot. I just don't care for the things that he does. He's been good to me, but at the same time I kno' that what I want may not always be what I need."

"You kno' that he ain't what you need. I'm a good dude, and I'm trying to rescue you. I guess you don't wanna be saved."

I paused for a minute.

"Who's to say that you ain't gon' do me wrong? You always tell me that you don't have a woman, only female friends. Yet, I kno' you got to be screwin' somebody, right?" I interrogated.

"I got a friend, that's it. I ain't gotta lie to you. My word is solid," he answered, avoiding my last question.

"You are fuckin' at least one of 'em, right?" I re-asked only a bit differently the second time around.

"To answer yo' question, yeah. It ain't nothin' serious, though. I guess you could call us friends wit' benefits."

"Why aren't you in a committed relationship, yet?"

"I feel like I need a special connection to a female before I claim her as my girl. You kno' what I'm sayin?" he added, "I just can't fall in love wit' any ole lame ass broad. She gotta be special."

"Yeah, I understand exactly whatchu trying to say."

"I'm feeling you a lot. It's something about you that I'm really diggin'. Maybe it's your determination, 'cause I see how you keepin' yo' head up. Even after the death of yo' mama. That tells me that you're a survivor."

I let out a deep breath.

"Dealing with my mother's death has been hard. Knowing that somebody killed her, and is still lurking out there, makes me even more depressed. I try to keep my head up and stay strong. It's a hard thing to do," I acknowledged with heartache.

"If you don't mind me askin'...where was she when she was murdered?"

"At the lakefront, and that really bothers me, because that's where she always took us when we were younger. My daddy is in prison and has been for a minute. So, Mama was all that we had."

"When's the last time you saw your daddy?"

"About four years ago. I'm not in any hurry to see him anytime soon. It hurts too bad to see him behind bars. He's supposed to be released in about eighteen months."

"Did your mama ride wit' him through his bid, or did she move on?"

"She was down with him for a long time, but she eventually moved on. I guess over time she just loss interest. But I kno' that she always had love for him. My mama was on drugs real heavy so maybe that contributed to her not visiting." I felt a need to justify her actions.

"I'm sorry to hear that," he consoled, rubbing my back.

"It's okay. She's gon' to a betta place. I miss her, but I kno' life gotta go on. I'm gonna do my best to make her proud, and not go down the road that she went down."

"I just had an idea," Young King announced.

"What is it, baby?" I asked, looking up into his eyes.

"You want some paper so you can move into yo' own crib?"

I excitedly replied, "What's up?"

"Where yo' man keep his stash at? We can hit a quick lick and split the money down the middle, baby."

I stalled before answering. "I'm not sure if I want to do that. I'm scared to do that, even though I'm sick of the dirty ass, cheating, bastard. I don't know where he keeps his money."

"Man, I got this, baby. We gon' map this shit out and have some loot in our pockets when we're done. The question is, are you down fo' it?"

After a few moments I responded, "Yeah." It was time for Choppa to reap what he had sown. I was fed up with him and his handful of ho's.

The Following Morning
Choppa

Last night, I didn't get no sleep. My mind wouldn't let me rest. I tossed and turned in my bed, wondering why the fuck Kay-Kay didn't bring her red ass home last night. That right there told me that she was a snake.

It was killing me how I had been there for her when she didn't have no place to go. Her family wasn't really fuckin' with her like that 'cause of how her mama was. Her dad's side didn't have shit to do with her and Alize either. Out the kindness of my heart, I got a crib with her, thinking that I'd invest my time into her. I couldn't blame anybody, but myself fo' believing in what we had. Yeah, I crept with a few, but at the end of the day, she knew where my heart was.

I had love for Kay-Kay, 'cause when I met her she was cool, and I saw a lot of potential in her. She didn't have much as far as materials, but I felt like if I showed her another side to life, and spoiled her, that she'd always have my back outta love for what I had done fo' her.

I rested in my bed, thinking back on all I had put her through. Maybe I did do a lot of grimy shit to her, like fuckin' wit' other ho's behind her back. I never once thought that she would up and split. Maybe I had taken her for granted one time too many.

I shoulda been at the point in my life where I was trying to become family oriented and ready to settle down. I couldn't, though. I was too young, and the streets was all I knew. I wasn't feelin' gettin' married, I had wifed the life of a hustler and there wasn't no turning back.

My bedroom's clock read 10:00 a.m. I let out a loud yawn and stretched to wake myself up. My room had chilled up a bit. September was peeping around the corner. Before I could step my foot onto the floor my cell was blowin' up. The caller I.D. read Carla.

"Whad up?" I uttered, my dry tone said that I didn't want to be bothered.

"Choppa, I don't want to talk to yo' triflin' ass no more than you want to talk to me. Anyway, I was callin' to let you kno' I'm pregnant."

"Whad the fuck you callin' me for? It ain't my baby. Bitch, you must be smokin'," I roared and sat up on the side of my bed in nothin' but my boxers.

"It's yours. I kno' who I been layin' down wit'," she shot back.

"I ain't got time fo' this and stop callin' my phone. Peace."

"You kno' what? Yo' gon' get exactly what you deserve. I hope you get everything that's comin' to you." She was fuming. But I wasn't allowing her to baby trap me. Not that crazy ho.

"You sucked me off, I dicked you real good, and I kno' fo' a fact that I didn't nut in you. What you think, I'm slow or somethin'? That mufucka in yo' stomach ain't mine. Now, get the fuck up off my phone," I barked.

She hung up in my face after I finished checkin' her. Damn, ho's think you stupid and don't kno' if a baby yours or not. They'll try to toss they shorty's on anybody wit' a bankroll.

But I wasn't goin' out like that. From that point on, I made up my mind that I was done wit' Carla's scandalous ass, too. I wasn't gon' be dippin' and dabbin' in her, and she was lettin' some other drop his soldiers off in her.

I wouldn't let Carla's bama ass throw me off track. I had only one thing on my agenda; murk three clowns that night. I wasn't gon' rest 'til they were in black bags.

*

When Gully hit me up, I explained to him what had gon' down yesterday. He had been released from the hospital along wit' Nine. I also gave Nine the scoop and they both were gassed up and ready to go to war wit' the three that had violated me. We all got together at my crib, came up wit' a plan, and mapped er'thang out. Those Chi-Town fools were about to see how niggas from Mil-Town rock.

Clubbin' Hard
Kay-Kay

My day with Young King had gon' smoothly. We'd had breakfast at Waffle House that morning, along with his two boys, and basically just hung out enjoyin' each other's presence.

That night we hit up the club called Club Fantastic where he'd be performing his hit song, "Drop It".

The club wasn't an enormous building. It was at least three hundred strong, which was a good number for its size. I was posted in the VIP, sippin' on my favorite, Grey Goose, lookin' like a video vixen in my white booty shorts, and white skintight shirt, with the Dereon logo on the front. My hair was flat-ironed straight, and there wasn't one person in there that could've convinced me that I wasn't the shit.

Three dudes sat at the table directly beside me.

"You kno' you lookin' good. You need some company?" a caramel toned dude with dreads asked.

"No, I'm good, sweetie. I'm here with my man. He's performing tonight," I politely dismissed him.

"My bad then," the dude replied.

Young King marched on stage like the king he was. Girls were dancing and droppin' their asses like hot potatoes. One-half drunken bitch standing in front of me bent over, wiggling her boodie in a short miniskirt. I felt like kickin' her dead in her ass 'cause her crack was showing.

She knew what she was doing. The dudes beside my table were definitely enjoyin' her nasty dancing. Every time the ho bent over, the dudes said, "Whoa."

Young King kept on performing even though I knew that he had seen Ms. Thang dancing. He couldn't have missed it. We were sitting close to the stage, and she was steady easing her way up closer to where he was performing. Young King's two hype men were jumpin' around.

"I want the baddest, sexiest chicks up in this mufucka to come up on this stage and drop that ass fo' me," Young King spoke into the microphone with a wide smile, exposing his grill.

He was fitted like a goon in his dark blue Ed Hardy jeans with a white Ed Hardy shirt and a fresh pair of all white MJ's.

Several hoochies ran to the stage looking drunk and horny.

"I want you, you, and you to come up here and get low fo' me tonight," Young King said, pointing at three females.

All of them got on stage, rolling their torsos. One dark-skinned chick did a split and made her butt cheeks bounce.

The dudes beside me stood clappin' and cheering. I could tell from their actions that they were a bunch of ho's.

A tall, yellow dude from their clique started throwin' dollars on the stage. Another short chick with micros, which was up there, strutted up to Young King in a yellow tube-dress with yellow stilettos. She did a seductive dance in front of him then leaned over touching her toes, and made her ass cheeks clap together.

Young King was bowing his head with the music, spittin' lyrics and watching that broad's ass. She dropped it down to the floor and came back up. Might I add, and started twirkin' all up on his dick. I felt like draggin' all three of 'em off the stage and punchin' them in their faces. I knew I didn't have any right to do that. He wasn't my man. All I could do was watch and pretend that I didn't give a flip. Inside I was burning up with jealousy. He could've had a little more respect for me than to let a strange hooker shake her ass all up on him, in my face. What kind of shit was that? I had to keep reminding myself that he was being paid to entertain the crowd, and that's what he was doing. Until it was over, all I could do was sit and look.

When Young King's performance was over, the dude next to me favoring Omarion asked, "Was that yo' man that just finished performing?"

"Yep," I said knowing he was trying to be funny since Young let that girl dance on him. I was close to losing my cool.

"You ain't mad at that chick fo' dancing on yo' nigga?" he asked with a smirk.

"She ain't fuckin' him tonight . . . I am," I replied.

That made him leave me the hell alone. I took another sip of Goose before realizing that it was gon', when Young King tapped me on the shoulder. "Kay-Kay, lets bounce. I'm done."

I slurred, "Okay, baby."

"You aight?" he asked, after noticing how unstable I was.

"Not really," I responded and reached for his hand. He grasped my hand and led me out the club.

A cool breeze hit me in the face, when we stepped outside. It helped to ease my high. Young King held me around my waist and guided me to his ride, with his boys behind us. The two of them got in their ride and rolled out. After Young helped me into the passenger's seat, we headed back to the room. He was bumpin' the latest Drake CD. I let my window down so that the wind could help sober me up.

"You need to eat something to calm yo' high down," he told me.

"Yeah, just stop at the first fast food place and let me get something," I said.

"It's a McDonald's up the street from the hotel. You want that?"

"I'll take that. As long as I get some food, I'm good. I'm not gon' be choosy. I'll take the number one."

"Thanks for choosing McDonald's. What can I get for you tonight?" the female on the intercom asked.

"Let me get two number ones and one coke and one..." he glanced over at me. "Whatchu wanna drink?"

I told him to get me a root beer.

"And one root beer," he finished.

"Can I offer you an apple pie with your order? Or will that be all for you tonight?"

"Yeah, I'll take two apple pies with that. That's cool."

"Alright, drive around for your total."

A woman who looked in her mid-thirties, and had a manager's shirt on, was at the first window where he paid. After paying for the meals, he drove to the second window where two young girls were. One was fixing the customers' drinks while the other asked if we needed condiments, and she put our orders in the bags. The two of them were just smiling at him, and checkin' out his wheels. I didn't crack a smile at either one.

The light brown girl with thin lips, clear-skinned, and a long weave ponytail gave him his drinks first. Then she handed him the two bags.

"I like yo' ride," she flirted.

"Thanks, Li'l Mama."

"You kno' you got this car lookin' good, and that black tint looks real good, too 'cause the car is black. I love this right here," she complimented.

I shifted my body toward the window. "Look, li'l' girl, don't nobody got time to be talkin' and tryin' to entertain you. We got shit to do. I'm hungry and drunk. Now, stop flirting with him before I get out and get retarded on yo' ass," I snapped.

"I don't kno' who the fuck you think you talkin' to. I will snap yo' neck. I was only complimenting his car, but now if you wanna take it there we can," she blustered.

"I promise you don't want this right here. Bomb ass bitch. I'ma snatch you up out this window," I threatened and reached over Young King, climbing over him, attempting to grab that heifer.

"Wait a minute. Stop it," Young King demanded, holding my arm with his right hand and rolling the window up with his left.

The restaurant's manager came to the window. "Whad's goin' on here?" she asked.

Young drove off, shaking his head in disbelief. "What's wrong wit' chu, baby? Why you spazzin' out on folks?"

"'Cause y'all were getting on my fuckin' nerves," I responded witha eye roll.

"All she said was that she liked my whip. That wasn't nothin' fo' you to go off 'bout," he said with fury.

"Well, y'all two can have each other. I promise it'll be fine wit' me."

Young calmed his voice down. "All I'm sayin' is that you ain't gotta go postal. I don't want that girl. I'm with you, so be easy."

I gave him a sideways glance. "You been very disrespectful tonight, and I've had enough of you and your shit. You was at the club lettin' that slutty hoodrat bounce her booty up on you. You did that shit right up in my face. Now, I kno' I'm not yo' woman, but damn give me a li'l' respect."

He rubbed the back of his neck and said, "You kno' I'm a rapper and bitches gon' do shit like that. They do that all the time. I don't pay that no attention."

"Anyway, you just pissed me off tonight. You and those others from the club, and that Mickey D's asshole."

"I twisted that pussy and made you come, and now you sprung." He smiled. "You think somebody else gon' get this?"

I giggled. "It ain't all that good, nah."

"I can't tell, you ready to murk somebody fo' giving me a nice comment 'bout my ride."

I reached over in my McDonald's bag, pulled a few fries out, and ate 'em.

"Give me a kiss, baby. I'm making it all betta when we get back to the room," Young

King said leaning, over toward me offering me his sexy lips.

I gave him a kiss and we headed straight to the hotel room where I ate and crashed. I was high as a skyscraper.

Vengeance Is Mine
Choppa

"Where this nigga at?" Nine asked from the backseat, strapped with his nine milli in his hand, gangsta grippin' the trigger.

"We gon' get these muthafuckas, don't worry. Just be ready to drill 'em full of holes when you lay eyes on 'em," I said, comin' through the block in an old beat up white Buick Skylark. I had copped that ride earlier in the day for a stack and five hunnid. The sole purpose of it was only to get the job done, then get rid of it.

The scenery was crowded with people. Cars were parked alongside the street. He musta been doing it big on his b-day. Chicks were outside in fly threads with cups in their hands, sippin'. Dudes were choppin' it up among each other. A few people were sitting in the yard, in lawn chairs, around a big black grill. The smell of barbecue roamed the air.

I crept down the street, slowly. Gully was on the front seat with his banger quietly observing. I stopped in front of a crowd of females and pulled my fitted cap down lower over my brow.

"Ay, where my nigga J-Roc at? I wanted to wish him a happy birthday," I yelled out the window.

"He's in the house. I can go get him for ya?" a peanut butter-skinned, thin chick volunteered.

"Go get him fo' me, and where Dip and Freddie at? I ain't seen them niggaz in a minute."

"They just left about ten minutes ago. They s'pose to come back. Dip had to go 'roun' the corner for some smokes."

"They walkin'?"

"Yelp," she said and paused. "Whad's yo' name?"

"I'm his boy," I answered dodging the question. "You a sexy ass chick, you kno' that?" I was spitting game to throw her off.

"Preciate that. You got some good eyes," she said.

I smiled and tossed another compliment her way. "You a model?"

"No, I wish." She giggled, eatin' that comment up.

"Baby, go get J-Roc for me. Tell 'em I'm gon' be parked up here in front of that green Taurus."

I pointed toward the end of the street.

"I'm gon' park and get outta the way. Come back with him so I can get yo' number. I'm just bustin' blocks in this old hooptie, but later on I'ma jump in my Hummer," I lied, stunting.

"Yeah, right. You ain't got no Hummer do you?"

I pulled my bank out with a rubber band around it, and flashed it before her thirsty eyes.

Her eyes widened with excitement. "That's what I'm talkin' bout. Let me go get J-Roc for you."

She started off, and then stopped in her tracks. "Here come Dip and Freddie now. They comin' down the street."

"Go get J-Roc first, then tell my dudes to come holla at me," I said and drove off and bent the corner before comin' back around again. I gave all three of them time to meet up.

We got ski-masked and click-clacked one in our chambers. It was time to turn the block into a mufuckin' fireworks show.

I made a left down the street and spotted all three of 'em talking to the chick from earlier. She pointed at our car as we approached.

"Nine, grab that choppa that's on the floor back there and give it to Gully. Hurry up," I demanded.

Nine hurried and handed Gully the long-clipped choppa. We got right up on all four of 'em.

"Touch my people, and I'm touchin' you," Gully shouted into the crowd and let loose with the choppa.

Screams mixed in with the cacophony of the AK-47.

A female's voice rang out with a piercing cry, "J-Rooooc."

Nine's twin glocks coughed out a rapidity of instant destruction. Bodies hit the pavement and remained there in a grotesque and bloody twist. I mashed the gas and split the scene.

"We dropped all four of 'em," Gully boasted.

"Hell, yeah. They won't jack nobody else," Nine said. From my rearview mirror, I saw him take his ski mask off.

I laid back in my seat and uttered, "Damn, it feels good to put yo' enemies to sleep."

"Now, I'm ready to blaze me up a mile long blunt," replied Gully, pulling off his mask.

Niggaz thought this shit was sweet. Now they gon' to the other side where they ain't nothin' but a soul. Fuck wit' me, and that ass get dealt wit'. Now, I just needed to find Kay-Kay, and she'd be another one to bite the dust.

Ain't Over Choppa

After bailing out, the tune of Webbie was in the background. I was headed to Gully's crib. Nine and Gully started recounting how the bodies had dropped and were leaking a short while ago.

"Man, I hit one of them niggaz in the head and it exploded like a pumpkin," revealed Gully.

"Yeah, I saw that shit. Did you see me spin that one cat around and bust two more in him before he hit the ground?" bragged Nine.

I wasn't as amped as the two of them were. I had so much shit on my mental at the time. Like, gettin' the old car to the junkyard. My cousin, Lance, owned a junkyard and that's where I bought my cars from, and dumped 'em off when my jobs were done. I would buy 'em from him, if I needed to get in some trouble, and I'd let him crush 'em as soon as I finished handling my business.

I clutched my cell and told Lance that I was on my way to drop the hooptie off. The junkyard was only three blocks up the street from where my mama lived.

I was a block from Mama's house and stopped at the stop sign. A green Ford Taurus swerved alongside of us on my side. In a flash, our car was filled with unexpected gunfire. I snatched the wheel to the right to avoid some of the shots, but they continued to pelt the car.

Gully swiftly reached on the floor for the AK. Tat.Tat.Tat.Tat.Tat. He fired back at the car as they sped off. I placed my foot on the accelerator with force, headed to my mama's.

"Dammit. That was that same Taurus that I was parked in front of at that barbecue," I recalled with a grunt of frustration. How had we not noticed anyone following us?

"I didn't even pay that car no mind when I saw it come up behind us. It had been trailing us for a few minutes," Gully answered my unspoken question.

Nine made no comment.

"Nine, you good?" I asked, glimpsing in the rearview mirror while I drove. I didn't see him.

"Li'l bro, you gucci back there?"

Still he didn't reply.

Gully peeped over his shoulder. "God dammit. He's down on the seat, and he ain't movin'."

Gully got on his knees and leaned over the seat shaking Nine. I pulled the car over and turned around and noticed Nine lying on the seat with his mouth open, with a bullet hole in his temple. Blood drizzled from the bullet puncture down his cheekbone and on the seat. I gasped; hurt like a mufucka. I felt like the world was on my shoulder, and my life was over.

"Nine, wake up, man. C'mon now, bro', don't do this shit to me. I need you. Say something," I wept.

I felt his wrist for a pulse. He indeed had one. I turned back around, put the car in drive, and sped to Mama's.

"Whatchu gon' do?" Gully asked.

"Man, I don't kno'," I responded, my voice cracking up.

"You kno' we can't take him to no hospital. We just did a drive-by, and prob'ly deaded some muthafuckas. We in this car and it's hot. Po-po's gon' be lookin' fo' it soon. And, I ain't goin' up to no hospital. Too many questions that I can't answer."

"Whad the fuck we gon' do then?"

"I need to get him some help. I just can't let him lay on the backseat and die. That's my brother."

"He my brother, too. We need to come up wit' somethin', or we gon' be under the jailhouse if the cops see us in this car, real talk."

My hands were trembling; mouth was dry as a bone, and Nine's life was in my hands. If I didn't get him to a hospital, he was a goner.

"Check this," I said and stalled for a second. "You gon' take Nine to the emergency room, and I'ma get this car over to my cousin so he can crush it."

"Man, what am I gon' tell 'em 'bout him gettin' shot and shit? White folks make me nervous. I don't mingle wit' 'em, and you kno' this."

"Take him," I fumed, rapping my steering wheel with my knuckles, emphasizing my point.

"Aight," he mumbled, reached on the backseat in Nine's pocket, and got his keys to his Beamer out.

It was in our favor that nobody was outside that night. Nine's car was parked alongside the street. We both got him in the passenger side of his car and that shit wasn't easy. It was more like lifting lead; picking up dead weight ain't no joke.

I watched as Gully took off to the hospital wit' my bro. Only thing I could do at that point was send up a prayer for him. It hurt me deep in my chest to kno' that he was ridin' hard fo' me, and got hurt behind it.

I got back in the hooptie and drove straight to my cousin's junkyard. He crushed the car and brought me back to my crib. I hopped in my ride and took off to the E.R.

On my way, I called Alize. "What's poppin', Alize?"

"Shit. What's jumpin' witchu?"

"Shorty, Nine got shot, and it's bad. We was beefin' wit some dudes earlier and they crept back on us."

"Whatchu mean he been shot by some dudes you all was beefin' wit? Who the niggaz that y'all got into it wit'?" she asked, in a panic-stricken tone.

"Just some mufuckaz who we don't really kno'. That's all, but I hope bruh gon' be aight. I'm on my way to the hospital now."

"I'm on my way too," she told me. Her voice was trembling.

"Don't tell Mama 'bout this right now. I'm gon' call and tell her later when I find out more 'bout his condition. I ain't trying to get her all upset. She goin' through too much now, not being in good health."

Alize breathed heavily. She responded, "Yeah, aight," and hung up her cell phone on me.

I whipped in and outta traffic, trying to make it to see how my brother was doing. Two seconds later, my cell rang.

"Yeah, Mama," I said.

"What the hell is goin' on? Alize said you called her, and it's an emergency. She took off like a streak of lightening."

"Yeah, we got an emergency goin' on," I replied after shaking my head, dreading telling her the truth.

"Well, tell me what the hell is going on then. What y'all hiding? Where's Nine, and why is Alize runnin' up behind yo' black ass?" she drilled.

"Nine..." I said and got silent deciding how I could tell Mama without gettin' her all upset, but it wasn't no way to say it without her blowin' up.

"What about Nine. Just tell me."

"He got shot tonight."

There was a long silence.

"Who shot my baby?" she cried.

"We got into some beef. I can't really talk 'bout it right now."

" You gon' tell me more than whatchu sayin' now," she screamed.

"All I can tell you is that we were beefin', and some dudes creeped up on us and started shooting," I said.

"Where is he now?"

"At the hospital. Gully took him."

"Why didn't you take him. That's yo' brother, not Gully's."

I couldn't explain to her that I had to drop the car off at the junkyard. And, just like Gully didn't want nobody interrogating him, I didn't either. I couldn't even tell her that I had just murked people, and that she could have a son in prison if I was caught by po-po's. I had too much on my chest to be having her hollerin', cussin, and fussin' at me.

"I'ma have to explain the situation to you later. I'll let you kno' how he's doin' when I get there."

"You ain't gon' let me kno' nothin'. I'm callin' a cab to bring me right now, since Alize left. You always gettin' my baby caught up in some shit. You never look out for him. You just let trouble come his way while you sit back and watch."

"You tellin' a lie. I ain't never let no shit go down wit' my brother and didn't try to help him," I exploded.

"Boy, you must be losing yo' damn mind to be sitting up there yelling at me."

"Naw. I ain't losing my mind. I'm checkin' you 'cause you wrong."

"Nine just got out the hospital yesterday, and I'll be damned if he ain't right back tonight fuckin' wit' you," she harshly blamed.

"I'm tired of arguing back and forth wit' you. You done said some foul shit to me tonight. I'm through talkin' to you fo' now. I'll holla at cha later."

"Boy, dontchu hang — up — this — phone," she spoke catching her breath in between words.

That's why I didn't want to upset her. She would get too mad, and it was hard for her to speak without starting to have an asthma attack. Along with her sickle cell condition, she just wasn't in good shape.

"I'll see you at the hospital. Let's pray for my baby. That's all we can do now," she said sniffling.

I was aware that she was crying and it hurt me to kno' that.

"Don't cry, Mama. Be strong, and we gon' make it through this. Nine strong, he gon' be alright."

"I hope so," she responded and dismissed our call.

I told Mama that Nine was strong, but I wasn't sure if he was strong enough to take a bullet and survive. All I could do was talk to the man above and be hopeful that he'd listen to a sinner like me, and spare Nine's life.

Shocking News
Kay-Kay

I was shocked when I received word that Nine had been shot. I was on the highway, back to Mil-Town, when Alize called me, hysterical. I told her that I would head straight to the hospital as soon as I was dropped off at my car.

"Why you ain't been answerin' yo' phone?" she asked.

"I'm so sorry. It went dead on me last night. I woke up early this morning and put it on the charger," I told her.

I could tell in her voice that she was somewhat mad at me for being outta pocket. Yet, I could also feel the neediness in her voice that said she wanted me by her side.

"Well, how is he doing?"

"He's in surgery now. They goin' to remove the bullets. Doctors say there's a fifty-fifty chance that he'll make it."

"Just pray for him. I'll be there shortly."

I entered the hospital's waiting room where I spotted Alize, Choppa's mama, Choppa, and Gully waiting. The gaze that Choppa gave me had me consumed with fear. Alize rose to her feet as I approached her. We embraced as she shed tears on my shoulder.

"He's goin' to be okay. Just keep the faith," I whispered.

"I'm doin' my best to be strong, but it's hard."

"I kno'."

We released each other and I sat beside her. Choppa and Gully sat directly in front of us. I simply ignored Choppa. I knew he was heated with me, and I wanted no parts of him. I happened to glance up at him, and his stare was terrifying. I directed my attention to his mama who sat on the other side of me.

"Hi, Ms. Elaine," I greeted as I conjured up a smile.

"Hello, baby."

"Are you holding up okay?"

"Yeah, I'm just doing the best that I can."

"If you need anything I'm here for you."

"Thank you, Kay-Kay. That's mighty nice of you," she said with sadness in her eyes.

I turned away and looked up against the walls. There were at least six more people in the waiting area. Two white women were half-asleep, with pillows behind their heads, sitting in chairs. The other four people were watching the flat screen television on the wall. Three women and one man, waited in the room.

"Where you been in them short ass pants and that li'l' biddy shirt? Lookin' like a li'l ho," Choppa spat.

"Who you talkin' to like that?" I kept my voice low but it was terse.

"Who I'm lookin' at?" he howled and cocked his head to the side, gritting his teeth.

"Boy, you got me messed up. You can't tell me what I can and can't wear."

Choppa stood up and made his way in front of me. He pointed his finger right in my face.

"Ho, I ain't seen you in two days, and you come switching yo' ass up in here like it's all good. You actin' brand new and like you Hollywood. Musta been out wit' yo' new nigga all night."

"I'm only here because my sister needs me. Now, forget what you up here talking," I scowled.

"You broke and ain't have shit befo' I started fuckin' wit' you. Now, you want to shit on me?"

The whole room grew quiet. The other people inside of it were gawking. I was embarrassed as hell. And I sho' as hell wasn't gon' sit there like a wimp and let him chump me off.

I sprung to my feet, annoyed by his actions in front of a room full of folks.

"Choppa, if you kno' what's good for you, you'll get yo' finger out my face. You can't be mad at me when you the one who tricks off with a new trick every week. So you can miss me with this dumb shit you jabbin' about."

Wam. He struck me with his fist, in my mouth.

"That's fo' gettin' outta pocket wit' me."

And that's when I lit into his ass, throwing blows. I was well aware that he was much larger and stronger than I was. That meant that I'd need to bring it. We got into a physical brawl.

"Y'all should be ashamed of yourselves," his mother seethed.

She was right, too. We shoulda been ashamed, but we weren't. Choppa grabbed me by my hair and threw me into a few empty chairs. I landed dead on my ass.

Gully grabbed him and escorted him outta the waiting room saying, "Damn, Dawg, you gon' fuck her up bad hittin' on her like that."

"Fuck that bitch," Choppa rumbled.

I regained my composure and sat up on the floor that I had been thrown on. Alize was standing not far from me frowning. She came over and helped me off the floor.

"You aight?" she asked.

It was then that I closed my fitted tee with my right hand, after I saw that my shirt had been ripped in the front. Thank goodness not all of my cleavage was bursting out being seen. A bit was noticeable, but nothin' serious.

"Yeah, I'm good, I guess," I returned.

"Choppa is stupid. You need to leave him alone before he kills you."

I ran my hand down the side of my face. It was tingling, stinging, and swollen.

Choppa's mama turned toward my way. "Kay-Kay you okay, darling?"

"Yes, Ms. Elaine, and I apologize for the way I just got through acting. I should have been the bigger person and walked away."

People were continuing to gawk and stare at me as I placed my butt down in a seat beside Ms. Elaine. Alize did the same, on the opposite side of Choppa's mama.

"Don't worry about it. You two need some time apart. You need to go your way and let him go his, before someone winds up hurt behind some shit."

"I totally agree with that," I acknowledged.

One white woman shot me a look of disgust.

"I don't know whatchu lookin' at. I'm quite sho' that yo' man has gotten on you before," I blurted.

"No. I've never let a man put knots on my head or physically try to harm me. Furthermore, it's a disgrace for you to take that off of him. You make the female gender look bad. You're a sad excuse for a woman," she blasted back.

"You can kiss my ass. If you keep saying shit, I'ma show you how I get down."

"You little whore. Do somethin' if you think you're bad," she raged. Her facial color went from pale to a brick red.

"Bring it then," Alize threw her two cents in.

"You're ghetto trash. I'll fuck both of you up, if that's what you want."

"Let's do it," Alize urged, and almost went over to confront the woman when Choppa's mama jerked her back down.

"Stop this shit," Ms. Elaine ordered. "My poor son is back there fighting for his life, and here y'all are keeping up confusion. All of you should be thanking God that you're blessed to see another day. You all don't have to walk around wit' this oxygen tank and struggle to breathe, so shut up; all three of y'all."

The white woman stared at Ms. Elaine with sympathy.

"Yes. We are all blessed. I shouldn't have given her the look I gave her, but my cousin is here and having surgery to remove a brain tumor. So, I'm really going through an emotional battle right now. Looking at my cousin, and his situation, makes me more appreciative and grateful for my life," the woman expressed.

"I'm sorry to hear about your cousin, and I'll surely pray for him, and you pray for my son, too," Ms. Elaine assured. "Kay-Kay tell her that you apologize for what you said to her," Ms. Elaine demanded.

"Why?" I asked. "She gave me that look first."

The woman interrupted, "I'll be the bigger person. I am older, and I shouldn't have eyed you the way that I did. I apologize, sweetie," she told me with a slight smile exposing her deep dimples.

"It's okay. I apologize to you for calling you outta your name."

I was still mad at her. I only told her that I was sorry because Ms. Elaine asked me to do it. If Ms. Elaine had not been there, me and that old woman would've squared up.

I had gone into the ladies restroom to take a good look at the damage Choppa had done to my face. As I was viewing my swollen up and bruised cheek, the white woman entered the restroom where I was standing. My first initial thought was that she had plotted to do something crazy to me.

"Hi. Honey are you okay?" she inquired.

She was elegant. Her hair was pinned up perfect, jet-black. Her acrylic nails were red. I observed her hand that showed off a huge diamond on her index finger.

"Yes, I'm okay. My face is hurting," I explained, still half-curious as to why she had followed me into the restroom. Unless, it was a big coincidence.

"Honey, I'm Grelza. You're so young, beautiful, and attractive. Look at you, girl. Yo' body is the body of a goddess."

Annoyed and uncomfortable, I responded, "Why you telling me all this?"

I watched her through the bathroom's mirror before facing her.

"I'm saying you are worth so much. I would love to introduce you to some men who'll give you time, attention, and put lots of money in your pocket. You don't have to accept somebody bruising your body up with ugly marks. I'm the owner of an escort service. I will work with you. You could live the life of a queen, and live comfortable, along with your family."

She stepped from behind me and strutted beside the hand dryer up against the wall.

"How would you like to make at least seven hundred and fifty dollars a night?" she asked, gazing directly into my eyes without a blink.

"For real?"

"Yes, I'm very much for real. I have no reason to stand here and tell you a lie."

She opened her medium sized purse with Dolce & Gabbana on the left side. I watched her take out a small pocketbook and offer me a card.

"Thank you, "I said and took it. The card had the picture of a naked Caucasian female on the front. The name, Grelza, was at the bottom along with her cell number.

"Think about it, sweetie, and if you're interested give me a call."

She gave me a wink, and left out the restroom, leaving me baffled. I was interested, but undecided. I didn't want to end up the way Mama had, nor did I want to live the life that she lived, but if push came to shove, I'd do what I had to do.

Another Burden To Bear
Choppa

Gully and I talked a good while outside, and he had calmed me down by the time I went back in the waiting room. The most important thing was that I wanted Nine to live.

When I got back to the waiting room, Kay-Kay was still in there. I couldn't understand why, though. Alize was her sister and all, but Nine was my blood and best friend. I felt that she shouldn't have ever shown up there in the first place. That ho knew that I'd kick off in her ass the second that I saw her. I didn't kno' what made her get bold and test me to see if I was weak. What made me even madder was not once did she try to explain where she had been. That right there said to me that she'd been lettin' some dude play wit' her insides. That alone tampered wit' my pride and ego. To kno' that yo' main' girl is fuckin' off wit' some other, fucks witcha bad. Many dudes don't like to admit it, but yo' main chick is the bitch that a dude will put more trust in than the other chickens he dicks down. Hell, that's the point of makin' her yo' main one. Er' thug needs a lady as Ja Rule stated in his lyrics.

Kay-Kay was beside my mama, and Alize was on the other side. I was plopped down in front of Mama, facing Kay-Kay who wouldn't look into my eyes.

"*Bitch, guilty,*" a voice in my head said. "*Kill this ho,*" another voice rumbled.

I didn't give in to any of it, and that wasn't easy to do.

I placed my face in the palm of my hands, stressed.

"Well, I guess I'ma go," Kay-Kay proclaimed.

I never looked up or bothered to say anything else to her. If I opened my mouth, the wrong shit would've come outta it, and I would've been ready to dig in that ass all over again. She leaped up after sayin' her goodbyes to her sister.

"Are you all the family of Kemarion Brown?" a male's voice vocalized.

I raised my head to see a tall, black doctor, with salt and pepper hair, clothed in a blue scrub. Kay-Kay re-seated herself.

"How's he doing, doctor?" my mama questioned.

"I'm so sorry, ma'am. We did all we could, but he didn't make it through surgery. You all can go back and view the body. And again, I'm sorry for your loss," the doctor said and turned and walked away.

"Oh, Jesuuuus. Oh, Lord, please help me right now. Please, God," Mama cried.

Alize and Kay-Kay comforted Mama by wrapping their arms around her.

"Get yo' hands from around my mama ole' low budget ho," I yelled. "This is family time right here. Mama just lost a son, and you ain't part of this family. So step, get on down," I dictated.

"You kno' what? I'm just gon' leave and go on. I ain't got time fo' this right here. You take care, Ms. Elaine, and if you need anything, I'm here for you. You got my number," Kay-Kay told Mama, and kissed her on her cheek.

Mama nodded, steady wailing and boo-hooing. Her cry told us all that she was hurtin' and in pain after the loss of her baby son.

"Choppa, I done had it wit' you. You just messy. If it hadn't been for you and yo' beef, Nine would still be living. Leave my sister alone, and stop fucking wit' her. She ain't did shit to you. So what if she didn't come home. I wouldn't have either, after fighting one of yo' cluckers in the street," Alize blurted out.

"She kno' that I don't play that 'bout her not comin' home."

Alize screamed, "I wouldn't come home to you either. All you do is drill every female in Milwaukee that will sleep wit' ya. Now, the pot damn sho' can't talk about the skillet, 'cause both of yo' asses belong on the stove."

I didn't reply, she was right. I kissed my mother on the cheek.

"Mama, I love you, and I'll talk to you soon," I uttered. "Kay-Kay, you can come get all yo' stuff from my crib, or I can meet you somewhere. We done," I told her.

"Are you gon' go to the back and view Nine?" Mama requested as her tears slowly dripped down, one after the other.

"Mama, I ain't goin' back there. I can't look at him like that. Make sho' you tell him I love him. Tell him I'll see him in Thug Heaven."

Next, Gully stepped forward to Mama.

"I'm sorry that this happened, Mama. I love you, and holla at me if I can do anything fo' you. And tell Nine I said I'll see him on the other side, when my time is up."

Mama simply nodded and she and Gully embraced.

We broke away. I had to hurt J-Roc's fam as much as he had hurt mine. And, I knew exactly how I'd do it.

Ain't To Be Trusted
Kay-Kay

Young King saw my face and was enraged. That's when he wanted to jack Choppa. At first, I wasn't down for it, but shid, two blunts later I was down for anything.

Later that night, he persuaded me to call Choppa and ask him to meet me to get all of my clothes from him. And that was exactly what I did. Young King told me that he would show up at the secluded spot and do the rest. My only request was that he didn't kill Choppa. It didn't make me a bit of difference that Choppa had knocked me around earlier. I couldn't help it if I had a few feelings for him. It's just that I felt rejected, and we women become vindictive when a man doesn't want us. Especially, when we take unnecessary bullcrap off 'em. Then, as soon as we make one mistake they just say, fuck it all. That's what really hurt me about Choppa. I couldn't understand why it was okay for him to cheat, and show up at the crib when he was ready. Yet, it was wrong for me to do the same thing to him.

But nooo. He wanted to play hardball, and that's how I landed in the spot where I was setting him up. Young King and I would split the profits. *Hell, yeah. I'd spoil myself off of my half*, I happily said in my head.

Choppa drove up in his whip, and my heart was racing so fast it felt like it would bust outta my chest and take off running. My hand was quivering, and my palm was sweaty. I had never been involved in any type of robbery in my life. Now, I was in my car anticipating and anxiously waiting to set a man up to be jacked. *Oh well.* I was ready to make it happen.

Young King parked in a secluded area where he could see Choppa pass through and not be noticed.

Choppa got outta his car. He came over to where I was parked and I let my window down.

"Whad's good?" he spoke with a bit of hostility.

I could tell from his tone and expression that he was still salty with me.

"I just need my clothes outcha car, and I'ma go."

"Where you been these past couple of days, Kay-Kay?"

I wouldn't look directly in his eyes. I checked out his outfit. He was wearing a black t-shirt, a pair of dark blue jeans, along with some all black Adidas. He was lookin' all handsome and G'd up, but I had to remember why I was there and not fall for his appearance.

"Why? What's up wit' all the questions and shit? I needed to free my mind and get away from you, that's all," I responded hoping he bought the lie that I was trying to sell.

"Why yo' eyes lookin' funny and shit?" He wanted to kno'.

He stepped closer to examine me.

"Yeah, I been smokin' a li'l' green," I bashfully went on and confessed.

"What. Get the fuck outta here." He laughed. "When you start that, this weekend?"

"Yep. It's the only thing that keeps me relaxed."

"Why you ain't never smoked wit' me?"

I shrugged. "I don't kno'. Back then I didn't want to. I was trying to be a good girl."

Gully swung the passenger door open. "Dude, I got to take a leak. I'ma duck out behind one of these buildings," he told Choppa, and slammed his door shut, walking off.

For the life of me, I couldn't figure out how I was going to get outta this situation. I couldn't call Young in front of Choppa. I was hoping that Young King was on top of his game and saw Gully's li'l' peanut head laid back in the cut. Maybe that was why Young King had taken so long to arrive.

"I kno' we been havin' our share of problems. I been wrongin' you. Overall, you kno' that I love you, and you didn't have to run off. Was you wit' a nigga?"

"No," I lied, keepin' a straight face.

He nodded a few times, satisfied with my answer.

Changing subjects I verbalized, "How's your mother?"

"Missing my baby bro'. And I'm missing him, too."

His eyes watered, head dropped, and whole attitude changed. He was sad and I could feel his pain. No longer did I want to be involved with the robbery. I wanted to hug him, tell him that I loved him, and go home with him.

A ghetto bird flew over our heads, light beaming down on us. I was certain that I was about to be arrested for a crime or something. My eyes were squenched tight while watching it. Then after a few minutes, it left and went in the opposite direction. A fugitive was normally on the loose when we saw that. The helicopter's loudness vanished the further it got away from us.

Choppa said, "They must be lookin' fo' somebody."

Just then, Gully yelled from behind the building, "I'm throwin' up and tipsy as a mufucka. I can't fuck wit' that Hypnotiq like this no mo'. That shit done made me sick, and I feel like I'm 'bout to have a tore up stomach in a minute, too."

Choppa and I burst out into laughter, and then Young King's lights pulled up in front of us.

"Fuck this is?" Choppa asked, suspicious.

"Prob'ly just somebody 'bout to make a U-turn and turn around," I answered, remaining as calm as possible, sittin' in my car.

Young King parked and quickly got out, ski-masked with his heat and pointed it at Choppa's dome.

"You kno' what it is. Come out 'cha pockets now, befo' I put some lead in ya," Young King cautioned Choppa.

I wanted so badly to tell Young King to stop. I couldn't, though. There was nothin' I could do except pretend to be startled and surprised by what was happening.

Choppa closed his eyes for a second, as if he couldn't have dreamed that this would be happenin' to him again. Especially, not now after all that he had gon' through with the passing of his brother and all.

When he reopened his eyes, he emptied out pockets full of money onto the ground. Young King also ordered him to take off every piece of bling that he owned. Then, Young King eyed

Choppa's ears. "I see yo' ears on froze. Take them earrings off."

Choppa took off all his jewels, including his diamond earrings.

And to keep his act going, he aimed his burner at me. I figured so that Choppa wouldn't think I was a part of it.

"Get out the car and I mean right now and you betta come correct," he ruled with his attention goin' back and forth from me to Choppa.

I sighed hard. "Please, don't kill me. I'll do whatever you want me to," I bargained and got out.

Young King told us both to get down on the ground, and he checked my pockets and didn't find nothing. I was sayin' to myself, *Hurry up, fool, and go on so we can break bread.*

Young King pointed his iron at Choppa's dome and threatened, "I should bleed you."

Pop. Pop. Pop.

I covered my eyes in my hand, scared that maybe he was dead from the shots that were fired. And if he was, me and Young King were gon' be scrappin', 'cause that was part of the plan; not to kill Choppa.

Choppa's head was resting flat down in the opposite direction from me, when I glanced over.

"Dumb ass. I told you not to kill him," I whispered.

Suddenly, Young King fell flat on his face. I frantically gazed around to see Gully coming toward us with his weapon in his hand.

"Whatchu mean you told him not to kill me?" Choppa's voice damn near made me pee on myself.

"Oh, shit you ain't dead?" I screeched.
"You set me up?"
"Uh, no…"
"Yes, you did," he growled.

I scrambled to get up, but Choppa grabbed me, throwing me back down on the ground. Wam. Wam. Wam. His tightened fists went up against my skull. I threw my hands up to protect my face when I felt two more stings.

Gully finally got him off me. "What you whoopin' on her like that fo'?" Gully inquired, holding Choppa down.

"She set me up, man."

"Whad the fuck," Gully said, and let Choppa get up.

"You tried to set me up, huh?" His size twelve shoe came crashing down on my stomach several times. He gathered up lots of mucus and spit in my face.

I could hear the police helicopter from earlier coming back toward us.

"We gotta jet, fam," Gully suggested. "It's too much heat 'roun' here. We'll catch her somewhere and finish her."

Choppa took his advice, and they both darted to Choppa's vehicle and raced off. I laid next to Young King's bloodied body crying for help. I was too weak to even want to live at that moment, and dying would have been easier.

"Fight, Kay-Kay," a feminine, all too familiar voice encouraged. I cracked my eyes to see a vision of Mama standing over me. She was beautiful.

Another Fallen Soldier
Choppa

I dreaded this moment. Being at my li'l' brother's funeral was a hard thing to cope wit'. The church was full. We were stuffed in there like sardines in a can. Mama was beside me, along wit' Gully and other close family members who sat on the front pew.

Nine's casket was a shiny, silver color, and loaded down wit' flowers. I ordered five thousand dollars' worth of flowers, and I still felt like that wasn't enough. Even though they were almost on top of each other. My bruh deserved the best 'cause he went out for me. He was loyal 'til his death, and I was gon' miss that nigga like crazy.

The preacher was doin' a short sermon, and I really wasn't listening to a damn thing he was sayin'. Me and Nine hadn't been to church since we started hustlin' in the streets. It was just that I didn't feel very comfortable bustin' up in a church knowin' what type of life I was livin'. And the things that I was doin' out in the streets, put lots of guilt on my conscious. I prayed, just not in nobody's church. Mama used to be a regular member, never missin' a Sunday, 'til her health issues stopped her from goin'.

The preacher was going on, on, and on 'bout how it's time for us to get our ducks in order and live right. I swear the preacher favored Redd Foxx from the old television show, Sanford & Son. He was the same skin color and er'thang, wit' some kinky, smoky gray hair.

The preacher put the microphone to his mouth and said, "I'm beggin' and pleadin' fo' anybody who ain't saved to get saved, and believe the son of God as your personal Lord and Savior. 'Cause, as you can see, you ain't got to be old to be called home, and when you get called, you need to be ready."

He wiped sweat from his forehead wit' a handkerchief that was inside the top pocket of his suit jacket.

He carried on, "You ain't gotta be old to die, and you ain't got to be doin' nothin' wrong to die. 'Cause, now a day, they even shootin' the preachers and tryin' to fight up in these church houses."

A few people accepted his statement wit' an "Amen." As much as I tried to block out what went on last night, I couldn't get rid of it. Especially, when the preacher kept goin' on and on 'bout doin' right and bein' righteous so that when death came knockin' I'd be ready. A vivid picture of what I had done entered my brain. I took in a deep breath and exhaled.

See, last night 'roun' eleven o'clock I rode by J-Roc's sister's crib. I promised myself that after ridin' by this last time I would drop somebody wit' gun spray. Even if I had to shoot up in there. I couldn't ever catch nobody outside slippin'. Until last night when Gully and me wheeled by her crib where she lived. Ole' girl was just makin' it home from somewhere. I guess it was work, 'cause she was dressed in professional attire. She had on a dark blue suit wit' some heels on and was unlocking her front door.

"Pop off on that bitch," I told Gully.

Gully pulled down the trigger on his burner and let off six rounds in the chick's back. The bullets knocked her down, and I sped off.

J-Roc's fam shot Nine, and I wasn't gon' squash the shit. I took out his fam like they had taken away mine. The streets were talking, saying J-Roc survived the drive-by, but he was paralyzed from the waist down. The streets said that his boy Dip and Freddie was body bagged. His sister just got mixed up in her brother's war. I had assassinated his boys, and that chick went down wit' 'em.

My mama kept sayin' that God would handle it, and that whoever killed Nine would suffer 'cause God don't like ugly. Well, in my opinion, God wasn't movin' fast enough, so I helped him out.

The preacher got my attention when he raised his voice with, "God ain't pleased with all the killin' that's goin' on in the world. The good Lawd is the only one who can give life, and he's the only one who should take one. People ain't got no right to slaughter another human being. Leave it to God to fix our disagreements."

He ended his sermon by saying, "I can't help this child lying in this casket, and my sympathy goes out to the family, but I can help the living in this congregation today. If you ain't right, my brothas and sistas; you betta get right. And er'day that you live is another opportunity to make things right befo' you leave this ole' world."

The church choir had at least seventy-five people in it dressed in cherry red and gold robes. They sang the saddest song that they could sing and slowly rocked from side to side to a tune called, "Heaven."

Mama burst out into tears. Alize followed her wit' an outburst, too. The church's usher comforted the two by hugging and fanning them. They later calmed down.

The funeral home opened the casket for one last view of the body. We remained on the pew and people who wanted to view the body were instructed to go around and see Nine.

Nine was laying there wit' a face full of makeup on. He didn't look no different other than the thick coat of foundation. I could see him perfectly from the front row. My bruh looked like he was sleepin'. That's what I kept tellin' myself, to keep from actin' a fool in the church. I wanted to hug Nine and bring him back to life, but I knew that I didn't possess that type of power.

As the folks were comin' 'roun', a few stopped to offer their condolences to Mama. I looked up to the alter and saw a recognizable face peering down into my brother's casket. It was our father, and he had his wife wit' him. A teenage girl and boy followed behind them. My daddy stood at Nine's casket, for a good minute, wiping his eyes. His wifey rubbed his back as they viewed Nine. That shit had me wanting to go ham on my daddy. He hadn't done shit fo' me or Nine. In fact, I hadn't even seen the nigga since I was fifteen. Now he was here at the funeral shedding tears like he had love for Nine. Had the audacity to come up in the church with the same bitch on his arm that he shitted on my mama for. The same bird ho who turned him against his own sons. *I ought to murk his ass.*

My daddy meant no more to me than a complete stranger did. I had too much hatred built inside of me to want to ever forgive him for what he had done. Mama was much different, though. She forgave him, and never spoke a bad word about him to me or Nine. I glimpsed over at Mama, and she had no expression.

"I don't kno' what he showed up fo'," I whispered in Mama's ear.

"Let it go, Choppa. Judge not less he be judged."

I let it go. This was neither the time nor the place, but one day he would have to answer to me for abandoning us.

The funeral was over after an hour and a half. They rolled Nine's body into the white hearse and Mama got into the limo. Alize got in, too. People were outside the church mingling, shakin' hands wit' folks they recognized, and some had gotten in their rides to follow the hearse to the cemetery two blocks up.

Me and Nine were marching to my vehicle. I had to get away from the crowd. I was sick of folks tellin' me that they were sorry for my loss and huggin' me. That sorry shit couldn't bring li'l' bruh back. I was sorry that he was gon' too, and I didn't feel like associating wit' nobody. My mind was occupied wit' gettin' to the cemetery to see Nine be laid to rest and say my final goodbye.

"Keyon," somebody uttered. I hated when people called me by my real name. Gully and I glimpsed over our shoulders to see who was callin' me when I didn't want to be bothered.

"That's yo' pops calling you," Gully said.

"Yeah, I'm just gon' keep walkin'. Don't feel like talkin' to that nigga," I snarled.

I kept on walking puttin' on an act that I heard and didn't see who had called me.

"Keyon."

"Fuck that nigga," I mumbled.

"You ain't gon' see what yo' pops want?" Gully pried.

"Man, fuck that faggot. I ain't heard from him since I was fifteen. Now, he wanna show up on the scene and try now," I gnarled.

"Aight," Gully said, seeing my point.

"Keyon." My pops called again.

I stopped in my tracks this time and turned around. "Damn, what you want?" I roared.

"I need to talk you, Keyon," he declared, drifting toward me.

"Bout what? I ain't got no talk fo' you. Don't you see I'm leaving? I'm headed to the cemetery to put my brother to rest. You ain't *been* wantin' to talk to me, so why now?" I cross-examined.

"I want to make things right between us. I kno' I ain't been in your life for years. I was wrong for not reaching out to you more. I just lost one son and I feel bad for not comin' around like I should have."

Gully asked for my car keys, and left pops and I standin' there talking.

"I really ain't got nothin' to say to you, man," I said and shrugged, not knowin' what he wanted me to say to him.

"Kyree," a woman uttered.

My dad turned, and his wife was standing there wit' their teenage kids. "Honey, are we goin' to the cemetery, also?" she wanted to kno'.

"Yes, baby. Just give me a minute with my son," Pops answered.

"Okay, no problem," she told him.

"Hi, Keyon." She waved from a short distance.

"What's up?" I replied.

My sister and brother waved also. My sister resembled her mama more so than she did my pops. And my li'l' brotha was the spittin' image of my pops and Nine. I hadn't paid a lot of attention to him the first time I saw him. Now, I could see it.

I waved back at the both of them, too. My li'l' sister walked away wit' her mother, but he stood there. I assumed that he wanted to holla at me, or get to kno' me or somethin'.

"Whad's they names?" I questioned Pops.

"Who?"

"My sister and brother."

"Your sister's name is Kalondra, she's fourteen. Your brother's name is Kydrick and he's seventeen, and just graduated from high school. And my wife's name is LaMonica," he added.

"First, tell me why you dropped me and Nine like we wasn't yo' blood, and never stopped by to even say hey."

I glanced at Kydrick who had started holdin' a conversation wit' some young chick that I didn't recognize. She was a red-boned cutie, too. I had to laugh. It showed that he had some playa in him.

"Whatchu laughin' at?" Pops interrogated.

"Lookin' at li'l' bruh over there mackin'," I smiled.

"He got some swagga like me I see," I credited myself.

Pops chuckled. "Yep. He thinks he's a mack daddy."

Kydrick stood about six foot one, nice build. Like my dad, Nine, and me, he was handsome. I recognized that all of our names started with a K, like his. One thing that I had to give my dad his props for was that he didn't make ugly kids. All of us, except for my sister, were dark-skinned. My sister must have taken after her mama 'cause she was fair-skinned with shoulder length, jet- black, silky hair.

"Keyon, I attempted to stay in touch with you two. I called several times after your mama and I separated. She wouldn't put either one of you on the phone. I sent birthday cards for the first two years. After I never got a response from you all, I gave up. Your mother told me every time I called that neither one of you wanted to talk to me. And I asked her why. She told me that it was best if I just quit callin'. She promised me that she'd never speak badly about me to you all."

I frowned. I was disappointed that Mama never told me that he tried to contact me. All these years I had been thinkin' that he pushed on and forgot 'bout us.

Pops added, "After that day she changed her number and the third year that I sent birthday cards they were returned. At first, I figured your mama was being evil and returned the first one. So, on Nine's birthday I sent one and the post office stamped that no one resided at that residence, she had moved."

"Yelp, we did move a few years after that," I acknowledged. "Mama never spoke bad about you; she kept her promise to you. She only told us that you had gotten married, and she heard that you and the lady had kids together."

My neck twisted toward Kydrick, who was puttin' the phone number in his cell. He said a few more lines to her befo' she walked off. Kydrick watched her backside move 'til she was outta sight, and shorty had cakes like Betty Crocker.

"Come here, Ky," Dad ruled.

Ky came over and stood.

"This is your big brother, Keyon, and Keyon this is Ky." Ky and I embraced.

"Good to meet you, big bruh. I always wanted to kno' you," Ky mentioned.

"That's the business." I chuckled.

I told them that I was on my way to the cemetery. I didn't ride in the limo. I let Mama, Alize, and a few of my aunts ride in it.

I saw the preacher getting in his car. The street was filled wit' cars, along wit' the church's parking lot. I knew that the preacher was headed to the graveyard, too. A long line was forming behind the hearse and limo that Mama and Alize were ridin' in. People were ready to see Nine be laid to rest.

"Can I ride wit' you, Keyon?" Ky inquired.

My dad and I looked at each other for a minute.

"Yeah, fa sho'," I answered without hesitation. "Pops is it okay wit' you?"

"Of course, it's cool."

My dad went to his vehicle with his wife and daughter to get in line. Ky and I strutted to my ride, and he got on the back seat. I introduced him to Gully.

"Goddamn, boy, you sho' they goddamn brother. You look just like my nigga Nine. I'm just like they brother, we all grew up together," Gully said to Ky. Ky gave a huge grin. I also told Ky to please stop callin' me Keyon and call me Choppa.

"Is that yo' nickname? And why they call you that, big bruh? You must put yo' choppa on niggaz when you mean business."

"Hell, yeah. I be bringin' the noise." I laughed.

"When you gon' let me bust some blocks in this whip, Choppa? This car is bangin'. You go hard, huh?" Ky said, admiring my car.

"Yeah, bosses do boss shit," I boasted.

"Well, you need to put me on. You gotta be bankin' that long money to push this. I'm tired of workin' at Checkers flippin' burgers."

"I might be able to put you on to a li'l' somethin'. We'll chop it up 'bout that shit later."

"Good," Ky stated.

The hearse drove off, and all the cars followed behind it, including us.

The cemetery was well kept. Nine's casket was slowly placed in the ground. I sat on the front row, holdin' my mama's hand, comforting her. Tears flowed freely from her eyes as she watched her baby son go further and further down into the dirt.

Pops' walked toward us once the dirt was on top of Nine's coffin.

"Elaine, I want to say to you that I'm appreciative and grateful for everything that you've done for our boys."

Mama removed her oxygen hose from her nose and blew into a Kleenex she had in her other hand. "You're welcome. Thanks for comin'," she said and refocused her attention back to Nine's grave.

"Elaine, if there's anything that you need me for, you can contact me. I'll exchange numbers with Keyon before I go," he proposed.

Mama nodded, never takin' her eyes off the grave. My pops and I exchanged numbers, hugged, and I said a few words to Kydrick. My pops' wife ambled over, wit' my sister.

"Hi, Elaine," she voiced. "My heart goes out to you. I kno' that this is a tragic situation. I'm going to keep you in my prayers. I'm so sorry about the passing of your son."

Mama shot her an evil expression, shook her head, and waved her off. Like, bitch get outta my face, 'cause I ain't trying to hear a damn thing that you sayin'. Mama leaped up from her seat, and wanted to go home.

My pops' wife quietly crept off, embarrassed. I guess, Mama was still holdin' a grudge against her for stealing my dad. Pops pushed on, too.

Gully and I got on both sides of my mama, assisting her to my car. I told her to ride with me and I'd take her home, instead of the limo. The limo driver drove off with my aunts inside.

I wanted Mama around me. We were all we had now. She always needed help walking long distances. It would almost take all of her breath from her. Alize trotted behind us. It was wrong, but I kinda had a li'l' animosity toward her for what her sister had done. Maybe I was accusing her of being like Kay-Kay, they were sisters. I didn't even like Alize being in my mama's crib without Nine bein' there. It wasn't no tellin' what she was up to. I didn't trust her either. I didn't trust her, like I didn't trust her sister.

Kay-Kay knew not to show up at the funeral after that plot of hers.

"Take yo' time, Mama," I advised, grippin' under her arm and leading the way.

"I don't have any other choice," she said, taking slow steps. A chilly breeze started blowing, making me slightly cool.

"That damn wretch of his got a lot of nerves sayin' something to me. What did she think I was gon' say to her? If I was not sickly, I woulda knocked fire from her ass. I shoulda wrapped my oxygen cord 'roun' her neck and choked her to sleep."

"Mama, why you mad at her instead of Pops?"

I curiously wanted an answer to that question.

"She stole my damn husband from me, that's why."

"Mama, she couldn't have gotten him if he wasn't ready to leave."

"Who damn side you on? Are you defending that homewrecker?"

"I'm not defending her, or on her side. I'm only stating facts."

"I don't need you to state your facts nor do I want to listen to the shit."

"Mama, my dad told me that he tried to reach out to us, and you blocked it every time. All these years I had been thinkin' that he didn't give a damn 'bout me. Why'd you do that?"

"It was easier for me to get over him that way. I didn't want him comin' around. He hurt me too bad, and I couldn't stand to look at him. He left me for her, and that was a slap in the face. I had two babies for that man, and for him to walk away, broke my heart."

I forgave Mama for that. I wasn't a woman, and I understood that women were more emotional than men. He did peel off and leave all the responsibility of raising us on her. She took good care of us. We never missed a meal, and she kept clothing on our backs.

I pressed down on the remote and unlocked the car doors. We helped Mama in wit' her portable oxygen tank. Alize had already got on the back. Gully and I opened our doors to get in when the preacher strolled over to us.

"Sister Elaine, I'm goin' to be prayin' for you, my sister. Just keep the faith and stay strong. God ain't gon' put no more on us then we can bear. And if you need me to do anything to make your load lighter, contact me at the church."

Next, he looked over at me. "Son, I hope to see you at church one Sunday. Maybe, all of you could get together and come visit us. We'd love to have y'all."

"Thanks, Reverend. I may take you up on that offer one Sunday," I remarked. I wasn't goin' to go anytime soon. I didn't believe in playin' wit' God. I knew what type of life I lived, and wasn't ready to just turn it loose, yet.

"Y'all take care and God bless," the preacher said, and trotted away.

I cranked my engine and was 'bout to drive away, when several gunshots rang out.

Er'body dropped low. I was fumbling under my seat for my burner, to grasp it, when I heard close shots firing near us. The preacher fired back.

I leaned up, opened up my car door, and let off two rounds at the Ford that was swerving in the street. I saw it heading for a big tree off the street. Boom. It crashed. Over on my right the preacher was holdin' a .357.

"I hope I killed that son-of-a-bitch," the preacher swore. I guess the Good Book hadn't diminished his gangsta.

The car was smokin' and nobody was attempting to get out. It sat wit' the hood smashed into the driver's seat. The preacher took off behind a bush and was reloading his strap. Mama remained on the seat, taking cover, Alize too. Me and Gully got locked and loaded and ran to the car.

"Hold up. I'm comin', too," the preacher said and caught up wit' us. "If one of 'em move, I'ma smoke his ass."

We peeped inside the car. The passenger's air bag was smotherin' his face. His knees were pushed in by the car's hood and blood was oozing from his brain. The windshield had cut his head wide open. Meat from his skull dangled open, exposin' his brain.

I saw a young woman wit' long curly hair wit' a spot of blood in the center of it. She was tilted over, with a gun in her hand. She looked like I knew her from somewhere, I just couldn't think where. Her head had swayed from her neck. That whole sight turned my stomach.

Gully and I pried the female's door open, reached over her petite, thin body and I held the dude's head back to see if I recognized who it was that wanted us dead so bad. Brain bones seeped down on my hand.

"Ugh, this shit nasty," I jabbered.

Me and Gully never thought that it was the person whose face was revealed. It was my boy, Dirty Red. Then it registered who the chick was. She was his bitch that was s'pose to deliver my dope the day J-Roc robbed me. She was one of the bitches who was in that car that drove off.

"Dirty Red," I said, shocked. "I fucked wit' him the long way."

"Dirty mufucka," Gully screeched.

"Y'all kno' these fools?" The preacher asked.

"Yep," Gully and I remarked. "He's a homeboy we been knowin' a long time. I thought he was a cool cat. All this time he been my fuckin' enemy."

I observed where one of the bullets pierced the back of his neck and that's prob'ly when he lost control of the car and crashed. I aimed my burner at Dirty Red and shot him in the face. Then, I aimed it at the bitch and shot her, too.

"I just preached on this shit today. How these evildoers will even try to kill the preacher. I stay armed. Especially, when I preach at a funeral that I find out the person was a drug dealer or gangbanger. Thank God I protected myself today. They could have killed one of us and got away scotch free," the preacher said.

I stood at a loss for words. Dirty Red had me set up by J-Roc to be jacked; that's when I was robbed. They took my ride, money, and er'thang, and it hurt a nigga through his chest to kno' that he was the mastermind behind it all.

"We'll handle this," the preacher said. "I'm a retired cop. I was on the force for forty-three years. I'm also a Veteran and I did security work for the V.A. Hospital for twelve years. I got some pull. I'm gon' get a Captain that I'm best friends with to help me clean this mess up. I'm licensed to carry a weapon. I'll explain that they drove through here and tried to kill us. They'll ask a few questions and that should be the end of it."

I went to my car and gave the Reverend all the cheddar I had on me for helping me cap them clowns. I handed him two stacks.

"Ooh, thank you, boy," he sang, smiling. "I hope to see you at church one Sunday."

"You will," I replied.

Gully and I got in my car and sat. Everyone was sittin' up straight. Mama and Alize were both frightened and hysterical.

"Choppa, my chest is hurtin' and my left arm is tingling. It feels like my chest is about to cave in," Mama complained, then stopped responding.

I mashed the gas all the way to the hospital. They say when it rains it pours, and they sho' didn't lie.

Nine was buried, and an hour and somethin' later Mama was pronounced dead on arrival. Her heart had taken all that it could stand. The cause of death was determined as a massive heart attack. Death seemed to be lurking around me a lot and had become a member of my family.

Three Months Later
Kay-Kay

Being a female escort contributed to Alize and I livin' ghetto fabulous. We resided in a nice house with two bedrooms and two bathrooms. I'd gon' through storms and rains to get where I was in my life. No more wonderin' where Choppa's ass was and who he was fuckin'. No more dealin' wit' that drama with those crazy, weak-minded bitches that he dealt with. He almost killed me the night the cops found my body. If it had not been for the police helicopter flyin' over me that night, I would have been in some deep shit. Young King died from the gunshots. I was the least bit shocked when I found out he was dead. I learned a valuable lesson from that whole incident.

After the death of Nine and Ms. Elaine, Choppa told Alize that she had to find a new place to live in, and he sold the house. That's when Alize started living with me and taking classes to obtain her G.E.D. I'm proud of her.

When Choppa and I first parted ways, I was in tears and real hurt behind it. Oh well, er'body knows that life goes on, and I was happy to be makin' my own money. No longer did I have to wait on him to throw me some paper. All those ho's who wanted him when we were together, could have his sorry ass. Pretty bitches don't stay down forever. He prob'ly thought I wouldn't make it without him, like I would die or stop breathing. Nope. I'm breathing just fine. Hell, prob'ly even betta now that I didn't have to sniff up behind his two-timing, cheating ass, wonderin' what bitch he had suckin' his dick when he wouldn't come home. I hated the way things ended between us, but I was glad that part of my life was history.

Lastly, I heard Choppa went downhill after selling his Mama's house. I hadn't seen him since the night he attempted to beat my brains out, and I didn't care to see him, either. We heard, through some peeps in the hood, that he was nothin' more than an alcoholic and cocaine addict. The loss of his baby brother and his mother must've really taken a toll on him for him to stoop to that level.

I was in my bathroom gettin' ready for my date. Grelza called earlier and informed me that I needed to be dressed and ready to spend a night out on the town with a surgeon named Joseph. It was so easy to be in this business. All I had to do was parade on the dude's side, go out to dinner or wherever they wanted to go, and give 'em some good sex. And bam. I had a good amount of money only for that. Better than being like most of these young ho's now and lettin' a nigga fuck 'em and won't even feed 'em. At least I was getting paid to go on dates, get fed, and fuck. Some were well-paid, wealthy executives who simply wanted a pretty companion on they hip, and didn't mind payin' for the service.

Grelza told me that Joseph and I would enjoy each other's company over dinner and next would be a suite at the Hospitality Hotel.

I was dressed to kill in a tight, shiny, black leather, mini, Dior dress and black leather Dior pumps. My hair was neatly placed in a bun. I glided past Alize's room door. She was doing some studying for her G.E.D. class.

"You lookin' all cute. Where you goin' tonight?"

I backed up in front of her doorway. "I got a doctor tonight. He's a surgeon, and we're supposed to be havin' dinner and prob'ly get nasty later."

"Well, have fun and watch yo' back."

I reached over in my purse hanging from my shoulder and disclosed my steel. "You must have forgotten that I keep some heat on me? I ain't takin' nothin' off nobody now. I wish a mufucka would try some grimy shit with me. I guarantee you that I'll murk 'em without thinking twice 'bout it."

"Wake me up if I'm sleep when you get in, to let me kno' you made it in safely."

"I will," I promised.

"By the way, is Joseph black or white or what?" she pried and put her ink pen down for a second.

"Hell, if I kno'. As long as his paper is green, I wouldn't care if he was purple or blue." I laughed.

"Just be careful. Remember, I want to hear details when you get back," she stated and picked her ink pen back up, and focused back on her studying.

I left to go meet with Mr. Joseph.

*

"Damn, I wish this damn light would change," I impatiently grumbled. Glancing over at the clock, I had about ten minutes to get to my destination with Joseph. Boy, was my ass excited 'cause I knew that if I put this body on him right, that he'd become a regular and that meant more bread in my bank account. The light eventually changed to green, and I mashed my accelerator. I'll be damned if I didn't soon have to stop for another traffic light.

"Maybe I will learn to start leavin' the house a few minutes early now," I admonished myself. I was pleading on the inside for the light to hurry the hell up.

While impatiently waiting, I watched a few people go inside a liquor store on the corner. An old, beat up red Ford Focus drove in the parking lot blasting Al Green's tune "Love and Happiness." Two skinny, nappy-headed fiends jumped out who looked like walking beanpoles. I shook my head, appalled at how bony they were. The bitches should have been somewhere gettin' a meal instead of alcohol. I had a good idea what they wanted outta the store, too...211. Dope heads loved that beer. Prob'ly 'cause it was cheap.

When the light changed again, I took off. A car drove alongside me and my eyes locked with Choppa's. His face looked very thin, indicating that he had lost weight. Bags resided under his eyes; a sign that meant lack of rest. I abruptly turned my head, putting my attention on driving. For some bizarre reason, I turned and looked at him again. A female was beside him. She peeped her head over to see what had gotten Choppa's attention. That ho was ugly. She was black as tar, and pop-eyed, and had a twisted up mouth. I was astounded by what I saw. I flipped them the bird and sped off. Those two dummies looked bad.

I was flawless and sittin' behind the wheel of my new Benz. My chromed shoes were glistening. A month ago, I threw some twenty's on it. I was now able to buy the things that my heart desired. That was a pleasing feeling to see him and let him check out how I was flossin' on his bitch ass. He got the opportunity to see how I had up-graded. He, and that heifer with him, looked like they were on some kind of drug. Guess it was true 'bout what the hood had put out 'bout him being on that shit. And that pop-eyed, twisted mouth female he had wit' him mouth must have been fucked up from her drug , unless it was from her suckin' a new dick seven days a week. He and that nasty ass garbage deserved each other. Nigga used to walk around like his shit didn't stank, and now he was just another dopehead.

*

Joseph was supposed to be waiting for me outside of Omega's Restaurant. I was approaching the entrance, when I spotted a man I thought was Joseph. He was the only person outside, and he was smokin' a cigarette. *Oh my God*, I said to myself. The creamy, cocoa-chocolate brother I rested my eyes on was so good looking and fine. I wanted to run up to his ass and sink my teeth into him. I'd say he was all that, plus some more. Dude was clothed in nice, black slacks, a long-sleeved copper shirt, and copper colored shoes. I added a little sugar to my switch and glided where he took his position.

"What's up? Are you Joseph?" I smiled displaying my pearly whites.

My kitty-cat was turning backward flips from the sight of him. I prayed that a stream of wetness wouldn't dribble down my leg, making it evident that he was turning me on.

"No, sweetie. I'm not Joseph." He grinned. "Sorry, I'm waiting for my fiancé."

My lip poked out so far with disappointment that you could have walked across it.

"Oh, my bad."

I moved several feet from Mr. Sexy Ass, waiting for Joseph to show up. I gave Grelza a ring and let her kno' that I made it to the restaurant and was waiting for him to get there. She told me to text her back when he arrived. I always had to check in with her coming and going. She wanted to make sure that all of her escorts were safe.

"Excuse me," a voice said behind me. "Are you Kay-Kay?"

The guy asking me the question was a white, short, stubby older guy. His thin, gray hair was combed backward. I was goin' on a date with somebody's granddaddy. I'd have to put my game face on, and go with the flow. At least I was gettin' paid for it.

"Yes, I am. Are you Joseph?" I smiled, phony as hell.

"Yelp. I'm Joseph. I may not be what you expected, but here I am."

I wanted to blurt, "No you're not. You're old enough to be my great grandpappy." Rather than saying that, I purred, "I'm happy to meet you, baby."

"You ready to get this date started?"

Joseph opened the door for me like a gentleman. I allowed the lady comin' toward me to exit the door before I entered. I glimpsed over my shoulder to see her grab Mr. Sexy Ass's hand and pace away. *Lucky bitch.*

We treaded inside for dinner, and no matter how his appearance was, I was ready to make the best of this night. My fingers were crossed for good luck.

Sugar to Shit
Choppa

I used to be That Nigga. The nigga all the young cats in the hood idolized, but after a few misfortunes, I went from sugar to shit.

Gully still ran one of my dope spots. I had to shut the other one down 'cause the po's had started comin' through the block sweepin' the block boys up. They were trying to clean up the community, and I couldn't risk gettin' jammed. So, I shut that shit down. Two houses had already been bulldozed and the law was boarding others. Most of the houses in that area were dilapidated anyway.

Me and my girl, Toya, were sittin' in her low-income crib ready to get high. I had lined a line of cocaine on the table and straightened it wit' my razor. Yeah, it's true; I'm snortin' powder now. Toya handed me a rolled dollar bill.

"Are you gon' tell me who that chick was that you was staring at like a hawk earlier?"

"That was a girl from the past. We use to kick it. Ain't shit shakin' between us no more, though," I explained.

I inserted the butt of the bill in my nose and inhaled the line. Seconds later, I was on top of the world. Physically, I ain't feel shit. My body was numb. My heart began beating rapidly and my pupils widened.

Toya got some of the powder outta a bag on the small table in her living room. She formed a straight line, too. But, her straightened line was longer than mine. She clenched on to a dollar bill I left on the table, and held one nostril closed wit' her fingertip, and exhaled the powder into the other nostril. When the line was gon', she sat back on her sofa wit' a biggo Kool-Aid smile. We were high and feelin' amazin'. That blow was fiyah.

Twenty minutes later, we crashed. The high was over. The intense pleasure that I got from that shit had vanished and I needed some mo'. I wanted to smoke a longer line to get even higher. My mucosal membranes were slightly damaged, but I couldn't stop. This was my short cut to paradise. I redid the procedure again wit' the cocaine. As I lined the shit up on the table, I couldn't help thinkin' bout Kay-Kay's triflin' ass. The way I beat her ass, I was surprised to see that bitch moving. I regretted not puttin' a few shots to her dome. And I used to actually love her. I was heated on the inside after thinkin' bout that ho. She was pushin' a Benz and tossed some chromed shoes on it. If it hadn't been fo' me, she would be in the ghetto somewhere suckin' dicks, assuming her mama's role.

Anyway, I'd been foolin' wit' Toya fo' bout three months. She wasn't dymed up, yet her head game was the truth, and that in 'tween her legs' was somethin' special. Toya had a hot body. Her ass was soft and phat. She owned a stomach as flat as an ironing board, pretty tits, and a beautiful personality. Her mouth to some extent twisted from a stroke she suffered when she was a teenager. She wouldn't go into details about it, and I didn't ask any questions. Her heart was gold, and she understood me. She listened when I spoke 'bout my problems, and how bad I missed my li'l' nigga, Nine.

I met her when I rolled through her hood after Mama died. We started conversing and she understood how much my family members' deaths had pained me. So, she introduced me to some shit she called Paradise, which was cocaine. It kept me from worrying and wantin' to say fuck the world and er' mufucka in it and committing suicide. The pain was so extreme.

Ready to snort or toot my shit I snorted the longest ass line. I'd rather snort than eat. That's how I lost a couple of pounds. Hell, runnin' behind the powder.

I was feeling the effects of the powder only minutes afterward. Next, I began feeling a strong, irregular heartbeat followed by respiratory problems. My breathing grew shorter and weaker. I held my chest, gasping for breath.

"Baby, what's wrong?" Toya queried, and darted over to me.

"I can't breathe," I whispered.

"Baby. You need help. I can call the ambulance if you need me to."

"Call 'em," I murmured.

I heard Toya speakin' to paramedics on the phone, hysterically. I musta overdosed and from the severe chest pain and abnormal heartbeat, I knew that this shit could possibly be fatal.

My thoughts that I was dying were confirmed when everything got blurry and I exhaled my last breath. All I could see after that was darkness.

A loud voice that I didn't recognize screamed, "Welcome to hell."

Then that li'l' jet black bastard standin' in front of me tossed a ball of fire on my ass. I had come face to face wit' Satan himself.

Following Morning
Kay-Kay

Goodness gracious. The date I had last night went just fine. That is until we got back to the hotel, and I had to suck grandpop's almost dead, half-soft wiener. He knew that he had a problem gettin' hard. Still, he wanted some brain and I gave his old, worn out ass exactly what he asked for.

He laid back on the bed shivering and shaking. He almost died trying to get a nut. He didn't do nothin' but shoot a blank. He promised that he'd be givin' me his business as one of my regular clients, and that was fine with me. There wasn't any hard work involved with him really. The hardest part was convincing that soft as cotton dick to rise. I still couldn't believe after he got a super duper head job that he attempted to sex me. When his gray-haired chest, and naked butt got off the bed and came toward me with his shriveled up penis and balls, I wanted to burst out laughing. Whew. Was that stage show ever funny. Every time he put it in me, it fell out. It couldn't get hard enough to stay in. After five or six tries, I kindly suggested that we lay down together and enjoy each other's company. Wasn't no need in letting the ole' timer steady make an ass of himself.

Before we went our separate ways, Joseph told me that he would be referring me to his best friend, Luke.

I smiled and replied, "Okay, Big Daddy." When I referred to him as Big Daddy, every tooth in his mouth was showing. He swallowed those words whole.

I had given Alize a rundown of what had gon' down. She laughed so hard that tears formed and fell down her face.

I was sitting on her bed that morning while she was sprawled across it. She loved to hear about my clients and laugh at some of the things some of them said and did. She worried about me a lot, worried about my safety and if I would be murdered like our mama had. I constantly assured her that nothin' would happen to me, and that I would always be careful.

"Sis, do you ever wonder where Choppa and Gully at?" Alize asked.

"No. I try not to even think about them. I hate that things went sour between Choppa and me. I really did care about him. Girl, he wanted me dead that night he attacked me. I was praying. I kept praying that God let me live."

"I'm glad you got a second chance."

"Me too."

I paused thinking about how blessed I was to still be living, after the pain I suffered when Choppa did his best to kill me.

"I saw Choppa last night. I was on my way to meet my client and saw him at a stop light. He had some twisted mouth bitch on the other side of him. Girl, I could've puked when she leaned over and showed her face."

"Ooh, wee, that's so sad." Alize chuckled. "That nigga done went from the top straight to the fuckin' bottom."

"Both of 'em looked like their on dope."

There were two knocks on the front door. We got off Alize's bed and proceeded to the door.

"Who is it?"

"Shay."

I opened the door and let her in." Whad's up, Shay?" I was excited to see her. It had been a long time since we kicked it.

She came inside and plopped down on the plush leather sofa. "Damn, I'm tired. I walked over here to get to y'all. I didn't have no money fo' a bus ticket. I ain't trippin' bout it tho'. Walking is good fo' the body. I needed the exercise."

She appeared tired. She fell back allowing her body to rest.

"Well, we sho' glad to see you, girl. Sorry, we still got our pajamas on," Alize expressed.

"Why y'all ain't been answering yo' cell phones? I been hittin' y'all all morning."

"My cell went dead on me, and I got it on the charger," Alize explained.

"Mine is in my car. I forgot to get it out," I responded.

"Well, I came over here to let you all kno' that Choppa dead."

"What?" I screamed in shock.

"Yes, girl. The hood says that he had an overdose on that cocaine. He was already gon' by the time he made it to the hospital."

"I just saw him last night with some ugly chick. Dayum, he got his payback fast, huh?" I said.

"Yelp, and that ho he was wit' name Toya. She was wit' him just so she could get high fo' free, that's it. She been on drugs for a hot li'l' minute, too. I would say 'bout a year or two. She a stripper, I heard," Shay gossiped.

"Who would actually pay to see that tramp take her damn clothes off?" I snorted in disgust at the mere thought of it.

"Maybe one of these ole' hard up scrubs. She had a nice body. It's her mouth that's damaged. I don't know what happened to it."

We continued on talkin' and got the skinny from Shay on what was goin' on in our old hood. I never imagined that payback would have bitten Choppa in his ass as fast as it had. He did good to run from dying as long as he had.

Justice Prevails
Kay-Kay

Joseph didn't lie when he said he'd be referring me to his friend. My next date would be with Luke. We scheduled to meet at six on Saturday evening. After rejuvenating with a long, hot bath, I explored my closet. I slipped on a blushing pink, low-cut, long-sleeved Mark Jacobs top with some carbon-black leggings, and a pair of Adelaide leather, lace up, black, zipper boots. My naturally curly hair swung down my back. I applied my eyeliner, mascara, and lip-gloss. I glanced over my shoulder to get a view of my ass in my full-length mirror, and to make sure I was divafied. Lastly, I dabbed on my new Poppy by Coach and dotted the door.

The only thing that kept haunting my mind were thoughts about Choppa as I was driving to the Hospitality Hotel. I kept wondering why he chose to start using cocaine.

My mama passed too, but I damn sho' didn't run to get a hit of crack. Guess I was stronger minded than he was. I would forever be thankful to him for saving me from the streets when Mama died. Our relationship wasn't all bad, and it sho' wasn't all good either. He was young and hadn't gotten all of that playa outta his system when I met him. Not only that, I have to take responsibility for my actions as well. He had an ole' lady at home when I got with him. That shoulda told me to step back; I didn't. I continued pursuing him so I got what I deserved, too. Common sense should have told me that if he cheated on her with me, then he would cheat on me with somebody else.

I parked in front of the hotel, killed my engine, got out, and toddled along inside. I used the elevator to get to Luke's room on the second floor. I text Grelza letting her kno' that I made it.

I knocked two times and was quickly satisfied when a handsome, blue-eyed, devil appeared on the other side of the door resembling the actor, Tom Cruise.

"Come on in, gorgeous," he said after hugging me.

The smell of his cologne turned me on. He went over to a small table in the room and sat down. A tall bottle of Moet was on the table. He grabbed his glass and carried on drinking.

"Can I offer you a glass of Moet?" he offered.

"Sure."

I joined him at the table, and we drank like two goldfish while watching the show "Cheaters" on cable. We giggled and were highly entertained by the people on the show who got caught slippin' by their partners.

"These people are hilarious." He laughed.

"I would be too embarrassed to go on a show like that, and let the world kno' that my man is cheating on me."

He focused his attention toward me. "If you don't mind me asking, do you have a man?"

I crossed my legs. Before answering him, I sipped from my glass. "No, I'm not involved with anybody at this time. I'm just solo, and I like it this way."

"I totally understand," he nodded. "You're so picturesque," he complimented.

"Awww, thanks."

No Win Situation

I stopped drinking after my second glass. The tipsy feeling was easing up on me, and I knew that I needed to slow down and pause. Luke was an absolute alcoholic. He was throwin' his drinks down his throat like it wasn't nothin'. Six of 'em to be exact.

"I'm feelin' good," he slurred. "Now I'm ready to fuck."

He staggered over to me, and almost fell on me until he caught himself.

"Oops, my bad, baby," he chortled with a smirk.

He snatched my shirt up and grabbed my titties so hard I started to slap fire from him.

"Ouch. That's a damn tittie. You can't handle my shit any kinda way."

He ignored me, and dropped to his knees putting sloppy kisses above my breast.

"Take this bra off before I rip it off," he ordered, rudely.

In silence, I removed my shirt and bra. He sucked my titties hard and held them rough.

"Open your legs up."

I opened my legs, and he dove his head on my jewel suckin' on it through my pants. This asshole was two cards short of havin' a deck, with his odd ass.

"Would you like me to take these leggings off and let you taste my honey," I asked, before he tried to rip my leggings off, wanting to get to my kitty.

He never responded. I stood, removing my shoes in order to get my leggings down. Luke got off his knees, went over, poured another glass of Moet, and swallowed it down before my leggings came off. *Damn drunk.*

He edged up to me, unzipped his pants, and let his pants drop to the floor; his navy blue boxers were showing. He unbuttoned his shirt and tossed it on the bed that was behind us. His chest was beautiful; smooth and buff with no chest hairs and that six-pack was nice, too.

"Are you into Dominatrix?" he sluggishly asked.

"Domi who?"

"Dominatrix."

"What's that?"

"Hold on, and I'll show you." He went over into the closet, came to me with a tiny backpack, and emptied stuff out on the table. There was a black whip, rope, handcuffs, and an enormous dildo.

My first initial thought was that this white idiot was gon' kill me. My mouth dropped.

"I don't kno' what kind of sick-minded shit you into, but I don't get down like that. I'm not no slave, and you not gon' be tying me up and whippin' on my black ass. Another thing, you ain't bout to hang me from no tree, either. So, you can put that whip and rope right back in that bag that it came outta," I seethed with my hand on my hip.

"I want you to use all of this stuff on me, silly." He snickered. "All accept the fake cock," he further said. He placed his hands behind his back.

"Put the handcuffs on me," he ordered. I reached over on the table, got it, and locked it on him.

"Now, get the whip and beat me, and call me dirty names," he requested.

I didn't kno' whether I would be thrown in jail or not behind this silly shit.

"Am I going to get in trouble for whipping you? And what's the purpose of me doing this?"

"It turns me on. I like to feel pain mixed in with a little pleasure. Treat me like I'm a filthy rag, Kay-Kay."

If he wanted it, I'd give it to his sick ass.

"Turn yo' stupid ass around and let me see that ass," I bossed.

He turned around, dropped his boxers, and let his ass face me. I grasped the whip from the table and splapow. Splapow. Splapow. Splapow. I was whipping that ass good. His boodie was fire engine red.

"Beat me, Kay-Kay. Beat me," he begged.

I kicked him right in his ass with my foot, knocking him to the floor.

"Yessss. Yessss," he howled, enjoyin' it.

"You just poor, white trash. You ain't shit. You're filthy, dirty, stupid and a sorry piece of shit, and I'm gon' beat you to death," I raged, steady whipping him.

"Beat me, honey. Do whatever you like. Please make me hurt, baby," he pleaded, and laid out on the floor with his legs gapped wide open, laying on his back.

I reached over, grabbed his prized possession, and squeezed it as hard as I could. His dick was no bigger than my big toe. I always heard that white men didn't have any size. He loved every second of me hurting his lollipop. I grabbed one of his gigantic balls and squeezed down on it. He squinted his eyes tightly.

"Ouch. Stop, that's hurting," he yelled.

"Naw, you said you like pain so take it. Stop being a pussy and man up," I roared. I slapped him in the face.

"I said, stop," he bossed.

"You gon' take it. You shouldn't have asked for it if you knew you couldn't take it."

"You look exactly like another black prostitute bitch that I killed, and if you don't stop, I'll kill you next. I killed that street whore, and her friend, and my friend."

I quit. "Where did you kill her at?"

"Up on the lake on Wisconsin and you're next," he said, panting.

It was somethin' how the liquor had him spillin' his guts and admitting to the murders. I locked my hands around his throat and choked him so long and hard until his eyes waddled back in his head, and his tongue was hanging from his mouth. I stopped right before I choked him out, and sat on the floor. He was gasping for breath. This man committed the crime. I ordered him to open his mouth and inserted the fake dick in it.

I got up off the floor, got the rope, and tied his feet together so he couldn't move. Next, I called Grelza and told her that this was the person who murdered my mother. I asked her what I should do. She advised me to call the police, and tell them what Luke admitted to then break camp before they arrived. And that was exactly what I did.

I called from a payphone in the area, and informed the police that he had admitted to killing Tamela Jean Butler and her friend Lacey Ann Montgomery. I gave them the room number and hotel name.

On my way home, I kept thinking about how I came face to face with Mama and Miss Lacey's murderer. I only hoped that the police would find enough evidence to charge him with the murders so that Mama could rest in peace.

Final Words
Kay-Kay

Police arrested Bruce Lucas, aka Luke. He was shown on the ten o'clock news being escorted and placed in a patrol car by local authorities. A former, white, prostitute named Becky Sojourner, who had been clean for six months came forward and admitted that she had seen Mama get in the car with Luke up on Wisconsin. At first, Luke lied to authorities about even knowing or ever meeting Mama. But after a hectic grill from detectives, which lasted for hours, Luke broke down and confessed to all three murders. He is currently serving three life sentences at the Waupun State Prison.

Alize has made me proud. She acquired her G.E.D., is taking classes at Milwaukee Area Technical College, and taking pharmacy tech classes. In one year she'll be done completing the class, and hopefully obtain certification as a Pharmacy Tech.

Shay recently finished her last year of high school and received a scholarship to the University of Wisconsin Milwaukee, and is going to pursue a career in Elementary Education.

As for me, I'm not goin' back to anybody's school when I can work my money maker that's cuddled between these thighs. I'ma keep paper chasin' and breaking dudes wallets in the escort business. Like my mama once told me, pussy rules the world. And, I'ma continue being a high priced ho and enjoying the fine things in life. You kno', I once thought that if I got with a street dude who had major dough that all of my problems would be solved. I had to learn that it's best to have yo' own shit and be an independent bitch. 'Cause flockin' over a street nigga is a NO WIN SITUATION.

Contact the author at
www.facebook.com/AuthorJennifer
email: lovewriting1@aol.com

Mail
P. O. Box 30
Canton, MS 39046

Made in the USA
Charleston, SC
05 July 2012